THE
UNWRITTEN LAW
IN ALBANIA

A Record of the Customary Law of
the Albanian Tribes, A Description
of Family and Village Life in the
Albanian Mountains, and an Account
of the Waging of Blood-Feuds'

T0371501

THE
UNWRITTEN LAW
IN ALBANIA

BY THE LATE
MARGARET HASLUCK

EDITED BY
J. H. HUTTON

CAMBRIDGE
AT THE UNIVERSITY PRESS
1954

CAMBRIDGE
UNIVERSITY PRESS

University Printing House, Cambridge CB2 8BS, United Kingdom

Cambridge University Press is part of the University of Cambridge.

It furthers the University's mission by disseminating knowledge in the pursuit of
education, learning and research at the highest international levels of excellence.

www.cambridge.org
Information on this title: www.cambridge.org/9781107586932

© Cambridge University Press 1954

First published 1954
First paperback edition 2015

A catalogue record for this publication is available from the British Library

ISBN 978-1-107-58693-2 Paperback

Additional resources for this publication at www.cambridge.org/9781107586932

CONTENTS

Map: This map is available for download from www.cambridge.org/9781107586932

PREFACE

Margaret Hasluck was the daughter of a Scottish farmer, John Hardie. She was born in 1885 and spent her early years in Moray-shire. From Elgin Academy she went to Aberdeen University, where she graduated in 1907 with first class Honours in Classics. Continuing her classical studies in Cambridge, she took a first class in both parts of the Tripos. She then went to the British School at Athens where her future husband, Mr F. W. Hasluck, was Assistant Director. They were married in 1912 and continued to work in Athens till the condition of Mr Hasluck's health compelled them to go to Switzerland in 1916. Mr Hasluck died in 1920, and his wife returned to England to prepare his book on *The Monasteries of Mount Athos*. When this work was completed, Mrs Hasluck, who had become greatly interested in the folklore of the Balkan countries, decided to devote herself to the study of this subject, and, with the help of a Wilson Travelling Fellowship, she returned to the Middle East. After extensive wanderings, she decided to settle in Albania. She remained in that country for thirteen years, building herself a house at Elbasan, and travelling constantly, especially in the mountainous region of the north where she lived with the people and got to know them intimately.

With the threat of the Italian invasion of Albania in 1939, she left that country for Athens, where she worked for some time in the British Embassy. When that city was being heavily bombed she was taken to Alexandria and thence to Cairo. In Cairo she was given the task of briefing the men who were to be infiltrated into Albania by air and sea, in the manners and ways of life of the Albanian people. She was, of course, well qualified for this work by her long and intimate knowledge of the country and of the language. Unfortunately, she became seriously ill in Cairo, and was found to be suffering from leucaemia. In the hope of some improvement she went to live in Cyprus, but, driven to realize that she had not long to live, she came back to England determined to finish the book which she had been planning for many years and for which she had collected a mass of material. After some inde-cision as to a suitable place to live she went to Dublin, and during the short time left to her she worked there with great courage and persistence on her book. She died in 1948 with her task far from completed.

Mrs Hasluck appointed the writer of this preface as her literary executor, not because of any knowledge of Albania or of folklore, but as an old friend who would do everything possible to get the book ready for publication. Had she completed it herself or entrusted it to some authority on her subject, the book would undoubtedly have been free of some of its faults. When the material came into my hands, only four of the chapters had been completed and much of the remaining material was in a chaotic condition. But Mrs Hasluck had sketched out the plan of the book with the proposed chapter headings, and the preliminary inquiries I made as to her standing as an authority and her know-ledge of Albania and its language were very encouraging. Also the Leverhulme Research Fellowships Trust, from which Mrs Hasluck had received grants for her work, undertook to give me a grant towards my personal expenses and to make it possible to employ a sub-editor at a later stage of the work.

I am indebted to a great many people, both English and Albanian, who helped me at the early stages of the work with information and ideas. I cannot mention all of these by name, but I heard from several of the officers who were briefed by Mrs Hasluck for their work in Albania. I discussed with Professor Jopson of St John's College, Cambridge, Mrs Hasluck's knowledge of the Albanian language, and was assured by him that it was good and that her *Albanian-English Reader*, published in 1932, was a reliable and useful book. But at the early stages of my task I owed a very special debt of gratitude to Lord Haden Guest, who was then Secretary of the Leverhulme Research Fellowships, and to Miss Branney, the present secretary. Without their interest and encouragement I do not think I could have found the necessary confidence to persevere in what has proved to be a difficult and prolonged task.

One source of great difficulty was the spelling of geographical names, and it was natural to turn to the Royal Geographical Society for help. I am glad to have the opportunity of expressing my very sincere gratitude to Mr Aurousseau, Secretary of the Permanent Committee on Geographical Names, who gave much time and thought to this matter and whose advice was invaluable.

Brigadier Davies, who was head of the Military Mission with the partisans in Albania, and who had been briefed by Mrs Hasluck, read a great part of her book in manuscript, and was much interested in the chapters about the domestic life of the people in the mountains whom he had got to know well. He was busy at the time with his own book, *Illyrian Venture*, which, alas, did not appear until after his death.

My expressions of gratitude would be incomplete without a very warm tribute to the invaluable assistance given to me by my sub-editor, Miss Margot Holloway, M.B.E. She worked with me constantly for many months, and not only did she type the manuscript, prepare an index, and read the proofs, but I owe more than I can say to her constructive criticism and suggestions.

Finally, I must express my appreciation of Professor Hutton's help at the final stages of the work. It was a great relief to me to have the manuscript read by an anthropologist with his specialized knowledge, and Professor Hutton has also been good enough to read the proofs.

J. E. ALDERSON

June 1953

INTRODUCTION

There is a singular absence of ethnographical material in English which deals with either the Balkan tribes in general or the Albanians in particular. In fact, apart from handbooks compiled during the Hitler war and still inaccessible to the general public, almost all that the student of Albanian life and custom can consult is the work, admirable indeed but of a single author, the late Miss Durham—*High Albania* (1909), and *Some Tribal Origins, Laws, and Customs of the Balkans* (1928), and two other works more nearly concerned with politics. In languages other than English there are the valuable *Albanesische Studien* of J. G. von Hahn (Jena, 1854), the same author's *Griechische und albanesische Märchen* published in Leipzig ten years later, the *Contes Albanais* of Auguste Dozon (Paris, 1881), and possibly passages in Strabo and other ancient authors with regard to the Illyrians from whom the Albanians in the main derive. More recently the Reale Accademia d'Italia has published an Italian version of Gjeçov's *Code of Lek Dukagjini* (Rome, 1941) and a number of other studies on Albania have been published in Italian as a result of the Italian interest in and occupation of that country under Mussolini's régime.

This volume of Mrs Hasluck's therefore constitutes a very important contribution to ethnography in English. Principally, it is true, it is concerned with the customary law of the Albanian highlands. But, as a means of understanding the fundamental logical basis of that code and how it works in practice, the author has been under the necessity of explaining the manner of Albanian life in considerable detail, and of illustrating it from time to time by the details of specific cases which illustrate the working of the unwritten law. We are thus given a great deal of information as to the composition of the Albanian family, and its mode of life, the general set up of the village and tribal life, and the nature and working of tribal assemblies. We are shown the methods of dealing with crimes against property or person, the conventions that govern, for instance, trespass, travel, and the feeding of flocks, or the guarding of houses by watch-dogs. We have detailed accounts of the administration of oaths, and of the imposition of penalties; and finally the conventions which govern the blood-feud. For the blood-feud has occupied from time immemorial, and no doubt still occupies, a very important place in Albanian life, providing the ultimate sanction in all cases in which personal honour is concerned, and on points of personal honour the Albanian is particularly sensitive; and the blood-feud is regulated by a number of very well understood even if unwritten rules and principles.

It is interesting to compare Albanian customary law with that of other headhunters, for the Albanians (see p. 230 below and Miss Durham, *Tribal Origins, etc.*, pp. 172 ff.) till recently at any rate were headhunters. The belief underlying headhunting generally is that life is a material substance residing *par excellence* in the head, and that the abstraction of an enemy's head enables the life-substance in it to be carried off to the head-taker's home to replenish the stock there and increase the fertility of its inhabitants, its crops, and its livestock. Incidentally a surplus of life-substance is necessary to beget children, and hence comes the importance of head-taking as a preliminary to marriage. The tuft left on the head by Albanians (p. 230), as by many Indian tribes and castes, by Chinese, American Indians and others, was probably left originally to shelter life-substance regarded as residing, as in the case of Samson, in the hair. Some Naga tribesmen of Assam give the same account of the purpose of this uncut tuft as do Mrs Hasluck's Albanians, that it is kept to carry away the head by. But this explanation has no doubt arisen from the fact that it is so used in practice. Among the Assam headhunters the vendetta is a communal or a village affair rather than a family one, and there is no taboo on taking the heads of women in pursuance of it, but quite the contrary. In this respect the Albanian practice is more suggestive of that of the Pathans of the North-West Frontier of India. Otherwise the unwritten law of Albania has much similarity with that of south-east Asia and Oceania. The communal destruction of an offender's house at which all members of the community must assist, for instance, is widely distributed from Assam to New Zealand; the banishment of a murderer for life or for a term of years according to the circumstances of the homicide, the association of compurgators with an accused person in the taking of an oath, the assessment of blood-money, are used in the Assam hills much as in the Albanian mountains, and probably in many other primitive areas also. But Albanian customary law is of particular interest in that we now have it reported in detail when at a stage half way from the purely customary stage to that of enactment and a written law.

Sir Henry Maine in his *Ancient Law* traces the development of jurisprudence from a stage at which 'it is certain that...no sort of legislature, nor even a distinct author of law, is contemplated or conceived of. Law has scarcely reached the footing of custom; it is rather a habit....The only authoritative statement of right and wrong is a judicial sentence after the facts, not one presupposing a law which has been violated.' This is the stage of culture reflected in the Homeric poems, or seen in Iceland as described in the sagas, in which is found no sovereign ruler, nor any legislative command, nor any definite sanction, but justice is effected by the pronouncements—θέμιστες, or 'dooms'—of individual chieftains. Maine regarded this stage of law as changing with a decline in the kingly office to one in which an aristocracy, or at least an oligarchy, whether secular or religious, became the repository of all juridical knowledge. The 'accurate preservation of the customs of the race or tribe...was...insured by confiding them to the recollection of a limited portion of the community'. Except for such customary law, entrusted thus to a privileged order, 'there is' said Maine 'no such thing as unwritten law in the world'. English case law, of course, is as much written law as codified and enacted law, though the method of writing it down is different. Customary law may of course continue to exist as a body of unwritten law alongside a body of divergent enacted law, a condition familiar enough in India under British rule. Maine goes on to point out that 'when primitive law has once been embodied in a code, there is an end to what may be called its spontaneous development'. A new era begins with the codes, in which modifications are to be attributed to a conscious desire for alteration.

It is unnecessary here to discuss the precise extent to which Maine's theory of the nature and origin of primitive law can still be regarded as valid. At best it is incomplete for he takes little or no account of taboo on which early codes such as those of Hammurabi or of Moses were based, and the taboos which preceded early codes of law seem to have been in the main rather social or communal in origin than arising from the individual pronouncements of chieftains or deemsters. Maine however was no doubt right enough in pointing out that when primitive law has been embodied in a code there is an end to its spontaneous development. But to reach this stage the code must be an enacted code, written and recorded, and this the pronouncements of the Albanian law-givers failed to achieve. On the contrary their codes seem to have remained in the verbal custody of the village or tribal elders and subject to modification or reinterpretation from time to time by assemblies of clans or villages. It is at this stage that we have Mrs Hasluck's account of Albanian customary law—law primitive enough in many ways to be compared with the customary law of tribes much less civilized than the Albanians; but it reached the point, and that some five hundred years ago, of becoming codified verbally by the efforts of individual law-givers, Skanderbeg in particular and the famous Lek Dukagjini, without having reached the stage of enactment. This was principally due to the fact that there was no one able to enforce sanctions over the Albanian community as a whole; individual Albanian chieftains had not the power, and Turkish rule interfered but little outside the towns.

It was no doubt this absence of any such sanctions as those provided by an enacted law and enforced by a settled government, or merely even by the continuity in administration of a single ruling family, which was the primary cause of the firm establishment of the vendetta as the real sanction for all Albanian law and custom. At the same time, however, economic conditions have probably contributed to this result, for in a richer country the administration of justice might have been made profitable to any ruler strong enough to provide it. Thus Albanian customary law not only reflects an economic stage through which most nations have passed before the establishment of enacted codes, but also a condition, by no means unique but very far from universal, in which poor and isolated communities have resorted to the vendetta for the sanction of their law, and that in spite of any influence that Christianity or Islam might have had to prevent it. The etiquette of the vendetta itself is likewise a customary code not dissimilar to taboo in nature and origins; and without any more definite sanction, or naturally any sort of legislative enactment, regular and almost technical forms of procedure have come into existence in what virtually are regularly constituted courts. In this the Icelandic practices, as described in the sagas of Njal and Kormak, for instance, afford a near parallel to those of Albania, and Mrs Hasluck's account of Albanian custom will prove of importance not merely to ethnologists and social anthropologists but also to those concerned with the early history of jurisprudence.

Apart from that the contents of this volume are likely to be of no little interest to the general reader as giving an account of the unfamiliar way of life of a people of very distinct and individual culture, who have throughout history taken pride and pleasure in their separateness. For the Albanians, direct descendants of the ancient Illyrians, still retain something of their ancient form of Aryan speech very distinct from that of other branches of the family; they still retain an ancient tribal system; and they still have that passionate love of independence which caused many of them to forsake their native mountains and form settlements in Greece, Calabria, and Sicily when their country was occupied by the Turks after the death of their leader Skanderbeg (George Castriota) in 1467. As a result of the Turkish conquest several of the Albanian tribes changed from Christianity to Islam, and there are now many Muslim Albanians as well as both Greek Orthodox and Roman Catholic Christians. The Mirdite, who constitute the biggest tribe, were perhaps at one time Orthodox, and are now staunch Catholics. But their profession of faith seems to have affected but little the adherence of the Albanians to their ancient customs.

J. H. HUTTON

New Radnor
June 1953

CHAPTER I

THE GEOGRAPHICAL FRAMEWORK

A book on the Unwritten Law of the Albanian mountains must needs begin with a short survey of Albanian geography. Without some knowledge of the fantastic physical features which have moulded the way of life of the mountaineers, it is difficult to understand that way of life and the Unwritten Law by which it has for many centuries been regulated.

The material used in this book was gathered in the northern half of the kingdom over which King Zog ruled until the Italians invaded Albania in 1939 and sent him into exile. This area, which includes all the country north of the River Shkumbî, stretches from the Adriatic Sea on the west to the Yugoslav frontier on the east. It consists of a narrow plain along the Adriatic coast and, inland, a vast complex of mountains. The coastal plain, from 5 to 25 miles in breadth, rises so gradually from the water's edge that when it ends it is not much more than 100 feet above sea-level. Low hills cut across it, dividing it into four compartments as separate as rooms in a house. The Plain of Zadrimë (*Fushë e Zadrimës*) in the north, between the towns of Shkodër (Scutari) and Lesh (Alessio), is 15 miles long by 3–6 miles broad. The next section, measuring 18 by 5 miles, extends from Lesh to Cape Rodoni (*Kep i Rodonit*), and the third centres in Durrës (Durazzo). The Myzeqe plains (*Fusha të Myzeqes*), which constitute the fourth 'compartment' between the Rivers Shkumbî and Devoll, are 37 miles long, over 25 miles wide in parts, and less than 6 miles wide in others.

The mountains are less easy to describe. Between the latitudes of Lesh and Durrës three great ranges run parallel to each other from north to south. The most westerly rises perpendicularly from the coastal plain, the most easterly forms the boundary between Albania and Yugoslavia, and the middle one separates the plateau of Mat from the plateau of Dibër. North of this central region, in north Albania proper, and to the south, in the district of Martanesh, no pattern can be discerned. The whole is a jumble of lofty ranges that strike off from each other at every conceivable angle. Those in north Albania throw up a multitude of peaks from their jagged crests; numerous valleys lie between them, each surprisingly narrow and steep-sided, some 3000 feet deep, all watered by a winter, if not by a perennial, stream, and many branching off right and left into side-valleys. In the district of Martanesh the ranges are rounded in outline, the summits are spreading instead of steep and sharp, large tracts of ground are comparatively unbroken, and in place of the countless valleys and streamlets of the north there are only a few deep ravines, each with a river on its floor.

These geographical characteristics have influenced the tribal cleft which still survives in the population. The main valleys in the north, such as Shalë, Shkrel or Orosh, are each capable of supporting a small unit such as a tribe, but seldom more. Appropriately, then, each is inhabited by a single tribe, which jealously prevents strangers from settling in its territory. The broad spaces farther south, such as the plateaux of Mat and Dibër, or the heights of Martanesh and adjacent Çermenikë, can carry a much larger population, in which no one tribe could hope to maintain its racial integrity or its political supremacy. Consequently, they are non-tribal and peopled partly by indigenous families, partly, at least in the case of Mat and Dibër, by immigrants, all of whom came in small numbers and many within recent memory. To quote only one example of each type, the Kadije family of Lis in eastern Mat is indigenous, and its neighbours at Burgajet, the Zogolli family, are immigrants.

More than the forms of social grouping have been affected by the physical features of the country. The number and height of the mountains have made stock-raising as important as agriculture to Albanians. Both parts of the range that rises sheer as a wall and green with forests from the coastal plain are over 3000 feet high, that of Krujë to the north being 3280–3940 feet and that of Dajt, which forms so beautiful a feature of the scenery round Tirana (Tiranë), 5290 feet—nearly 900 feet more than Ben Nevis and 1720 feet more than Snowdon. The parallel range which bounds the plateau of Mat on the east runs southwards from Mt Nezhdë in Lurë to Mt Dêjë and on to Mt Allaman at a height that is in few places below 5000 feet and is often above 6000 feet. The frontier range is still higher, composed as it is of Mt Gjalicë (8150 feet) and Mt Korab (9070 feet), the former in Lumë, the latter in Dibër. The topmost summits of the Martanesh area, Mt Kaptinë and Mt Lopë, are respectively 6145 and 6630 feet in height; the surrounding ranges average 5000 feet. As seen from Shkodër, the welter of northern mountains begins modestly with ranges 2000–2600 feet above sea-level, surpasses 7000 feet in several peaks of Lower Shalë, and culminates in the Accursed Alps (*Bjeshkët ë Nemuna*), where the close-set summits of Radohinë (8690 feet), Jezercë (8790 feet), Rosh (8270 feet) and Kolatë (8370 feet) wall off Yugoslavia from Upper Shalë in spectacular fashion. East of Shalë, the monster Peak of the Irons (*Majë e Hekuravë*, 8530 feet) divides the tribe of Mertur from the open plateau of Krasniqë. The passes across the mountains are often lofty and arduous. To take an extreme example, the only way from Shalë to Bogë, its western neighbour, is by the Sheep Track Pass, to the northern frontier by the Pejë Pass, and to Nikaj on the east by the Ndermajnë Pass, which are respectively 5900, 5600 and again 5600 feet above sea-level and take a day to traverse. It is self-evident that the tribesmen of Shalë have never seen much of their neighbours. Elsewhere geographical conditions are less formidable, yet generally severe enough to limit intercourse between communities.

It is clear that agriculture and permanent habitations must stop far below the summits of many mountains, and that on the highest slopes there can be only summer grazing. Throughout the area as a whole, however, there is so much summer and winter grazing that many Albanians live entirely by pastoralism and many others combine it with their agriculture. In this connexion it is essential to remember the part played by the immense forests. These spread over the grim mountains as well as the plains, saving Albania from the desiccated look of Dalmatia and Greece, and making its scenery agreeable to the eye at all seasons. The forest trees are of many kinds, with a large proportion of evergreens. Since they grow at different levels according to their kinds, three zones, named the shrub, oak and beech, or pine zones after their predominating tree, have been distinguished.[1]

Shrubs grow all over the plains near the coast and up to a height of 600 feet in exposed regions like Shkodër and Durrës and 1600 feet in sheltered spots like the gullies on Mt Dajt. They include tree heather, hornbeam, arbutus, wild olives, broom and the terrible Christ's Thorn (*Spina Cristi*), which, withered or green, tears the flesh so savagely with its spikes that it is popularly said all over the Near East to have been used for the Crown of Thorns. There is rough winter grazing among the shrubs, especially for

[1] See Gashi, *Shqipnija*, pp. 51–60.

goats and cattle, and some agriculture in clearings, but the zone derives its chief riches from the many acres of fertile alluvial soil that adjoin the rivers.

Oaks, tall or dwarf, begin sporadically among the shrubs and continue as thick forests up to a height of 2900 feet near Shkodër and 3300 feet in warmer districts. Among them grow ash, aspen, chestnut, cornel, elm, hawthorn, hazel, hornbeam and limes. The majority of the 1140 villages in north Albania are found in this zone, for it best provides for Albanian needs. Though the soil is dry on the whole, it contains a sufficiency of springs. On the plateaux and gentler slopes there is enough arable land for subsistence farming, all that is possible among these rugged mountains. The copses and woods furnish winter grazing for small flocks and herds; an adjoining mountain furnishes the requisite summer feed. The copses and woods also provide fuel for the log-fires that in Albanian phraseology are 'the poor man's wealth'. Leaves lopped from the oak trees in autumn supply winter fodder which livestock eat with almost as much relish as they do hay, a scarcer commodity. It is this supplement to the grazing in the copses and woods which makes mixed farming possible in this zone; without it many animals could not get through the winter, and their number would have to be reduced. If it is sometimes hot in the forest in summer, the heat is never unbearable, and in winter the cold is never excessive. In general the zone is healthy. A little wheat is grown, but—as everywhere in Albania, the Myzeqe plain excepted—the staple crop is maize. The grain provides food, and the livestock luxuries and government dues as well.

In the next zone beeches grow singly, in small clumps, or in mighty forests such as those between Çermenikë and Martanesh where one may walk for seven hours in the daytime and never catch a glimpse of the sun. Still without roads to carry modern woodcutters and their tools to them, such forests are in the virgin state, the trees self-sown, the strong killing the weak, and the survivors growing bigger and bigger until they succumb in extreme old age to some winter blast, when they lie and rot where they fall. When communications are developed, this waste will stop and these forests become a very valuable asset. No grass grows in them or under isolated beeches, of course, but there are usually grass meadows in the clearings, some of which are enormous. Well watered from the same sources as the beeches and fat with humus from decaying beech leaves, these meadows make magnificent grazing in summer.

Where the underlying rock is serpentine, the forests in this zone are of pitch pine, not beech. Following the rock formation the pines may continue above the beech limit as on Mt Munellë in Mirditë, Mt Nezhdë, and the Peak of the Irons in Shalë. Or they may grow as low as the oak zone, adding to its amenities with their timber and pastures. In certain districts they cover whole mountain sides, while beeches fill the intervening, moister valleys; for beeches like a damp soil, and pines a dryish. Whether among the trees or in the clearings, these forests are a paradise for animals. They have other values, too. Their lower reaches are accessible enough for the peasants to cut their timber, load it on ponies, or slide it down the mountain side to their villages, there to be used for building or other simple purposes. Pine slivers are the only form of lighting in many village houses, and they also bring in a little money, finding a ready sale in towns as kindling for fires.

The pine and beech zone is mostly too high for winter use. Near the coast its tree-limit is 5200–5600 feet above sea-level. Farther inland, where one range shelters another and the soil is damper, it may be 6000 feet, as on Mt Bukanik in Shpat or Mts Munellë and Nezhdë. On Mt Gjalicë it is 7000 feet. Between the tree-limit and the summits of higher mountains there is nothing but rock, scree and treeless pastures.

This pine zone is as necessary to Albanian economy as the oak zone. On much of the treeless ground above it the grass is so coarse that sheep will not eat it at all, and horses nibble it only at the beginning of the summer season and then with distaste. The grass of the pine and beech zone is sweet and palatable even to dainty sheep throughout the summer. On the agricultural side the zone serves as a great catchment area, not only for the huge, unharnessed rivers that traverse north Albania, but also for the myriads of invaluable little streams that flow down to the agricultural districts in the oak zone. Without these streams there could be little irrigation; without irrigation there could be little agriculture. Maize must have water, and there is never enough rain in summer to supply it.

In the two areas of summer pasturage, the beech and pine zone and the treeless slopes above it, many thousands of cattle, horses, goats, and especially sheep, graze from May to October. Their number is limited only by the amount of winter grazing available, which small owners find, and have always found, in the oak zone. In Turkish times, when Albania and Macedonia were both Turkish provinces and had no customs barriers between them as they have now, large owners sought it on the roomy plain of Salonica. Since Albanian emancipation in 1912 they have been confined to the more meagre pastures on the seaward side of the coastal plain at home, a restriction which has entailed a considerable cutting down of their flocks and herds. Nevertheless, in 1936–7 taxes were paid on 1,424,965 sheep, 773,969 goats, 144,763 cattle and 44,318 horses in the whole of Albania;[1] there are no separate figures for its northern half. Many more animals ran about the houses, unregistered and free of tax. For Albanians the importance of sheep lies, it should be noted, not only in their wool and meat as in England, but in their milk and the butter and cheese made from it.

If only the coastal plain were more spacious, it would be a perfect complement to the mountains for pastoralism on the grand scale. In the portion south of Lesh the rivers Drin, Mat and Ishm, entering the sea at points less than 6 miles apart, have created what is virtually one vast delta of mud and swamp, lush undergrowth, and trees that have come too quickly to maturity. Farther south, swamps of the same type cover much of the Plain of Durrës, and a great lagoon extends to the very outskirts of the town. Two more lagoons and a series of swamps mark the estuaries of the rivers Shkumbî and Seman on the coast of Myzeqe. More marshes and the lagoon of Kakarriq outline the course of the River Buenë in the north.

On the coast the average yearly rainfall is 39–47 inches, against 57 at Shkodër, 67 at Krujë and 72 at Pukë, an inland place 39 miles east of Shkodër. Albania is one of the wettest countries in Europe because so many of its ranges run from north to south and are high enough to intercept the rain-laden clouds that drift in from the west. The first rains fall in October when it is still hot on the coastal plain. The moisture and the heat combine to produce a luxuriant crop of new grass by the time that the sheep come down from the mountains.

This grass is found, not only in the hay meadows and swamps, but also, owing to the violence of the winter rains, on all the arable

[1] Gashi, *Shqipnija*, p. 117.

land. A high proportion of the year's rainfall falls in November and March:[1]

NOVEMBER	MARCH
Durrës 215 mm. (8·46 in.)	100 mm. (3·94 in.)
Shkodër 209 mm. (8·23 in.)	162 mm. (6·38 in.)
Krujë 337 mm. (13·27 in.)	157 mm. (6·18 in.)
Pukë 260 mm. (10·24 in.)	202 mm. (7·95 in.)

When a storm breaks over the mountains, every river and rivulet in the storm-swept area rises rapidly because the surface soil is seldom deep enough to retain much of the falling rain. In furious spate the rivers rush steeply towards the sea and, as they near the coast, spread far beyond their banks, engulfing many acres of arable land, and enlarging the marshes and lagoons so that they engulf many more. Because of this flooding, wheat cannot be sown near the coast. If sown in autumn, the November floods would wash it away, and after the March floods the ground does not dry in time for a spring sowing. Maize is, consequently, the only crop that can be raised. While awaiting its planting in late May, the fields lie fallow and grass-grown. The March floods are also responsible for the striking size and number of the hay meadows; much land never dries enough to grow even maize and must be left permanently under grass.

Climatically, too, the coastal plain dovetails into the high pastures. Whereas the mountains are deep in snow all winter, the temperature at the coast never falls quite to freezing-point. In January, the coldest month, the average recorded for Durrës and Valona (Vlonë) is respectively 47 and 48 degrees, with 40 and 41½ degrees at inland Shkodër and Tirana (Tiranë). Rain falls frequently and heavily, but unless a sudden rise in a river catches sheep unawares and sweeps them out to sea, neither animals nor shepherds come to much harm. By the end of May, when the rains cease, everything changes, and life near the swamps becomes intolerable for man and beast. Day temperatures rise swiftly towards their summer maximum of 86 degrees and the nights are hot, so that every movement is a burden. The dense vegetation of the swamps exudes odours as foetid as those in a tropical forest. Swarms of malaria-carrying mosquitoes emerge from the stagnant pools to attack man; swarms of gadflies, more savage than any

[1] Gashi, *Shqipnija*, p. 49.

known inland, attack beast; when thirst, a rarity in winter, drives an animal to forget its instinctive caution and to drink from a swamp, as likely as not a crop of leeches fastens on its tongue. So, as soon as they have sown their maize, the shepherds and their families and flocks desert the hot coast for the healthful pastures of the mountains.

CHAPTER II

THE UNWRITTEN LAW IN OUTLINE

To ensure for all, irrespective of their individual material wealth, a fair share of the essential grazing, arable land and irrigation, there has grown up a corpus of Unwritten Law. This was evolved at some unknown date by the mountaineers, as part of the legal framework which they had devised for every aspect of their life. They evolved all their laws—social, administrative, or pastoral—unaided. For many centuries before the Turks arrived in the fifteenth century, the country was split up into a number of principalities, none of which was strong enough for long to subject a neighbour to its rule. Though the Turks remained for four and a half centuries, they could never exert more than a nominal authority outside the chief towns. If they sent a punitive column into the interior, the people living in the mountains took evasive action, retreating to some peak until the inevitable departure of the intruders; their wealth was so small that they could carry or drive off most of it to their refuge, and so lost little from the raid. If the Turks sent tax or police officials, they fired on them at the first defile as a warning to return to their offices in town. There were no roads along which forces strong enough to be effective could march, in order to reduce them to real submission. The Turkish government, unable to enforce its will, accepted the situation and left the mountaineers to govern themselves, as they had presumably done under their native princes and chiefs. The first all-weather road to be built in North Albania was constructed in 1916 by the Austro-Hungarian armies during their temporary occupation; it ran from Shkodër to Durrës, with a branch to Tirana.

Every type of unwritten law has been constantly recast, added to, and restated down the centuries by a body of experts drawn from the rank of rulers. This rank exists because the mountaineers came to realize that an entity which is divided against itself cannot stand. Consequently, in every social unit—in house and village as in tribe or group of villages—the principle of subordination to a supreme head was accepted. In a household the headship is hereditary, with an important qualification. As the mountaineers are aware that a first-born may be inefficient, the mantle of a dead or dying head falls on the son who in the opinion of all the adult males in the household is the best fitted to keep it together, irrespective of whether he is the eldest or not.[1] This combination of birth and unanimity of choice gives these heads the strength of inevitability, so that they can be neither envied nor rebelled and intrigued against, but must be recognized and implicitly obeyed by their subordinates—a most important factor in keeping the peace.

Before the Turks left in 1912, the headship of a northern village or tribe descended in the same family, always to the head it had chosen for itself. Since 1912 successive Albanian governments have slightly modified this system. In non-tribal areas like Mat, Martanesh and Shpat there has been less need for a change; as far back as we can go, the head of the average village or group of villages has been elected by the community for his personal qualities in the same way as the head of a house. A few villages of Mat, however, had long been ruled by the landlords (*begs* or *beys*) who owned them; after 1912 the power of these landlords, the Zogu family excepted, was curtailed by the central government like that of the bajraktars of the north.

In the old days the laws were administered as well as enacted or revised by the ruling rank, who were collectively known as elders. The system was elaborate, with public trials over which elders presided, and at which evidence was taken from witnesses on oath as well as from the plaintiff and the accused, and a jury might be asked to render a verdict. Fines were the usual penalty for petty misdemeanours, and temporary banishment, permanent expulsion or death for serious offences; a modified form of imprisonment also existed. Offences against the cohesion of the social fabric, as understood by the mountaineers, were reckoned more serious than crimes against an individual. Thus parricide was graver than fratricide; the first struck a blow at parental authority, an essential part of the social structure, but since one brother had no right to rule another except in special cases, fratricide was little worse than an ordinary murder and hardly a public concern.[2] The murder of a neighbour or the theft of his property seldom entered the serious category until the criminal became an habitual offender. Then the community, regarding the man as a social menace from whom none of its members was safe, took whatever action the law laid down for

---

[1] See Chapter V.   [2] See Chapter V, p. 38.

his case. Since 1912 most of this administrative and penal legislation has been superseded of set purpose by European methods
and laws, whereas the social content of the old mountain code has
been left comparatively undisturbed, free to come into line with
the ways of the West in its own time.

The community sense was fostered by every art the mountaineers
knew. Each member of a household was encouraged to regard
everything in it and everything its other members said and did as
his own. The humblest man was encouraged to regard his village
or group of villages as his personal property. If home, village or
group of villages prospered, he rejoiced as if he had himself been
advanced. If they were insulted or injured, he burned to avenge
a personal affront. If they were disgraced by misconduct on the
part of another member, he felt his own honour to be smirched.
The patriotism so bred was narrow, perhaps, but it was genuine,
free from egregious self-seeking, and by its emphasis on the need
to keep the community's honour untarnished, a good deterrent
from crime.

This close relationship between individual and community was
also a curb on dictatorship. The ruling rank had always to respect
the individual's property in the community's laws. They could not
make any change in an existing law unless they obtained the consent
of a General Assembly of their village or tribe. They could impose,
but (except in the tribes which maintained fine-collectors) they
could not collect fines; social pressure was necessary for that. In
a very common punishment, social ostracism, they might play no
more than a subordinate part. They could not pass heavy sentences
like banishment or death unless a General Assembly demanded
them, and if it did, they could not resist its will. In short, the
elders voiced, but did not dictate, popular sentiment.

They were no privileged oligarchy either. They might sit in the
seat of honour or get the lamb's head and eye at a banquet, but
they had no official residences, horses or guards of honour
provided for them at public expense. They lived in houses that
were often meaner than those of their subordinates; they ate the
same food and toiled in the same way in their fields and among their
flocks. In fact, the self-government of the Albanian mountaineers
went far towards being true democracy in the Anglo-American
sense of that much-abused word. In its primitive way it was really
government of the People, by the People, for the People. It had

its defects, of course; sometimes a judge took a bribe or a man bore false witness in spite of the deterrents devised against such malpractices. Yet the legal system worked well on the whole, was often speedier and always cheaper than any European counterpart, and left few crimes unsolved. What chiefly precluded modern Albanian governments from adopting the unwritten laws, however, was their diversity. This was mainly due to the isolation in which the geography of their country compels the mountaineers to live, and the fact that they do not settle permanently at altitudes more than 3000 feet above sea-level, but live on the lower slopes of the mountains enclosing their settlement and in summer graze the upper slopes as far as the mountain crests, where a carefully demarcated boundary indicates the end of their property.

Communications were as dangerous as they were difficult. As a result the principle of delegating one man to represent a big geographical unit was not established until modern times. It was regularly practised in small units, where the delegate had to travel only a short distance, and that through known, if not friendly, country. It was enough that one man should represent his house at a General Meeting of his village or tribe, but it was unthinkable to the mountaineers to hold General Meetings at which laws for the whole area might be passed as in an English Parliament. At best two adjoining communities might meet to settle a dispute about their common boundary or a road or forest, and after much argument make laws about the matter that were binding on both. More usually, a village or tribe drew up or revised rules for its own governance without any regard to what others, ten, twenty or fifty miles away, were doing. The outlines of a law might approximate in different groups, especially if there had been some ancestral connexion between them, but the details of the law were as varied as the minds that shaped them in the various communities.

The isolation in which it lived bred a fierce individualism in each community. This prevented it from submitting to the laws of another, except in an emergency. Then it might call in an elder from outside to decide a case and afterwards consider his ruling law. Such an elder had to be specially renowned for wisdom and sound judgement, and with one known exception his influence never ran far beyond the distance he could ride in safety and comfort from his own community.

That exception was Lek Dukagjini, an ancient law-giver of such eminence that what he said is still as sacred as Holy Writ to the mountaineers of Mirditë and all the tribes to the north, including those unjustly incorporated in Yugoslavia in 1912–13. According to tradition it was he who framed the laws by which the mountaineers still live. More probably, like Solon of Athens, he revised and codified existing laws, though apparently without setting them down on paper. Numerous items in his code resemble those known among the Romans and other ancient peoples, and in the versions we have there are many signs of evolution from earlier forms. The code is said to be best preserved in Mirditë, where its items were collected about 1913 by the eminent Franciscan scholar, Father Shtjefen Gjeçov, though his book was not published until 1933. A few years previously he had been murdered by Yugoslavs, as is related in a brother Franciscan's preface to the book.[1]

Little is known of Lek's personality. He must have been a man of standing as well as genius and fine character to have imposed his will on the rude mountaineers of his time, so he may well have belonged to the princely medieval family of north Albania which took its name from Dukagjin, a district lying between the Great Mountains (*Malësi e Madhe*) of the far north and the river Drin, and inhabited by twelve tribes of which Shalë is the chief. Tradition represents him as an older contemporary of Skanderbeg, the national hero of modern Albania, who, born in 1403, died in 1467 after resisting the Turkish invaders of his country as gallantly and as unavailingly as William Wallace of Scotland resisted the English. The Mirditë tribes are also reported to have been living near Mt Bishtrik in north-east Albania when they learned Lek's code. As they moved to their present fastness under Turkish pressure in the fifteenth century,[2] we are fairly safe in maintaining that Lek's legislation has survived at least five centuries of oral transmission, a high tribute to its quality and to his personality.

Traditions gathered in areas as far apart in every sense as Moslem Lumë in east Albania and Catholic Shalë and Shkrel in the north say that Lek's main stronghold was the now ruined fort of Drisht near Shkodër. He had another in Has in east Albania which commanded the ford crossing the Drin at Spas, five hours below Kukës; it is perched above the water on the last of a line of

---

[1] An Italian translation of Lek Dukagjini's canon was published in Rome in 1941 by the Reale Accademia d'Italia.
[2] M. E. Durham, *Some Tribal Origins*, etc., p. 30.

denuded peaks linked by perilous natural bridges. The track, once paved in parts, which leads eastwards from Drisht to Shalë is still called 'Lek's road', and there is a 'Lek's rock' in several districts, notably Shalë, Berishë and Surroj. He fought on against the Turks for at the least twelve years after Skanderbeg died, and surrendered only when the Turks promised to respect the unwritten laws of the mountains. He then fled to Hungary, where he died.

These traditions are as persistent as they are widespread; those given here tally reasonably well with what Miss Durham heard among the Catholics thirty years earlier. The detail about Lek's conditional surrender is curious, recalling the similar terms given to the Greeks of Constantinople by the Turks in 1453. But there can be no proving or disproving the traditions, unless evidence is eventually found in the Vatican archives; the records in Albanian churches have been burned again and again, together with the buildings. It seems likely, however, that popular memory has confused Lek the law-giver with a warrior of later date.[1]

To mountaineers everywhere Lek the law-giver's code is known as his *kanún*, for which reason Father Gjeçov's book is entitled *Kanuni i Lek Dukagjinit* ('The Code of Lek Dukagjini'). The editor rightly derives the word from the Greek κανών ('rule'), but does not give its interesting pedigree. It came, not directly from Greek, for north Albania has never been under Greek influence, but through Turkish and Arabic. In the words of Professor H. A. R. Gibb, 'the Greek word was very early incorporated into Arabic as qānūn, pl. qawānīn. The Islamic jurists adopted it to designate an administrative regulation, as distinct from the Revealed Law (*Sharī'a*), and many centuries later the Ottoman Sultans adopted it as the designation of their legislative rescripts. The point of retaining this term was that it suggested no interference with, or modification of, the Revealed Law.' To Turkish officials stationed in Albania after its conquest, Lek's code was naturally a *kanún*. Aloof though the Albanian mountaineers held themselves from these officials, they learned a number of their technical terms, as will appear from other examples in this book. They made *kanún* so much their own that they still say something is illegal in pure Albanian (*ligja nuk e ep*, lit. 'the law does not give it') or in mixed Turkish and Albanian (*kanuni nuk e ep*). But,

[1] Perhaps Lek Dukagjini III, 1459–79.

curiously, they never call Lek's code anything but *kanún*, and so the Catholics amongst them are the only Christians in Europe who have a Canon Law that is not ecclesiastical.

Lek's power, says a tradition referred to in Father Gjeçov's book, extended as far south as the town of Lesh, which he made his capital. Overcoming every difficulty of geography and human obstructiveness, he used to convoke the mountain chiefs to parliament there and after discussion promulgated his laws. No less a personage than Skanderbeg was among the deputies. On p. 121 of Father Gjeçov's book there is a lively description of the argument between the two Alexanders—both Lek and Skander are Albanian forms of Alexander—which ended in their both proclaiming the important doctrine that all men are equal in the sight of the law.

Skanderbeg, if primarily a warrior, was also a law-giver, and it is his code which still guides the mountaineers of Dibër, Mat and Krujë, the three districts with which he was chiefly associated. His family took its patronymic Kastrioti from the hill-fort of Kastriot in Dibër; it was at Krujë that his stout resistance to the Turks made the Pope of the day hail him as the Champion of Christendom. His jurisdiction extended no farther, suggesting that without his military exploits his fame as a law-giver would have faded. In areas farther south where the mountaineers still obey unwritten laws, as in Martanesh and Shpat, no law-giver is remembered a generation or two after his death. The northern limit of Skanderbeg's jurisdiction was fixed by Lek with characteristic wisdom, according to a tradition prevalent in Milot. Once when Skanderbeg was at Dibër and Lek at Shkodër, the former suggested that they should come and meet each other, the point at which they met to be the boundary line between their spheres of influence. When Lek agreed, Skanderbeg set off at sunrise, the canonical time for beginning a journey. But Lek set off four hours earlier and so met his rival at the Kullë Pashaj ('Pasha's Tower') in Mat, which remains to this day the boundary between the two *kanúns*. In general Lek was too clever for Skanderbeg. Once, says another tradition from Milot, Lek, who had a he-goat while Skanderbeg had a steer, suggested that they should swop animals. When this had been done, Lek was heard to mutter: 'He-goat this year, he-goat next year; steer this year, ox next year.'

CHAPTER III

THE ALBANIAN HOUSE

At its simplest an Albanian peasant's house was very simple indeed—no more than a small, square room with walls of undressed stones from the nearest stream; a man so poor had no money or time to spend on transporting better materials from a distance. The stones were bedded in mud and bound together every three feet or so by horizontal beams; in their turn the 'belts' were strengthened, particularly at the corners, by cross-timbers. The roof was a steep framework of timber covered with stone slabs but never with thatch or boards, for the house would stand no chance if an enemy flung a blazing firebrand on these. The doorway was low, but the wooden door, emblematic of the insecurity that lasted until Turkish rule ended, was strong enough not to be easily broken down from outside. In most cases there was not even a hole in the wall for window, and there was never a chimney—a ring of stones in the middle kept the log-fire in its place, and the smoke found its own way out between the rafters unhampered by a ceiling. A kitchen-crook, a most important article, was suspended over the fire from a tie-beam. The floor was of beaten earth. In sum, the house was the most rudimentary type of stone and timber architecture.

The furnishings were in keeping. They consisted of a three-legged stool or two, a box or pile of bedding but no bedsteads, a rough shelf with a frying-pan and a few platters and pots, a big metal jug for boiling water, an earthenware pot for holding drinking water, a round dining-table on stumpy supports about ten inches high, a flour-bin, a pan for mixing bread, perhaps a pan for baking it, and nothing for washing—the nearest stream served for that. A metal tray with coffee cups inverted to keep them clean and a tiny pot with a long handle for making Turkish coffee rested by the hearth, a few satchels of home-dressed wool and a distaff hung on the wall, and a hen stared at the company from her nest under the eaves. The only ornaments were yellow maize-cobs, rosy pomegranates, and strings of onions or garlic, all hanging from the tie-beams. At meal times a cat took up a vantage point under the dining-table, to filch what it could. It was never caressed or deliberately fed; the whole Balkans believed that either indulgence would stop it from catching mice.

A man and his wife, with one or two small children, might live in this house. Of a kind hardly paralleled in the Balkans, except in the poorer parts of southern Greece, it was not common in Albania as a permanent dwelling. As soon as its master could scrape together the necessary money, he added a sitting-room. As he provided all the labour himself and needed to hire only one professional, a stone-mason who, like all his brethren in the Balkans, was also a carpenter, ten pounds sterling were enough. The sitting-room might be built on top of the kitchen (*shtëpí* or *shpi*, lit. 'house', from Lat. *hospitium*) or against one of its walls. It had a wooden floor, a chimney at one end, a window or two, a niche in the wall beside the hearth for the utensils for making coffee, and a few wooden pegs near the door on which to hang up rifles; it might also have a ceiling. It generally had a separate entrance, for sitting-rooms were men's apartments and Catholic, Moslem, and Orthodox Albanians all segregated their young women. The Catholics and Orthodox attributed this custom to plain jealousy, and the Moslems, less convincingly, to a desire to obey their Prophet's order. In the evening and when not at work outside during the daytime, the master of the house with his men guests reclined, ate and smoked in the sitting-room, while his wife and children remained in the draughty kitchen. But the men were less comfortable than might have been expected. Since Albanian chimneys seldom drew, acrid fumes from the wood fire filled the room and almost made them weep unmanly tears. But not quite, for if they succumbed, they would be derided as 'poor sticks' who 'would never see to shoot'.

Guests, in the form of family friends or strangers 'sent by God', often came for a night. Because there were no inns in the Albanian countryside except on the long-distance tracks used by pack-horses, it was the rule that a benighted stranger might claim supper and shelter till the morning from any house he saw. The hospitality was never refused or charged for, but travellers of standing were expected to give a sum proportionate not to the hospitality offered but to their supposed wealth.

As soon as the children in a two-roomed house grew up, its master must build again. His daughters went forth to live in their husbands' homes, but his sons brought their brides to his house and each couple required a separate bedroom. If he were very poor, he might be unable to provide anything better than a lean-to in the farmyard, but the average man built a proper house round the nucleus of sitting-room and kitchen. In the first of the two types to which this house might conform, a number of rooms were grouped together sideways, sometimes on one floor only, usually on two, but rarely on more. In the second type one room was built on top of another, as in a tower, for two, three or even four storeys. This type was always known as a *kullë* (lit. 'tower'), a description also often given to a two- or three-storeyed cluster, although, more usually, any clustered house was called *shtëpí*, the name of the original kitchen. Access to the upper floor in the clustered type was usually by an inner, fixed staircase, and in a tower by an inner ladder that could be pulled up if an enemy penetrated to the ground floor; a trapdoor hung over both staircase and ladder, ready to be closed in an instant, if necessary. The two types of house were found side by side. The clustered one was preferred because its rooms were easier of access, but a family with many enemies or little land fell back on a tower as it was more defensible and took up less space. Whereas a clustered house stood in a farmyard surrounded by a fence of withered thorn or, more frequently, a stone and timber wall of the same construction as that of the house, a tower had generally no farmyard. All its appurtenances—livestock, farm implements, hay or other fodder— were gathered under its own roof, on the ground floor, as being more secure. In a one-storeyed cluster livestock, farm implements, and probably dairy and kitchen as well, were housed in sheds in the yard to save space in the house. In a two-storeyed cluster they were more often accommodated on the ground floor as in a tower, but for convenience rather than security, which was guaranteed by the farmyard wall. Since the sitting-room in such a house was often over the cow-house, it contained an ingenious labour-saving device for use after supper. As soon as the table had been removed, the host swept the crumbs towards a small, unobtrusive hole in the floor in front of the hearth, removed its lid, and with a last flick of his broom dropped the crumbs on the animals below. In a tower the kitchen was over the cow-shed and under the bedrooms, and these in turn were under the men's sitting-room.

In a tower or a two-storeyed cluster there might, for security

reasons, be no openings in the ground-floor walls except the doorway, but square holes were left in those of the upper floor for
windows. Except in rich houses these 'windows' were not glazed.
At night they were closed in rich as in poor houses by propping
stone slabs against them or sliding wooden panels across them.
Those in a one-storeyed cluster were usually too high for the curious
outside to peep through or the hostile to shoot through. Nikollë
Gjetë Coka of Breg i Matit, putting his trust in the exemplary
peace which King Zog's government had established throughout
Albania, neglected this ancient precaution and was shot in 1938
by some Mirdites who thrust their rifles through the window of the
room in which he sat at supper. At the top of a tower there were
usually loop-holes, splayed to give a wider field of fire and low
enough to let a man kneel as he shot. When these were found in
a clustered house, as they often were, it was naturally on a vulnerable
side, where they might also be reinforced by turrets in the wall of
the farmyard. In the kitchen, where the women and children must
spend the day and evening, the hearth continued in the middle
because more people could sit round it in that position.

In planning his house the Albanian householder sought chiefly
shelter from the elements and his enemies, and took no thought for
beauty. When villages are picturesque, as many are, it is always for
such extraneous reasons as their site, the line of their roofs against
a lightly clouded sky, and the greenery surrounding them, rather
than for the architecture of their individual houses. A tower, it is
true, may have machicoulis over its door or under an upper window,
and these give it distinction; its elevation and its usual situation on
a knoll may also be attractive. The best examples, some of them
over two hundred years old, may be seen in Lurë. But few
clustered houses are more than an assemblage of featureless boxes.

In the bigger houses the furnishings altered little from those of
the simplest type already described. Mattresses and pillows were
probably added to the bedding, and the floor of the sitting-room,
instead of being left bare, was covered with mats made from reeds
grown in the swamps near the coast. In the cold north and north-
east there was usually a layer of earth under the mats; it made an
admirable shield against winter blasts. Chairs remained rarities
and stools were still confined to the kitchen with its chilly earthen
floor. Workers being more plentiful, enough animals to make butter
could be kept; the churn was made by hollowing out a section of

2-2

tree-trunk. A similar section, split lengthways and hollowed out, made two wash-tubs for laundry work. Toilet appliances, a basin and ewer bought in the bazaar, and paraffin lamps from the same source, completed the list of additions.

The above outline omits many small variations in Albanian houses and furniture as irrelevant to the main subject of this book. Mention must be made, however, of certain houses which differed widely from the average type. The first were found among the Highlanders (Alb. *Malësorë*, 'mountaineers'), the semi-nomads who wintered on the soggy plains at the mouth of the river Mat. These houses had walls of planking or wattle and daub, with roofs of tiles or strips of wood. They rested on vertical sections of tree trunks about two feet high which had been laid at close intervals on the ground but had not been driven into it like piles. In this way they kept snug and dry even during the winter floods. All over Albania granaries were raised some distance from the ground in order to keep out the rats, but so far as is known, there were no houses on stilts except at the mouth of the Mat.

A number of Highland houses also contained a child's play-pen which might be as little as twenty-five inches long, wide and high. A shallow porringer projected from one of the top bars, chipped from the same piece of wood as the bar itself. In this pen Highland children spent all their winter days from the time they could crawl until they were three years old. They had no toys, but practised walking round the pen, sometimes stopping to eat a little bread and milk from the porringer with the diminutive home-made, wooden spoon which was tied to the bar, or merely gazing broodingly at the fire. The mothers meanwhile cooked, spun or gossiped, each secure in the knowledge that her child was on the dry floor of the kitchen and not sitting outside in the quagmire of mud that reached up to the very doorstep. The Highlanders said they invented both the houses and the play-pen themselves, but it is possible that they were at least advised by the Austro-Hungarian troops who were stationed in the neighbourhood for part of the war of 1914–18.

In Shpat, near Elbasan, huts were built for many bridegrooms. In the higher villages trunks of young trees about as tall as a man's waist were planted in a rectangle of the size desired, their boughs, while still green and flexible, were laced in and out of these uprights, and cross-pieces of timber were nailed to the uprights to keep the structure rigid. When a light roof thatched with straw or more boughs had been nailed on and the inner walls had been plastered with mud, the hut was ready for occupation. Quickly built and costing only the price of the nails, it was often larger and more comfortable than the sitting-room in the adjacent house. A folk-tradition says it was long the handsomest dwelling to which any country Albanian aspired. At lower altitudes in Shpat the huts were flimsier as befitted the milder climate. They were usually made of reeds plastered with cow-dung, which was sufficient to keep out the wind.

Three houses of more splendid type, each containing about forty souls, exist at Dibër—Hysni Dema's at Homesh, Murat Kaloshi's at Kandër, and Cen Elezi's at Sllovë. The owners were rich and most hospitable Moslem notables. As some of the older generation were schooled in Constantinople, they complemented their culture and their position by building establishments of Turkish inspiration, with separate blocks of buildings for the men's apartments (Tk. *selamlik*), stables, granaries, storehouses, kitchens and women's apartments (Tk. *haremlik*). These are all enclosed within a high stone wall with defensive turrets at every weak point, especially near the one and only gateway. The women's apartments are really only a series of bedrooms, one for each married man and his wife and children, and the women, for want of a common sitting-room, sit normally in the kitchen like their poorer sisters. Softer mattresses, richer floor-rugs, and fireplaces in the bedrooms indicate the family's wealth, but European beds, tables and chairs are still barred, partly to avoid rousing envy in more backward neighbours. Cen Elezi's sitting-room was a magnificent oblong, warmed by a log-fire in a huge chimney at the far end from the door and softly lit on both its long sides by a row of short windows at the top of the tall walls; enemies outside had as usual to be prevented from shooting through the outer windows, and the men inside must not be able to look through the inner ones at the women's apartments. In this room a hundred travellers supped and slept every night, going their separate ways at dawn; a chef, working in a kitchen of his own and slaughtering a couple of sheep or an ox per night, provided the unvarying menu of soup, boiled meat, bread and rice pilaff. In their retired kitchen the women catered for themselves and the children, when there was no over-flow from the chef's.

A man's house, simple or elaborate, was his own, and he could do what he would with it up to a point. But he held it on conditions laid down by the Unwritten Law. This law defined a house as 'any hut or building of one, two, or more storeys that has a hearth and emits smoke', and insisted that poor house and rich house are alike inviolable. A stranger might not enter either without first hailing the master by name. If very discreet, he would call out from some distance; if bolder or on friendly terms with the family, he might lawfully enter the yard first. If no one answered his call, he must wait there or go away. On no account might he push the door open; that would make him a housebreaker. In the old days it would have cost him the usual penalties for theft, a fine of five hundred *grosh* ('piastres') for housebreaking, plus the obligation to send the family two of every article found missing after his visit, and even more recently it caused strife that might end in shooting. It was of no use for him to plead that he knew the master was from home; he knew also that somebody must have been left in the master's place.

The law allowed a man to erect a new house anywhere on his own ground, subject to the all-important provision that it did no harm to his neighbour's house and ground. In this connexion the term 'house' comprised, not only the dwelling, but also the farm-yard wall or fence, and everything that this enclosed. It followed that a new house must be kept at least the width of its eaves from the neighbour's boundary to make sure that the rain dripping from them should not damage his property. The method most commonly adopted to ensure this was to leave space enough for a man to pass on foot between the new house and the neighbour's boundary. If a man wanted plenty of elbow-room, however, he might build his house as much as two *pashë* ('fathoms') from the boundary. As his visitors were as free as members of his family to use the empty space, a sizeable road was soon trodden out. Sometimes, too, a man who looked into the future left room for a road that was still non-existent but might one day be wanted by the community, in which contingency his house would otherwise have had to be pulled down and rebuilt elsewhere.

There were also a number of minor rules to be remembered in building. According to the law in Fulqet, if several men had contiguous land, they must build their houses as near as possible to the point at which their land met. Otherwise their several dogs would not recognize them and when A came to till his field, B's dog would treat him as an intruder and bite him, and he would have no legal claim to compensation for the injury. It is not known if this law obtained elsewhere, but the common sense on which it is based makes it probable that it did. Again, in the Moslem villages near enough to Elbasan to conform to the rigidity with which Moslem townsmen secluded their women, it was not permitted to make windows in a wall overlooking a neighbour's farmyard; the latter's womenfolk must be free to move about their yard unwatched. This ban on windows—which was Moslem, not Albanian—hardly extended to remoter Moslem villages, as women there enjoyed almost as much liberty as did their Christian ancestresses.

A man's ownership of his house and land was so absolute that he and his might emigrate temporarily or for good without losing their title to either house or land. Even if the family absented itself for a hundred years, no one might squat on its property. If the emigrant, before leaving, sold his land 'together with all that is on it', and one leaving for good usually did so, the piece constituting the site of the house remained his in spite of the terms of sale, and so long as one stone stood on another, no one might use the site. In Mirditë, however, a fixed term was set to this law; if the emigrant did not return within ten years, his house might be occupied by whosoever wanted it.

Every dwelling that emitted smoke might have one or more of the following accessories—yard, vegetable garden, field, road, boundary and, in suitable latitudes, vineyard. Of these the boundary and road were the most indispensable.[1] Every owner of a dwelling that emitted smoke had a right to graze his animals on the summer and winter pasturage owned by his village and to cut firewood and timber for his own use in the public coppices and forests. If he cared to build a bothy for his shepherds on a summer pasture or to break in ground for a field or vegetable garden on a common near his village, he was welcome to do so. He must first secure the consent of the elders of the village, who generally put the common weal before individual convenience. Their permission given, no one could stop his tilling the ground, nor turn him out. Theoretically every dwelling that emitted smoke should also have a portion of irrigation water, but the right to sell water often made this provision a dead letter.

[1] See Chapters VIII and IX.

Obviously the crude and comfortless character of the Albanian house indicated a low standard of living and dire poverty in the ordinary sense of the word. But the Albanian had his compensations. He was secure in what he had, and unless he lived in an over-populated area like Dibër, he had the essentials. In alluvial areas like Myzeqe and in a few villages in the district of Mat there were big estates worked by share-croppers, but with these few exceptions the Albanian owned his house and land and need not think of rent or eviction. Since forests and commons belonged to his village or tribe and their products were free to him and his fellows, he need think only of the trouble involved in fetching his firewood and grazing his sheep. With luck he might have surplus animals to sell in a market town for money that would pay for his taxes, for clothing, for imported goods like coffee and sugar, and, costliest of all, for brides. With subsistence as his only possible aim, he need not work every day and so enjoyed a good deal of leisure. In short, although his comforts and amenities were few, so also were his worries.

CHAPTER IV

THE ALBANIAN HOUSEHOLD

Society in the Albanian mountains was patrilineal, and took so little account of women that whereas the names of ancestors in the male line might be known for as many as twenty generations, those in the female line were forgotten after two or three. In the words of the Unwritten Law 'a man has blood, and a woman kin', i.e. a man has a pedigree, and a woman her own relatives, and 'a woman is anybody's daughter', i.e. comes from anywhere and has no pedigree.

As usual in patrilineal societies, all property and rights were vested in the men. So when a man married, his house belonged to him exclusively and not at all to his wife, neither priest nor law having bound him to endow her with his worldly goods. The Unwritten Law states further that 'a wife is a sack for carrying' things, i.e. she was in her husband's house to bear his children. It was also understood, however, that she must take an active part in the work of both the farm and the house. In consequence, the wife in a household containing only a married pair and their small children led a life of almost unrelieved hardship, all the relaxations and leisure going to the husband. Since the Unwritten Law forbade her to have any dealings with the outside world until she was old, she stayed at home to work while her husband went to market to shop and sell, visited government offices to discuss the payment— or non-payment—of his taxes, and arranged the future marriages of his children. Whether it was a kerchief, a daughter-in-law, or nothing at all that he bought for her, he never consulted her wishes and she might not murmur openly at his choice. Nor might she remonstrate with him if he idled when at home; any such criticism would only make him beat her. The Unwritten Law said that the husband was the head of the wife and might punish her for indiscipline as well as misconduct. There was plenty of secret grumbling of course. Thus a pretty young woman in Mat was heard to complain that her husband spent all the money he could find on coffee and cigarettes for himself and left her, after five years of marriage, 'without a rag to her back'. 'And it's for him I toil and moil the whole blessed day', she ended, sadly rather than bitterly.

Toil and moil she did. The daily duties of every peasant woman in her position included fetching firewood from the forest and water from the river or spring, besides cooking, washing and baking for the household. At certain seasons she must also do farm work, so long as she retained a measure of youth. Her husband did heavy work like ploughing, scything hay, or cutting oak leaves for winter fodder. But she must carry the manure from the stable to the fields in spring, help her husband to sow and earth up the maize and, while he stayed indoors, reap it. She must carry home the hay and fodder and feed them to the animals. If grain was trodden out by horses or oxen, her husband drove them; if threshed with flails, she wielded them. If there was no miller, she conveyed the grist to the mill, ground it, and brought back the flour. Only if there were a miller did these tasks devolve on her husband, and then it was only in order to keep her virtue above suspicion. In poor families she was herself the beast of burden, and when young was expected to carry up to seventy pounds. In richer families she had a horse or donkey to do the actual carrying, unless her home was under snow in winter. Then she must brave the snow that confined the animal to its stable and bring in supplies of firewood and water, fodder and flour. Paucity of workers prevented her husband from having more than a couple of milch-goats or ewes, and these were tethered; it was she who tethered, watered and milked them. It was she, too, who turned their milk into curds (*kos*) or butter and cheese, arduous tasks in summer when milk sours easily. She also saw to the poultry and in her spare time knitted or span.

Fortunately for the women, there was almost no peasant household in which a young husband and wife were the only workers. The eldest child, boy or girl, began at seven or eight years of age to herd the goats as they roamed in search of food and saw to them morning and evening. This gave the mother some relief and provided the family with more food and, by the sale of the goats themselves or the kids, more money. When very small, the girl must spin or knit as she herded; when in her teens, she must sew her trousseau; but no extra tasks were expected of boy herds. Since, too, a man's mother and sisters never lost their legal right to share his home, a family might include the husband's mother and even his unmarried sister or his widowed, childless sister. In that event, while the younger women worked outside, his mother, if physically fit, remained at home to cook, sweep and bake, besides attending to the dairy and poultry. She also saw that any children who were big enough to walk but too small to follow their mother to the fields, did not fall into the fire or otherwise come to grief. She further entertained any men visitors who might come when her son was absent. She did not, however, wash her clothes or her husband's, should he be still alive, for even at the height of the busy season outside that was one of her daughter-in-law's duties. When she was no longer strong enough for her various tasks, she was sent out, complete with distaff, to herd the goats or plough-oxen and another woman succeeded her as housekeeper.

If the married pair had a separate bedroom, it was private property, as inviolable as a separate house would be, and no one other than the man and his wife and children might enter uninvited. Unless she was his wife, even the housekeeper was under the ban. It followed that when a wife worked outside, she must care herself for her bedroom, sweeping it, spreading the bedding at night, and picking this up again in the morning. She must also tend her children, and wash and mend their clothes, her husband's and her own, besides those of her mother-in-law. If she had a tiny baby, she carried it in its cradle on her back to the fields, left it in a shady place while she worked, and carried it home again in the evening.

If the house was too small to have a sitting-room, the husband ate in the kitchen. He never lingered over the meal, and in most districts ate alone unless his mother, privileged by having brought him into the world, wished to join him. A man who ate with his wife or sat much in her company courted public ridicule as unmanly and 'no class'. If there was a sitting-room, the husband probably took his midday meal in the kitchen and his evening meal in the sitting-room. Before supper he might invite his sons or even his daughters, if these were small, to share the comfort of the sitting-room for a little.

Peasant households with only one man in them were rare, since for economic reasons it was customary for several brothers or even several first cousins to live together until their children were of an age to marry. Then sheer pressure of population compelled the household to split up into smaller units, each with a house of its own.[1]

[1] See Chapter VI.

When the men in a household were numerous, three or more might be shepherds, one tending the sheep, another the goats, and a third the oxen; several might be farmers who ploughed and hoed and irrigated; yet others might be housemen, one keeping the house supplied with firewood, a second going to the bazaar, and a third grinding grain at the local mill for the household's bread. Each thus contributed his quota to the family wealth, and obviously the more numerous the quotas, the greater the general comfort. A well-to-do household which had only a few men might make up the number of hands available by engaging servants. 'Çota's tableful' is now proverbial in Çermenikë because eighteen men—ten relatives and eight hirelings—used to sit down nightly to supper in Sali Çota's house in the village of Fenars in that district. If, however, a household were poor as well as small, it could not risk having to pay servants in a bad year, and must restrict its activities—for example, by keeping only sheep or goats but not both. Since sheep eat grass and goats leaves, they must have separate herds.

Even in the richest of these multiple households the women lived much as they did in small, poor ones. A housekeeper, who was generally elderly, cooked and baked for the whole family, swept the kitchen, the men's sitting-room, and her own bedroom if she had one apart from the kitchen, but did not enter any room belonging to a married man, even if he was her son. The young wives worked out of doors when required and at all times looked after their children, husband and bedroom. They were often exempt from fetching firewood and water and were reasonably fed and dressed, but otherwise fared no better than their poorer sisters. By and large, even in these relatively more leisured homes, women worked much harder than men. The latter excused their comparative idleness by saying that in Turkish times, when blood feuds raged, it had been death for most men to show their faces outside in the daytime, and if the family was not to die of starvation the women had to work for its bread. They claimed that when blood feuds grew rarer, they became more industrious. But they could never produce any evidence that the women had gained by their new diligence.

Soon after sunset the men sat down to sup at the same table in the sitting-room, while the women and children ate at another table in the kitchen. The food was brought to the sitting-room by the housekeeper who remained discreetly out of sight behind the door where she handed it to the men. She must wash up but, warned by the proverb which says of work done badly by firelight because there are no lamps, 'Evening's work, morning's laugh', she waited till the next day. Then her task was much less formidable than one might think. At both the men's and the women's table everybody ate out of a common dish, fingers were used for a meat course, and one and the same wooden spoon dealt with soup and any semi-liquid food that followed. The men generally had their own spoons as they thought this more hygienic; they washed them themselves—rather sketchily—immediately after supper, and tucked them into their breast, ready for the next meal at home or at a friend's. If coffee was served, the master of the house or his deputy rinsed out the cups, for the precious utensils must never leave the sitting-room in case the women took to drinking coffee. Twenty men could sup on soup, meat, bread, curds and coffee without the housekeeper's having more than three centre dishes and the dining-table to wash.

A multiple household might contain as many as twenty persons, a goodly enough number but only a pale reflexion of past glories. All over north Albania it used to be the custom for brothers, first and even second cousins to live with their wives and children, and probably several aged uncles and aunts and young sisters, under the same roof. Enormous housefuls sometimes resulted. For instance, there were sixty-four people in Gjon Macaj's house in Perlat about 1900, ninety-five in Isuf Isaku's in Zdrâjshë in 1923, and seventy in Lushan Sadrija's in Shalë even more recently. The houses themselves, though conforming to the regulation pattern of men's sitting-room, kitchen, stables, store-rooms, and one bedroom for every family unit, were remarkably small by our standards. Quite a little bedroom suffices for seven or eight persons if they all sleep on the floor, and both the sitting-room and the kitchen often served as dormitories, the former for men guests and the unmarried or widowed men of the family and the latter for women guests and the widows of the family. The primary cause of this way of life was the lack of public security in former times. Enemies and bandits could wreak their will on a single-handed man, but had to respect one surrounded by well-armed guards, and these the trustiest possible, his nearest relatives. After Albania became independent, public security improved so much that the need for a family to see to its own safety disappeared, and with it the need for several generations to huddle together under one roof if they wished to survive. Consequently, immense households like that of Gjon Macaj disappeared.

In the families of the landed gentry of Dibër such as Cen Elezi, life followed rather different lines. Most of the young men went into government or army service and left their wives and children at home, visiting them when they obtained leave, and the farm work was done by hired servants with the help and under the supervision of any of the family who might have remained at home. The women were organized on the customary pattern, with some variation in detail. A housekeeper cooked, but only for the women and children, since a special chef was required to cope with the hospitable requirements of the *selamlik*.[1] Each young wife attended to her own room and children besides cleaning her husband's boots and helping him to dress when he was at home. No one was required to work outside, but each must in turn wash up after meals for a week at a time. The daughters of such families were often less fortunate in their lives than the daughters-in-law. For want of suitors of their father's standing they must often be given to men of lower rank and then they worked both in and out of doors as if born and bred in a poor family.

Every house containing two or more married men included a corresponding number of family units. Each of these looked on its own members as we should do—as father, mother, son, daughter, brother and sister—but in its attitude to the other units diverged from our practice. To us the oldest men may be brothers or cousins; to Albanians they were all 'brothers', irrespective of whether one father had begotten them or not. In the next generation instead of first cousins and in the third, second cousins, Albanians saw only 'brothers' and 'sisters' in both. The middle generation of Albanians regarded all its elders as 'uncle' or 'aunt' (though in some, particularly in Moslem, cases distinguishing between the paternal and maternal lines) and all its juniors as 'nephew' or 'niece'. It was only when some need to particularize arose that they defined the relationship according to the blood tie as 'father's brother', 'father's brother's wife', 'brother's son', 'cousin' or the like.

Not only did a man who was seen much in his wife's company lose face, but in a communal household his brothers, in addition to

---

[1] See p. 21.

railing at him, threatened to make him set up a separate home, which would reduce both him and her to a lower level of comfort. Custom, it is true, under the stress of hard necessity, sanctioned his working alongside her in the fields, but only on condition that he did not indulge in unnecessary or frivolous conversation with her. The only explanation which Albanians offered of these restrictions was that a husband and a wife felt 'ashamed' in each other's presence. The same feeling existed all over the Balkans until they came under strong western influences a generation ago. Before that every decorous peasant bride, whatever her race or religion, refrained for several years after her marriage from speaking at all to her husband in public and spoke to him in whispers only in private, meanwhile keeping her eyes modestly downcast. This behaviour seems to originate in an idea which is prevalent throughout the Near East. The Greeks say that since only the celibate life is really holy, the matrimonial state is one of sin and therefore of shame. In I Cor. vii, 8, St Paul voiced it when he wrote, 'I say therefore to the unmarried and widows, It is good for them if they abide even as I'. Moslems, too, believe this, in spite of many being polygamists. There is, for instance, a married as well as a celibate branch of the Bektashi Order of dervishes, but it has so few supporters that at the central monastery at Haci Bektas in the heart of Asia Minor its headquarters are little more than a poverty-stricken excrescence on the enormous, wealthy headquarters of the celibates, and in Albania it has only the monastery at Qesarakë in the south-east, compared with the seventy maintained for the celibates in different parts of the country.

Now the Unwritten Law of Albania ordained that every married woman had the right to visit her own relatives at least once a year. Since these frequently lived in a different village, she could not travel to or from them without an escort, which neither custom nor the law allowed her husband to provide in person. Since brothers were everywhere allowed to talk to each other's wives, no difficulty arose in a communal household, where any man except the husband could accompany a wife to her parents' home and fetch her back. In a house with only one man matters were more complicated. If his mother were alive and physically fit for the journey, she might go with his wife, but who would then cook his supper and prepare his bed for the night? If his mother were dead or incapacitated, one of his wife's relatives must come for her and bring her back, but that meant the extra trouble of letting them know that she was coming.

Each member of a household had a personal name. Though this was usually determined by the religion professed, Moslem first names were not uncommon among the Catholics. The usual cause seems to have been no more than a personal whim. Thus the junior bajraktar ('standard-bearer')[1] of Shalë, a Catholic, was called Avdi because his father was very friendly with a Moslem of that name at the time of his birth. Another interesting anomaly is found in the forty-three Orthodox villages of Shpat, near Elbasan, where the older men have two names, a Moslem one for public use and an Orthodox one for private. For some decades before Albania freed herself from Turkish rule these villages were pressed by the Moslems of Elbasan to abandon Christianity and, to save their faith and lives, camouflaged themselves as Moslems, giving themselves Moslem names, keeping the Ramazan fast, and so on, but evading circumcision. At intervals they fetched an Orthodox priest from Elbasan under cover of night so that in some dark stable he might marry the newly wed with Christian rites and baptize the newly born. So, to name only two examples, the apparently Moslem Tahir Baduri of Shelcan and Ymer Tullumi of Bujars are really the Christian Spiro Baduri and Vasil Tullumi. Religious persecution having ended when Albanian independence was attained, the Orthodox of Shpat shed their Moslem camouflage and gave only Christian names to their children. If Godolesh, the picturesque village north of Elbasan, had managed to hold out for only two years more against the pressure to 'turn Turk', it, too, might now still have been Christian. It failed to hold out, so that its middle-aged and young inhabitants are fanatical Moslems but the old still visit Orthodox churches in secrecy and grieve that they must lie in a Moslem grave. One sturdy old woman, who married soon after the conversion to Islam, boasted that she had had all her four sons baptized. One of them confirmed this to the author, saying he had often been told by Christian and Moslem alike that he smelt less than did other Moslems, an agreeable peculiarity which he attributed to his baptism. The Greeks too, who introduced Orthodox Christianity into Albania, subscribed to the belief that baptism takes away the smell from which all Moslems suffer.

[1] See Chapter XI.

Women, too, had a personal name, but after they married their husbands were too shy to use it, and others knew them in early life as 'Mark's (or Asllan's or Vasil's) young wife' and in later life as his 'wife' or 'old woman', so that their own name fell into disuse. This contributed to their seclusion from the outside world and at the same time avoided the superfluous; since descent in the female line did not count, their names were not thought worth remembering.

Surnames in the sense of family names were general among the Orthodox, comparatively rare among the Moslems, and non-existent among the Catholics. Both Moslems and Catholics, however, tacked on the name of a man's father to his own and so distinguished him from his fellows. Thus a Moslem called Sadik Asllan was Asllan's Sadik and different from Sadik Arif, the son of Arif. A Catholic called Zef Nika was Nikë's Zef, i.e. Zef son of Nikë—Joseph Nicolson in English—and Zef Toma was Tom's Zef, i.e. Joseph Thomson, quite another person. Nika and Toma are in the indefinite genitive, to mark possession. As Moslem names might also be put in this genitive in Albania, Sadik Asllani, an Albanian form, was as frequently heard as Sadik Asllan, its Turkish counterpart. The endings of the Albanian indefinite genitive, it should be said, are tricky and vary according to the final letter of the root word and also according to the dialect used. They are further liable to be confused by foreigners with the definite article which Albanians must suffix to the name when making a statement about a person or a place. Thus Zef Nika signed himself so, without any suffixed article, but if another Albanian reported that 'Zef had gone', he must add the definite article to the name, saying *Zefi iku*. Turkish influence also made Moslems stop at the father's name, but the Catholics, who seem to have preserved the oldest Albanian method of nomenclature, often appended the grandfather's name as well.

34

CHAPTER V

THE MASTER OF THE HOUSE

Some co-ordinating authority is obviously necessary when many workers, most of them occupied with different duties, live under the same roof. The Unwritten Law therefore requires that in each family there shall be a patriarchal system of government, with one man master of the house and everybody else subordinate to him.

When there was only one man in a house, he became automatically its unquestioned master. If he died while his children were small, his brother or, much less often, his wife's brother saw to the family until the eldest boy grew old enough to take charge as master. When there were two or more men in a household, the master was elected, not born, to his position. Most frequently he was chosen in early youth by his predecessor, but should the latter die prematurely, he was elected at a general meeting of the men of the household. The women were not invited to this meeting nor were their views ascertained. The former method was preferred because it enabled the future master to be trained by his predecessor with incessant talk about the matters that would fall within his competence—relations with the authorities, relations with neighbours, household management, laws on roads, field boundaries, pasturage rights and so on. If he had to be elected by the household, he must rely on his own good sense and experience, supplemented by consultations with his subordinates or neighbours. Since its publication in 1933 Father Gjeçov's book on Lek's Kanùn has become available for reference, but previously heads of households had only the unwritten laws for guidance.

When a new master was being chosen, primogeniture was one of the factors taken into consideration. Albanians regarded their elders with deference and, consequently, obeyed them more willingly. A very young master, however, such as might emerge from exclusive reliance on the accident of birth, could be a misfortune for his family.

Primogeniture, however, counted for nothing compared to administrative qualities such as knowledge of the law, shrewd judgement, even temper and fair-mindedness. A reigning master would pass over any or all of his own sons in favour of his younger brother or nephew if the latter promised to be a better administrator. Ymer Tullumi of Bujars in Shpat was a case in point. His father made him heir over the heads of his two elder brothers, and in his own old age, being childless, he selected as his successor, not his oldest nephew or the eldest son of his eldest brother, but the most intelligent among his nephews. For the same reason a master whose powers had been dimmed by years or illness generally resigned his position to his successor, although he was legally entitled to remain master as long as he lived.

In his relations with the authorities and the neighbours, the master had to do his best for the family. He tried, for instance, to get the burden of taxation and unpaid labour on government roads lightened, or, better still, shelved altogether; here he might find some degree of literacy useful, though it was otherwise superfluous. To keep on good terms with the neighbours he restrained his subordinates from provocative acts such as stealing or trespassing, and if a quarrel broke out he tried to settle it before it reached the shooting stage, which was always a nuisance to everybody concerned. At home he tried to keep the domestic wheels well oiled, soothing the quarrelsome, reasoning with the disgruntled, never showing anger real or feigned, assigning to each worker, whether man or woman, a daily task. In practice the last point seldom required thinking out, since each man had early specialized as ploughman, shepherd, cow-herd or odd man. If 'hands' were few, the master must work himself; if they were numerous, he confined himself to general supervision and planning of the work of the others. His chief duty was then to see that the fields were properly tilled and the flocks well cared for. In some districts, when temporary labourers had been hired for a special job, the master of a household so big that he did not normally work with his own hands ceased to supervise the workers and joined them as one of themselves. This was regarded as gracious condescension on his part and stimulated the hired men to greater effort.

The master's rule over his household was absolute and extended to every aspect of its life. Unless he first consented, no other man might stay away from work, leave the farm for a day's outing, accept employment elsewhere, or even call in a doctor to attend to his sick child; no boy or girl might be betrothed; no child might be hired out, apprenticed, or sent to school; no woman except his mother and others in her position, such as his uncle's elderly widow, might go to spend the night in her father's house. This gave him complete control over the time of the workers of the household. Whatever task he assigned the other men and the women must be performed without cavil; they must not only work as he said but go where he bade them and even marry when and whom he pleased. He spoke of them as 'my people' in English or 'my folk' in American parlance. When obliged to speak of them to the authorities or neighbours, he called any young man 'my son', any girl 'my daughter', and any married woman 'my wife' or 'my old woman'. No decent Albanian, it should be noted, ever mentions the women of his household to outsiders except under compulsion.

The master had also sole control of the family purse. Any money earned by the other men by the sweat of their brow or a windfall like a tip must be paid over to him and spent for the family's benefit. For, says the law, 'the earnings of a son are shared by his father and brothers'. Here the words 'father', 'son' and 'brothers' have not only the narrow application which we English give, but also the wider Albanian sense of relatives in the older or younger generation.[1] The farm was registered in the Land Office and popularly spoken of under the master's name, but this was only for convenience. It was owned jointly by all the men on it, and the master did not own a blade of grass more than the others did. Yet in virtue of his position he need not consult any of them if he wished to buy or sell a field, vineyard, wood or portion of irrigation water. The right to buy and sell was his alone. There were only two limitations on this right, both deriving from the simple good sense that underlies all the unwritten laws. He could not sell a sheep or goat without first securing the shepherd's permission, and if the latter preferred to give him another animal, he must accept it, for the shepherd knew the flock better than he did. Secondly, the farmer of the family, having sole charge of the plough-oxen, did not require to ask his leave if he wished to help a neighbour with his ploughing, to lend the oxen, or even to give them away outright.

As keeper of the purse the master generally went to market himself with whatever produce was for sale, and bought what he thought necessary with the proceeds. It was his duty to see that everybody in the house was as well shod and dressed as the

[1] See p. 30.

family's means permitted, and that there was a sufficiency of coffee, sugar and cigarettes to maintain its dignity with visitors. He must also pay government dues and instalments of the price of any bride who was marrying into the family. Until the newer ways of to-day came in, he had further to buy a rifle for every youth in the family who came of military age. If he sent another man to market in his stead, as he was entitled to do, he often put a reserve price on the produce and always instructed his deputy about what he was to buy. On his return the latter must give a full account of his stewardship, saying what he had received for the produce and what he had spent, proving that he had made no unauthorized purchases, and handing over the remaining money intact. If the master grew so physically incapacitated that he could no longer make the long, arduous journey over the mountains to market (*pazàr*), he usually appointed one of the others, preferably the future master, to the permanent post of 'bazaar-man'. The latter then kept the family purse, but in other respects remained subordinate to the master.

It resulted naturally from the master's hold on the family purse that only he could lend money or contract a debt recoverable in law. If any of his subordinates made a loan or pledged the family credit on behalf of a friend, the borrower might lawfully repudiate the debt on the plea that it was not lawfully contracted. Generally, however, the master first scolded the culprit well for transgressing the law and then told the borrower that the loan was made on his authority, so leaving him no option but to repay it. In the same way, when subordinates borrowed, both they and the master were within their rights if they said the loan was illegally contracted and refused to repay it. More often than not, for the honour of the family, the master paid up. Again, in such matters as going surety for a loan, a woman's chastity, or a man's life, which were great features of Albanian life, only the master might act, subject to one exception. Each man's rifle and revolver were his personal property—to keep, to barter, to sell or to pledge without any reference to the master. Consequently, each subordinate might go surety up to the value of his arms. He usually did so with circumspection, however, for if he lost them he must not ask the master to replace them. The master was also responsible for any material damage done to a neighbour by his subordinates. If, for instance, they had stolen or killed a cow, or had set fire to a haystack, it was he who must find the money for compensating the injured neighbour. He sought it naturally in the common purse according to the law that 'the mishaps of a son are shared by his father and brothers'. If however, a subordinate killed a neighbour, it was just as likely that he himself or another subordinate would have to pay the penalty of a life for a life as that the master would have to do so. Presumably this anomalous division of responsibility arose because if the master alone were responsible for a murder, he would be so closely guarded that there would be no catching him and the murdered man's death would remain unavenged.[1]

Though the master's authority, resting as it did on his customary and traditional acceptance as his predecessor's choice or on his election by general consent of the household, was essentially moral, it was also backed by certain powers of enforcement. He had the right to beat a culprit, to leave him hungry, or to tie him up in a room or cellar until he came to a more proper frame of mind. This applied equally to the women; in fact, the commonest victim of tying up in a cellar was a girl who had jibbed at a proposed marriage. When a subordinate was grossly at fault and seemed incorrigible, the master might threaten to give him his portion and turn him out to fend for himself, and if the man did not reform, he would carry out the threat. In Krujë the author was present when a father expelled one of his sons for killing the other. In Turkish times the master had another salutary form of punishment at his disposal. This was taking away a culprit's arms for a week or two, so reducing him to the status of women and greybeards. 'Once shamed, twice shy' was almost invariably the result. But the best of masters might be helpless with a shiftless subordinate who had grown too old to beat. So long as the latter avoided gross misdemeanours like murder, he might idle with impunity. For physical reasons the master could not force him to work, and except in extreme cases the Unwritten Law disapproved of turning him out to sink or swim as an angry English parent might do.[2] The law said

---

[1] It is perhaps more likely that this vicarious responsibility of any member of the family instead of the master only is the survival of the more ancient practice unmodified by more civilized conventions. It is typical of the blood feud in more primitive societies than that of Albania. (Ed.)

[2] In Montenegrin tribal law the disobedient son might be fined the first time, confined and beaten the second and third time, and only expelled after that, expulsion involving disinheritance. *Vide* Durham, *Some Tribal Origins, Laws and Customs of the Balkans*, p. 84. (Ed.)

it was the offender's birthright to remain in the house, to eat at the common table, and to have his wife and children maintained out of the family purse. A striking illustration of this weakness of the communal system was to be seen in Shalë in the 1930's, when Mirash Nue's family included his wife, his elder son Pal, Pal's wife and four children, and his younger son Gjon. Since he, Mirash, was too old to work and Pal was a wastrel, Gjon alone ploughed to feed the household and fetched firewood to keep it warm. To get money for government taxes and his father's coffee and cigarettes, he worked for the priest in his spare time. He had been unable to earn enough to pay for a bride and at thirty years of age was still un-married, a calamity in primitive Albanian eyes. Pal, not criminal, just lazy and selfish, and saved from beating by his father's ad-vanced years and his own age, paid no attention to either his father's upbraidings or the barely concealed contempt of the neighbours and turned up unfailingly for the meals he had done nothing to provide.

The master received no money payments for his services but enjoyed certain privileges. His clothes were often newer and of better cloth than those of his subordinates; more silver chains crossed his breast, and more silver rings glittered on his fingers. He was entitled to have his own bedding and coffee utensils and to keep them until he died. If he chose to buy himself a riding horse, a watch, or arms richly inlaid with silver and bright stones, he might do so. His subordinates, though left to walk while he rode, to learn the time from the sun by day and from the crowing of a cock at night, and to content themselves with the plainest of rifles and revolvers, did not seem to resent his magnificence. He represented the family, and the worthier he appeared in externals as well as in mind and character, the greater the glory reflected on each of them.

Indoors the master sat in the place of honour in the sitting-room, the right-hand chimney corner as one looked from the fireplace towards the door. Though marked deference was usually shown to old people, he never gave up this place to his aged father or elder brother except in the districts of Shpat, Çermenikë and Shalë, where age took precedence over social position. The other men grouped themselves cross-legged in front of the fire, the future master facing it squarely, older men flanking him, and younger men sitting behind him. The youngest of all, who had to do such work as shutting the door, bringing firewood, and carrying in supper, sat next to the door; he was described as the serving man. When the master entered, all rose to their feet and remained standing until he was seated. If he was armed, one of them relieved him of his rifle, hung it on a peg by the door, and turned to see if he wanted to keep his side-arms or to have them hung up beside the rifle. As soon as he settled down he made himself a cup of coffee, rolled and lit a cigarette, and perhaps pulled a small bottle of raw spirit (*raki*) from his pocket. If in a gracious mood, he might make a cup of coffee for the older men and the master designate and let them smoke or even suck at his raki bottle, but if he wished he might lawfully reserve these joys for himself. In any event the younger men might neither drink nor smoke in his presence, though they could do both elsewhere. If he chose to make conversation, the others must follow his lead; if he preferred to remain silent, they could not speak—like good children they must remain seen but not heard. When supper came, no one might put his spoon into the common dish until he had done so. When the time came to leave the room, he led the way as he did when walking through the fields. In the house this indicated his pre-eminence; in the fields it was also a security measure. The others strung out behind him at specified intervals, on the assumption that he could deal himself with a frontal attack but needed to have his back protected by friends.

Given his duties, rights and privileges, the master soon acquired an air of command, whereas his subordinates, condemned for ever to show no initiative, shrank progressively into complete nonentities as their youthful qualities atrophied for want of exercise. But the master must not be tyrannical or unjust, spendthrift or careless of the general weal, and above all he must show no favouritism. If he developed such faults, the other men might lawfully depose him and elect another in his stead. However, the care taken initially in selecting him made such action extremely rare. A good master preferred the spirit to the letter of the law. For example, he rarely sold or bought any family possessions without first consulting his subordinates. And he was always careful not to destroy his subordinates' feeling that the farm and everybody and everything on it belonged to each of them individually as well as collectively, that the welfare of each of them concerned the whole family, and that the general welfare concerned each individual.[1]

[1] Thus a youth who obviously had nothing of his own was yet perfectly in order when he stated that he had just bought a field or even a bride for his brother.

The master designate, who might be appointed 'bazaar-man' in the master's lifetime, sat in a place of some honour, and might be given coffee and cigarettes while other men went without. Often, too, he was deputed to make the coffee and to lead the conversation with a guest. This was training for him and practice in family manners for his future subordinates. When the master was not present, all the duties and privileges of headship were his. During wedding celebrations no one might join a ring dance, however much he wished to do so, unless commanded by the master or in his absence by the master designate.

There is little to add to what has already been said about the subordinate men in a communal household. Each was head of his own particular family, with full powers to chastise both wife and children, though not to direct their lives and work—that was the master's business. An older man was further regarded as a father by his juniors. This principle was carried so far in Mirditë, though not elsewhere, that he might lawfully reprimand and even beat a junior's wife and children. The junior could not retaliate in kind, for the law holds it criminal to strike a 'father's' wife. In other respects it was a subordinate's whole duty to obey the master.

As for the women in a communal household, the master governed them through the housekeeper: under her official style of mistress of the house she transmitted his orders to the other women or gave them her own and supervised their indoor work. When they were working outside, the master or a man deputizing for him must oversee them, for a mistress worked only in the house and farm-yard. She was appointed by the master and was not necessarily his wife. Like him, she must rule justly, moderately, and impartially, taking special pains to avoid favouring her own children, and if his wife did not possess these qualities, he passed her over and chose another. In no case did a mistress have as much authority as the master; she had none at all outside her own departments, and in these must at all times work under his orders. Nor might she buy, sell or barter so much as an egg on her own responsibility. Her tenure of office was also much shorter. Since strong young women must do farm work, she was seldom appointed until nearing forty, and since her duties were manifold and heavy, especially in summer owing to the absence of the other women, she was superseded about fifty when her physical strength began to wane. Her only privilege, but one for which she was much envied by the other women, was to work indoors. Her clothes were no better than theirs; indeed, if she had dairy work to do, they were usually dirtier. If she was unjust and ill-tempered, pilfered or sold family property, or fomented rather than composed the quarrels that were endemic among the other women, the men assembled in general meeting and deposed her.[1]

It only remains to describe a small domain with which the master had nothing to do. In astonishing contrast to the penniless men, all the women had their own money and controlled it absolutely. Called *pekul*, from Lat. *peculium*, and essentially pin-money, they spent it on kerchiefs, gewgaws, and even clothes and shoes. Each received the first of it on the morning after her marriage, when her men relatives filed past her in farewell and dropped money into a plate for her. Afterwards her father or brother might slip a coin or two into her hand when he visited her. In the tribal districts of the north her father also gave her on her marriage as much as half of the money which her husband had paid him for her. Later on she might occasionally earn a few pence by knitting socks in her odd moments or making the rough home-spun trousers worn by peasants. Debarred by law and custom from taking the finished articles to market herself, she gave them to her father or brother to sell, but never to her husband or grown-up son, for they would not let her even see the money. If near a market-town, she might gather walnuts or hazel-nuts in the woods and send these to market. In tobacco-growing areas she normally got the coarse bottom leaves of the plants, to smoke or to sell as she pleased. If she had none of these resources, she could only steal maize, eggs, wool or cheese from her husband's house and send a child to the shop to barter them for what she wished to have; she was bound to pay in kind or money, for the law forbade her to pledge either her husband's or her father's credit. On these occasions neither her father nor her brother would act as her agent, for if such connivance in her pilfering were discovered, they would be in serious trouble with her husband's family. If she chose to keep her *pekul* idle, she might safely lock it up in her dowry-chest in her room; her husband never seemed to make her give it up and no others might enter their room. Generally, however, she made the money fructify. In southern areas like Çermenikë she lent it at the usual rate of interest, which was 30% (enough to compensate

[1] The author never heard, however, of this being done.

lenders for the want of security), and in the less-developed north she invested it in sheep, plough-oxen, or even horses which she hired out on the 'half-and-half' system. Before a woman died, she gave a little of her *pekul* to her daughters and the major part to her sons, but nothing to her husband, so making a last comment on the curiously detached relationship between them during their married life.

Except in the towns, no Albanian woman ever went into domestic service. Each worked as a girl in her father's house and then in her husband's and, though never paid any money, was assured for life of whatever board, lodging and clothes these could provide. This applied even to families of the standing of Cen Elezi in Dibër. Consequently the Unwritten Law took no cognizance of female servants. On the other hand, men servants—mainly farm workers or herdsmen—were numerous enough to have been carefully legislated for.

Though such a servant ate out of the same dish as his master and slept in the sitting-room or elsewhere in the same conditions as the young unmarried men of the family, he had always to take a back seat—in the literal sense near the door and far from the fire; and, in the metaphorical sense, effacing himself. This befitted both his youth and his status. For his status was like that of a woman. 'It is for the master to command and for the servant to obey', said the Unwritten Law. If he were a shepherd, his views on the beasts under his care commanded his master's respect, but other servants were required to keep their opinions to themselves. In areas such as Martanesh where women could not be killed in a blood feud, a servant was as safe as they were from his master's enemies. 'Kill a servant? Faugh! As well kill a woman', was the sentiment.

There was, however, another aspect to his position: since he came from another family in his master's village or from another village altogether, he was not a member of his master's household but was its guest. As such he was entitled to protection by his master against all hurt from third parties. If he were hit, the offender must pay twice, compensating him for the personal injury of the blow and his master for the affront to his guest. If he were robbed, his master latterly complained to the police, but in the old days would have shot the robber out of hand in the north, but in Martanesh and farther south, not until he saw that the servant himself was too weak to resent the injury as honour demanded. If a servant were killed, a modern master again told the police, but nevertheless both he and the servant's family considered themselves at feud with the murderer, the former to avenge the death of his guest and the latter to avenge the death of their relative; more often than not, the master made it 'tit for tat' by killing the murderer's servant. In former times a servant was most commonly killed because he was mixed up in a blood feud of his own. In that event his master went to see his enemy and warned him that the man was now in his service and, consequently, under his protection. If his enemy disregarded the warning, his master never rested until he had avenged the servant.

Again in the old days, vengeance took a fiercer turn when the servant was from a different community. He was then counted as a stranger, and the guest of his master's tribe or village, as well as of his master himself. If he were killed by one of this community, the others rose as one man, burned down the murderer's house and destroyed all his goods. The modern Albanian government has repressed this custom, but the servant's master and family still try to shoot the murderer.

The same public vengeance used to await the murderer of a local servant who was working for a stranger to the tribe or village. But in such a case it was the injury to its stranger guest which the community wished to avenge; in itself the death of the servant was a matter for private vengeance by his family. In aggravated cases, as when the murdered servant as well as his master was a stranger, the community might order the execution of the murderer by a firing squad. This was done in 1944 in the village of Dukat, in south-west Albania.

No Albanian ever stooped to become a servant except from dire necessity. Most commonly he wanted to marry, and having no spare cash, must earn enough to pay for his bride. He was usually engaged on St George's or St Demetrius's day in the Old Style calendar, and so on 6 May and 8 November in ours, dates which correspond roughly to the beginning and end of the dry season. His engagement was for six months or, more often, a year. His wages and his work depended on the bargain he made with his master before being hired. In the 1930's his wages, including food only, ranged according to his quality from one napoleon (16s. at par) to half a napoleon a month, payable monthly. In late Turkish times, when clothes as well as food were given, the rates were from

500 to 50 *grosh* ('piastres') a year, payable in two instalments, the first after six months' service and the second at the end of his term.

According to a list from Shkrel where wages were still on an 'all-found' basis, a servant must be given a complete set of clothes —a shirt, drawers, cloth cap, scarf, cow-hide sandals, socks, trousers and sleeveless jacket. He got sandals as often as he needed a new pair, and a set of the other things three times a year: when first engaged, at the end of three months, and during his last month. On leaving he was given three okes of wool, which his female relatives could work up for him.

Disputes hardly ever arose over the servant's food or clothes, but were common about his work. As an Albanian of Koplik said picturesquely, 'Before a man is hired he talks like an angel, and then turns out a devil', so that 'half the men who lie in cemeteries have died of worry over servants'. The same speaker told a lively folk-tale of a master who was delighted to get a servant cheap and then found him come very dear indeed. Every time he asked him to do something, the man said it had not been mentioned in their bargain and he could not do it unless he got a rise in wages. Little attempt to get 'references' seems to have been made, perhaps because in the old days a would-be servant would have shot the giver of an adverse 'character' for slandering him. There was also a feeling that a servant's engagement was too temporary to take seriously. Once when the author inquired uneasily about a servant she had been urged to hire, an old mountaineer replied, 'What does it matter? you're not going to marry him'.

'Any gains made or any damage done by a servant are his master's', said the law. If, for instance, a servant somehow gained a horse, he could not send it to his own family, but must give it to his master. On the loss side of the ledger, if a servant unintentionally damaged a neighbour's property, say, by killing his horse, it was not he but his master who must make restitution, and his master could not keep back any of his wages for that purpose. Fining a servant was absolutely forbidden.

The relations of master and man with each other and with the outside world were regulated in detail by the Unwritten Law, using the servant's wages as its chief instrument. Thus if the two parted prematurely, the master being to blame, he must pay the servant his full wages for the year. When the servant was to blame, he had no right to more than the money for which he had so far worked, and must forfeit the rest. To us the pound or two involved seems too insignificant to matter to either, but to most Albanians it was an important sum. In the event, for example, of the master's moving from one district to another, he might not dismiss the servant unless he gave him a full year's wages. If, however, he asked the servant to go with him and the servant refused, he must let him go but need give him no more than what he had so far earned. In the same spirit the law forbade the master to dismiss the servant for a frivolous reason, such as not liking him, and forbade the servant to run away for a frivolous reason, such as boredom. If the master disregarded this law, he must pay the servant a full year's wages, and if the servant disregarded it, he must be content with the wages he had earned to date. By exception, in Krasniqë, in north-east Albania, the master sought out his runaway servant, and after making him find a man to guarantee his future behaviour, brought him back to stay out his time.

If the master had good grounds for dismissing the servant, he must warn and forgive him twice. If the warnings went unheeded, the master said the elders must now judge between them. The servant then went and told his story to the chief elder—the bajraktar in tribal areas—who next asked the master what he had to say. Thus in possession of both sides of the story, the elders sat on the case and pronounced judgement; this turned generally on what money was to be paid to the servant.

If the servant were lazy, an all too common occurrence, or otherwise unsatisfactory, without being criminal, the Unwritten Law allowed his master to reprimand him reasonably and bade the servant swallow the reprimand. But the master must not use foul language or hit the man. For his motive might be to force him to leave before his time, apparently of his own volition, and so deprive himself of his full wages. If the master transgressed this law, the servant had leave to appeal to the elders, not only for payment of his wages in full, but also for compensation for the injury of being hit or violently abused.

The more serious crimes with which a servant might be charged included theft, murder and seducing a girl or young wife in his master's family. In the case of theft the issue depended largely on whether the servant stole from his master, in his master's village, or in another community. If he were caught red-handed robbing his master or subsequently admitted doing so, he was immediately dismissed with only the wages due until then. Since it was in a sense his own house and his own father that he had robbed, he could not be given a second chance; he was too obviously devoid of ordinary decency to be trusted again. And since the law forbade his master to strike him, he could not be beaten, as a thievish woman might be, till he reformed.

Dismissal did not end his story. He had to pay the statutory fine for housebreaking and to bring his late master two of everything he had stolen. If he had no money for the fine, he had to find a surety for the amount and then go and earn it elsewhere. After European legal codes were introduced at the end of the 1920's, these unwritten laws lost much of their force, and it was rather by threatening to get the thief sent to prison that an injured master obtained restitution.

In less sophisticated days a servant who was only suspected of robbing his master could be tried by the ordeal of the oath. If this proved him innocent, his master had to pay him six *qese* ('purses') for unjustly accusing him, besides a full year's wages and clothes. If it was later found that he had perjured himself, the elders fined him twenty-four *qese*, of which half went to the church (or mosque) and half to the tribe; he had also to return to his master the six *qese* and the unearned wages and clothes which he had won from him by perjury. It sometimes transpired, however, that the informant who had disclosed his perjury had lied himself. Then the elders once more declared the servant innocent, ordered the church and tribe to return his twenty-four *qese*, and the informant to pay him a year's wages and clothes besides six *qese* for the false accusation.

If a servant stole in his master's village or another community, punishment depended on who had instigated the crime. If his master had done so, he and not the servant was in fault, and it was for him to make reparation to the victim. He must also dismiss the servant forthwith as a public nuisance; but since the man was only his tool, he must pay him a full year's wages. If, on the other hand, a servant stole on his own initiative, the fault was his and it was for him alone to make restitution. In addition, he might be legally dismissed with no more than the wages he had earned.

Much the same laws applied when a servant committed a murder. If he did so at his master's instigation, both were punished. He must be dismissed, but his master must pay him a full year's wages. The resultant blood feud was primarily his concern, but if he escaped from the district, his master might lawfully be shot in his stead. When, however, a servant murdered on his own responsibility, he alone should suffer for the crime. His master was entitled, in dismissing him, to keep back the portion of his wages for which he had not worked, and according to Lek's Kanùn ought not to be shot in his stead. Skanderbeg's law, however, held him as liable in this case as in the former.

The only available information about a servant's seducing a girl or young wife in his master's family comes from Martanesh and Shkrel and dates from past times. In Martanesh the law condemned the man to death for incest because his master was his 'father' and the young woman his 'sister'. In Shkrel he was killed at once if he had sinned with a young wife, but if with a girl he was dismissed with orders to hold his tongue, and only if he talked did the girl's father go and shoot him. As for the girl, she was married to her fiancé as quickly as possible. He was not told that she was pregnant by another man, and would not have cared if he had been. He wanted her as wife and worker and felt sure that he was man enough to keep her straight after marriage; beatings always worked wonders. The child was sent to the servant as soon as born; he never acknowledged it but either killed it or exposed it by the wayside. The father did not dare to beat the girl in case she ran away to the servant; at all costs he had to keep her for her fiancé, who had presumably paid a good proportion of her bride-price and would have killed him had he failed to deliver her. Presumably the fact that a servant was held to be of little or no account saved the wife or girl from the usual punishment for adultery.[1]

Sometimes, despite their being 'brother' and 'sister', a servant married his master's daughter. Thus an ancestor of Bicaj was a Catholic of Gjugjë in Mirditë who entered the service of Hysen Agë Shteki of Bicaj, turned Moslem, and married Hysen Agë's daughter. Even in modern times a servant may be given his master's daughter in marriage. This is particularly likely to happen if his master is Moslem and he a Christian who agrees to change his religion. His master then looks on his own consent to the marriage as an act of piety. Servants varied in importance according to the master they served. Thus the servant of a Moslem priest (hoxhë) had more power than an ordinary peasant's and less than a bajraktar's —at least in the days before most bajraktars were shorn of their

[1] See Chapter XXI.

power by modern governments. The value of the difference to the servant was that the more important his master, the better he himself was protected.

It is the rule in all denominations that priests may not carry arms. This is no drawback to anybody under a modern administration, but in Turkish times it meant that a priest's servant was more exposed to danger than an armed layman's. The Catholic church tried to make up for the deficiency by special legislation of which Father Gjeçov gives a full account. Thus, though a priest's servant had a certain freedom to attend to his own business, any message he carried to a house was treated as coming from the priest. Whoever molested him molested the priest, and might be fined according to the gravity of the offence but not less than ten lambs, which went, not to the servant, but to the church and tribe. Whoever killed the servant started a feud with his family only, if the servant were local, but with the whole parish if he were a stranger— here can be recognized the principle of the community's guest— and if the murderer was local, the parish burned his house and took a hundred lambs and an ox from him as fine. If labourers hired by the church were molested, the offender had to pay a fine, divisible between them and the church; the more numerous they were, the heavier the fine; on an average this amounted to ten lambs. If an offender refused to pay, the parish went in a body and took what it wanted from his sheepfold. In short, the church treated any wrong to a defenceless priest's servant as a major crime.

The retainers of great men were essentially a bodyguard, and were only maintained by men with blood feuds. Some lived at home and joined their patron for some special, and usually brief, occasion; others lived for long periods with him, constantly ready for whatever service he might ask. They occasionally received a gold piece as reward; more often they were paid in kind—by being lent money without interest for a funeral or a wedding feast, by being given grain in bad years, by having a useful word said in the ear of the authorities to extract them from some difficulty. While his own children were small, the Hereditary Captain of Mirditë had eight young relatives living permanently with him, brief holidays at home excepted. They waited at meals or carried messages to the servants with the lofty air of medieval pages of noble blood. Until exiled during the war of 1939–45, Shevqet Vërlaci, the formidable Bey of Elbasan, was guarded night and day by relays of peasants

4

from his own farms, who spent weeks at a time with him. During the same period every notable from Dibër who visited Tirana called at least six peasant neighbours to come and escort him there and back. If his stay in the capital were short, they saw him safely home; if long, they were relieved by others at intervals. Needless to say, all retainers were crack shots.

Finally, the protected might also be the protector. In the 1930's Hamit Callaku, an influential notable of Fulqet, had a notorious murderer from Çermenikë living with him for nothing except the assurance that so long as he kept Hamit's enemies at a distance the former would prevent the authorities from arresting him.

CHAPTER VI

THE SEPARATION OF BROTHERS

In spite of the modernization which Albanian laws had undergone since 1912, brothers still separated according to the laws they had learned from their fathers. The only change introduced by the civil code adapted from the Swiss models was that economic provision must now be made for the daughters of the family, who had formerly been given only a nominal sum when their father's home was broken up.

There were several reasons for breaking up an old home. When a communal household was already full of men, each with his wife and children, it could no longer spare a room for each boy as he grew up and married. Some of the men must hive off, although many disliked the idea of separating from their brothers. As the Albanian proverb says, 'When the hive is full the bees must swarm'.

Quarrelling was another cause of separation. Often the brothers themselves quarrelled, the younger resenting the elder's control of his person and of the family purse, or 'the devil entering both their hearts' they quarrelled about nothing. In the latter case climate might play a role. Theth, for example, lay so high that the peasants were confined to their houses for several months each winter. Then brother got on brother's nerves, high words were spoken and the younger demanded a separation or the elder threatened to expel him. When the milder weather came to release them from confinement, their tempers cooled, but each was too proud to retract the word he had spoken in haste. A financial cause operated in villages near towns, such as Godolesh and Shijan near Elbasan. With the bazaar at hand each brother wanted to control the purse, which he could not do unless he had a separate establishment. Often too brothers must separate because their wives quarrelled. The companionship enforced by communal life naturally bore harder on the women who lacked the blood tie and similarity of upbringing that might neutralize clashes of temperament among the men. Occasionally brothers separated while their father was still alive. If this was their own wish they lost face and were publicly mocked as 'low-class fellows'. Sometimes they had no choice, being so disobedient and unruly that their father compelled them to leave his house. Or they got on so badly with each other that he feared there would be murder done.

Three factors militated against separation. There was the sense of family which was so strong that four or five generations, numbering twenty souls or more, might live under one roof. Secondly, it was economically to the advantage of each man that the household should remain together. In a large household all branches of the pastoral and agricultural life were possible, but in a small one activities must be restricted; one and the same person could not tend cows and oxen, ewes and lambs. With good reason the proverb says 'Separation ruins a family'. In the bad old days too, it was strategically good for brothers to stick together; the more guns in a house the stronger it was.

When separation had been decided on, the family possessions were divided equally without any regard for primogeniture. Everything that could be eaten or drunk—dairy produce, grain, haricot beans, eggs, honey, raki—was considered food and divided equally among the mouths to be fed, and everything else—land, livestock, farm implements, house, household utensils—was considered property and divided equally between the brothers.

The law of food, as expanded, laid down that every living soul in the house on the day of separation, male and female, sick and well, greybeard and infant drawing its first breath, should receive the same share of food. Supposing one of the two brothers had besides his wife ten children, and the other two, the first received twelve portions of food and the second four. Then the age clause was variously interpreted. In Dibër even a child still in the womb was allotted a full portion, but elsewhere one born so little as an hour after the conclusion of the separation received nothing and the prospective father naturally tried to protect himself against this loss by delaying the separation, if possible, until the child had been born. In Lumë and Mirditë a child less than a year old was not given food, the idea being that its mother's milk would suffice for it throughout the coming year—partly to avoid conception Albanian children were everywhere suckled until they were three years of age. In other areas a new-born child received its quota on the assumption that before a year was out it would 'eat a little, spill a little and let the cat eat a little'. Separation generally, though not invariably, took place immediately after harvest when bins were full and a year must pass before the fields again yielded a crop.

Although food supply was divided in most areas into equal portions irrespective of total quantity, in the Malësi e Madhe each person received three loads of maize, which was considered to be enough food for a year. Any surplus was sold and the proceeds divided among the brothers. In other areas a surplus rarely existed, so the specification of quantity had never been made.

For the purposes of separation the term 'grain' included not only maize and wheat but also everything that grew in a field or garden, such as fruit and vegetables. Exceptionally, in Godolesh both olives and butter were regarded as property and divided equally, not among the number of souls, but among the brothers. In Perlat raki and wine were divided equally among all who drank; some of the men did not drink and some of the women did. Sometimes a woman tried to secure a double share of drink for her husband by alleging falsely that she herself drank. The attempt was usually frustrated by the other women, who, not wishing to see their husbands go shorter than they should, exposed her fraud. In rare instances where drinking water was divided, it was treated like food.

Property, said the law, was to be divided equally among the brothers. This applied only to property inherited by the father; the number of children belonging to each brother was not considered. One of two might have seven children and the other three, but each received exactly half the property. The only exception recorded is in Martanesh, where a brother with many mouths to feed might be given a little extra food on condition of accepting a little less land. It followed that the brother with the large family was much worse off initially, though eventually, as his children grew old enough to work, he might catch up the other because he would have more hands at work. No doubt it was this balance of initial poverty against subsequent wealth that led the old law-givers to enact this law of equal division of property among brothers. It was also immaterial that one of the brothers had a grown son; the son counted in the division of food but not in that of property.

A dead brother was ignored when the food was divided, but if he had left a son, his rights to an equal share of the property remained intact. It descended to his son, who, irrespective of his age, ranked on separation day as his father's representative and the equal of each of his father's brothers. Supposing the dead man had been one of four brothers, the three survivors and his orphan son each received one-quarter of the property. If he had left two sons, these became joint owners of his quarter share. Even if all the brothers in a communal household died before it split up, the principle of division was the same. Suppose they were three, and the eldest had ten male descendants, the second five and the third one, the property was divided into three equal parts, one for each of them, regardless of the disparity in the number of their descendants.

Division of food was relatively simple, a matter of arithmetic—so many souls, so many portions. The process of division of property was much more complicated, a thing of exact measurements and difficult calculations. As a first step the land was measured with a rope and divided into as many equal parts as there were brothers. Occasionally it was measured by pacing, the man who paced clasping his hands behind his back to steady himself and so to keep his paces equal.

When the quality of the land was uniform there was no difficulty about the actual partition by these methods. But it might happen that one field or one part of a field was better than another. Good and bad must nevertheless be shared alike by the brothers. To make this possible, what may be called the system of 'offset or compensation' came into play. Most commonly a smaller field or a smaller portion of the same field was given to the brother who got the better land, and a larger field or larger portion of the same field to the one who got the worse. The basis of calculation was the average yield of the land, this being common knowledge in the district. Size was thus offset against quality. Less often the portions were valued and the brother who got the better one paid compensation to the other; the latter was theoretically supposed to spend the money on buying himself a piece of land somewhere else.

The term 'land' included arable land, vineyards, vegetable gardens, orchards, hay meadows and enclosed lowland pastures, all of which must be divided up when the brothers separated. It did not include mountain pastures or woods and forest for firewood, fodder and timber. These remained undivided, common property for the common use of the brothers. It was rare, however, to find a joint household owning mountain pastures and forests, for these were generally held in common by a whole ward or even a whole village. In Çermenikë all the brothers were allowed to graze their sheep after harvest on a divided arable field as they did when it was whole and they were together; it was immaterial that one had a bigger flock than the other. At least it was immaterial in theory, but in practice they sometimes quarrelled over the grazing. Then each must set a shepherd on his own boundary to watch over his interests. Presumably the impossibility of providing shepherds enough to guard the wide boundaries of forests and mountain pastures has prevented these pieces of property from being divided up.

Two curiosities of land division are to be noted: if an arable field was very narrow, it must be divided short-ways, for if divided long-ways, the plough-oxen might not have room to turn when ploughing; sometimes, too, three brothers who were separating amicably might wish to have each of their father's fields divided in three rather than each receive one field apiece. A day might come when one of them might wish to sell his land, then there would be more inducement to keep it in the family if it immediately adjoined another brother's holding. They also wished, they said, to perpetuate the memory of their joint ownership of all the fields, and when one field was some way from another and in different hands, it was less easy to realize that once the same family had owned them all. If possible they would like to keep up their brotherly ties for a hundred years or more.

The division of the joint home was generally much more complicated. Supposing there were two brothers in a house consisting of only a sitting-room and a kitchen. By the partition method one was given the sitting-room and the other the kitchen. Since the sitting-room was manifestly superior it was valued together with the kitchen. The values were added, then divided into two, and the difference between half the total and the value of the kitchen was paid to the less lucky brother. The payment made, it was held that the old home had been equally divided between the brothers. Sometimes instead of money the offset system was used, a better portion of land being given to the brother who had received the worse part of the house. For this purpose the land as well as the house was valued, and if the former's total value was 26 napoleons, 14 napoleons' worth would go to the brother with the kitchen worth 6 and 12 napoleons' worth to the brother with the sitting-room worth 8, so giving each 20 napoleons' worth of property.

Alternatively, both sitting-room and kitchen were measured with a rope and divided into two. A partition wall of lath and plaster or, more probably, of lath and mud was then run up in both. This left half of each with the old door and, where it existed, the old staircase, while the other two halves had neither door nor staircase; a new door and, if required, a new staircase, were built for these, generally on the opposite side of the house. Each brother then took possession of his new home, a small poor place but his own with its own egress to the outside world.

In the Mohammedan villages near Elbasan there were regulations about windows which aimed, like the building laws, at protecting women from prying eyes. In Godolesh the brother getting the upper room in a two-storeyed house was told to blind the windows overlooking the yard if his brother's kitchen, as was probable, opened on to this; otherwise his brother's womenfolk would not have full freedom to move about the yard. The brother getting the middle storey in a three-storeyed house was given similar instructions, but the brother with the topmost floor might leave all his windows open as they were too high to overlook the yard. In Labinot all windows overlooking another's property must, irrespective of their height, be blinded. Such regulations were not enforced in Christian villages.

When the old house had two rooms as well as a kitchen the division was less complicated. To begin with, one room was assigned to each brother. If one was bigger than the other they were both valued and due compensation paid to the brother with the smaller one. As for the kitchen, either it was divided in two or it was given to one brother and its estimated value paid to the other so that he could build a new kitchen for himself on his own land.

Continuing to live under the same roof imposed certain mutual obligations on the brothers. If the flimsy partition wall or the roof needed repairs, both must share the expense in equal proportions. If one could not or would not pay his quota the other was entitled to repair only his own section of the roof, leaving his brother's to the ravages of the weather; or he might try to extract the money from his brother by force; until lately, he might even shoot him in truculent Lumë. As for the partition wall, he probably repaired it at his own expense for the sake of his personal privacy.

To avoid such quarrels and to secure more houseroom the buying out method of dividing the old home was preferred. The building itself was allotted to one of the brothers, almost every-where the youngest, who became its sole owner and master. But he must pay each of his brothers a proportionate share of its value, half if he had only one brother, a third if he had two and so on. Sometimes two brothers who had decided to divide the old house with a partition wall, according to the first method of division, quarrelled irreconcilably about the position of this wall. Then they might switch over to the second method, one buying out the other. If they could not afford to do this, one might legally pull down his own section of the house, take away the timber and stones, and build himself a new house on his own land.

Sometimes four brothers separated two by two, one pair remaining in the old home and the other going out. In that case the former paid between them half the assessed value of the house to the outgoing pair. Sometimes the four separated one by one, two remaining in the old home as before and two going out. In this case the old home was divided by a partition into two portions, one for each of the two brothers remaining in it and one-quarter of its value was taken from each of them and given to each outgoing brother.

In Dibër and Perlat, possibly elsewhere, the outgoing brothers received an extra portion of land as a site for the house they must build. In Perlat a distinction was made between irrigable and non-irrigable land. The extra portion given in the case of the latter, which was nearly worthless, might amount to as much as 120 *pashë*.

Almost everywhere the old home was valued as it stood, but a system not recorded elsewhere prevailed in Perlat. This took no account of the timber, stones and mud (for mortar) which went to the building of the house because these cost nothing but labour, and the labour had been provided as a joint enterprise by the family when still united. (But the brothers, remembering what the mason who built the house had been paid, divided that sum equally between themselves; it was generally no more than 6 or 7 napoleons.) As usual, the brother allotted the house paid cash to his outgoing brothers. The drawback to this system was that it did not provide for fluctuations in the value of money.

The old house was generally given to the youngest because he was thought too young to be able to build one for himself. 'The man who has not built himself a house or celebrated his daughter's wedding does not know what trouble is', runs the proverb. The older brothers had had time to acquire friends and could make their own way in the world, but the baby of the family knew nothing about anything except his father's house.

After the land and the house had been divided, the boundaries between the holdings were demarcated. The house, it should be said, included land round it and also any cattle or sheepfolds. When the land was under water, irrigation channels were marked out at the same time as the boundaries. Where the father had possessed one field with an irrigation channel running down its whole length, his sons tapped this channel without difficulty, each digging a small transverse channel from it on his own portion of the field. Where the stream was farther off the brothers jointly dug a channel to the point where their land met, after which each made a separate channel through his own ground; by preference each took this down his own side of the little path between his field and his brother's. When the water came from above a field so narrow that it must be divided short-ways, the brother getting the lower half was entitled to dig an irrigation channel down the side of his brother's land. But the area it occupied must be measured and an equivalent amount of land subtracted from his holding and added to his brother's. It was, of course, always stream irrigation that was in question.

The period for which each brother might irrigate was also settled when they separated. This was usually a matter of simple arithmetic. If, for example, the father had had the right to irrigate for two days, each of the two brothers was given the right for one day and each of three brothers for sixteen hours. In Mirditë, where few streams could be utilized, irrigation water was divided by the oke; unfortunately there is no information available as to how this was done.

Drinking water was seldom regulated; 'God has given it' and almost everywhere in excess. There was so little in some villages near Shkodër, however, that it was divided by the jugful, at least during the dry season. When brothers separated in these villages their portion of drinking water was decided. Division was as with food, by heads, so many jugfuls per person.

Milling rights varied from district to district. Where they were by hours or days each brother's quota was settled on the day of separation. It was again arithmetical, each of two brothers getting half the father's period and each of three getting one-third.

Generally one took over the others' periods and compensated them with an agreed quantity of maize per year.

In dividing the livestock the system of 'offset or compensation' was much used; four horses could not otherwise be divided equally between five brothers. By this system four of these brothers each took a horse and together subscribed the value of one for the fifth. Or this brother might be given another animal, such as a cow, plus the difference in money between its value and that of a horse. If there were five horses to be divided among four brothers, one received two horses and each of the others one horse and another animal or animals of the same value as a horse, plus any money compensation that might be necessary. In Çermenikë a house-dog was equated to a sheep and rules enunciated for its future service. If the old home was partitioned between the brothers, it must continue to guard this for their joint benefit. If they set up separate houses, it went with the one to whom it had been allotted and guarded only his house; the other must buy a dog for himself. As for the brandings or other marks on animals, the father's sign was assigned to one brother and new ones devised by the others. There were some exceptions to these rules. In Dibër livestock was divided equally among all the boys and men old enough to herd; this is said to be Skanderbeg's law. In Mirditë it was divided equally among the guns in the house. In Çermenikë if a brother had a very small family the sheep might be divided equally among the souls in the old home on the plea that a man with few hands could not tend many sheep. Everywhere sheep-folds and cattle-folds were divided, like the old home, equally among the brothers. Fodder, including wheat and maize straw, hay and leaves of trees, was divided on the same principles as the livestock, equally in Mirditë among the guns, in Dibër among the herds, and elsewhere among the brothers.

As for poultry, custom varied. In Lumë they were considered property, not food, and so divided equally among the brothers. In Çermenikë they were regarded, somewhat uncertainly, as food, and so divided according to the number of souls. In Mirditë the mistress of the joint household divided the poultry as directed by the person arranging the separation.

Farm implements included plough, sickles, saws, hatchets, hoes, etc. If possible one article of each kind was given to each brother. Otherwise an article was given to one and something else of equal value or money compensation to the other. In the cases, frequent enough, where each had had his own implements before the separation, he took these with him to his new home.

Beehives too were divided on the offset or compensation system; they were seldom enough to go round the brothers. Honey was divided on a food basis, equally among old and young.

Household utensils such as spoons, milk cogs, churns, wash-tubs, pots, saucepans and all wooden and earthenware vessels were also divided equally among the brothers. After being taken out of the house they were stacked in piles, one for each brother under the direction of whoever divided the property. It was almost never possible to find an article of the same type for each brother. So an article was laid on one pile and the offset on the others. Less often, an article of which there was only one was valued and a proportionate share of its value paid by its new owner to his brothers. There was never any furniture in the sense of tables, chairs and bedsteads to divide. At most, there were reed mats and straw-stuffed cushions in the sitting-room and some wooden stools in the kitchen. The stools might be divided equally among the brothers; the other things were generally treated as part of the house and left where they were.

Certain articles in the house were not subject to division. These included the portable oven, flour-bin, tongs, shovel and kitchen-crook, which were the symbols of family life; and the mill, caddy, pot and cups forming the coffee outfit, which was the symbol of guest-friendship. The former remained in the kitchen and the latter in the sitting-room, irrespective of whether these rooms had been separated or left to one brother. Above all, it was unlucky to move the kitchen-crook; it was almost as sacred as the fire on the hearth on whose continuance depended the continuance of the family. Very occasionally, however, it was allotted like the rest of the property. Other articles were considered individual property and excluded from division on that account. These included the jack-knife, gun and revolver carried by each man (at least in the not-so-distant past), the trousseaux brought by the married women or being made by the girls, and the married women's pocket-money, wedding presents, possessions and livestock, or money lent at interest. All these continued to be the sole property of their owners. Bedding too was individual property, each brother's having been brought by his wife as part of her trousseau. If the father was dead his bedding was divided in Mirditë equally among the brothers; presumably it was so elsewhere. There was divergence about his arms. In Mat and Mirditë, for instance, these were given to the oldest brother but in neighbouring Perlat and Dibër to the youngest. In Perlat the mother's jewellery also fell to the youngest.

With both the land and the house, it was only the father's property which was divided according to the number of brothers. Any land bought after his death was divided according to the number of adult men. All of these, it was considered, had shepherded the family flocks or worked in the family fields, so helping to amass the purchase price of the new land. Under this rule, when one brother had two grown-up sons and one small son, and the other brother had only two small sons, the small son of the former and his little cousins received no land at all, but the two grown-up sons received each one-quarter of the land bought since their grandfather died. In Perlat a son taking a share of bought land must be at least 20 years of age; in Mirditë he need not be more than 15, the age at which he began to bear arms. In Mat, if he herded sheep, he need be only ten.

So with the house: this went to the youngest brother only if built or inherited by the father. If built by the brothers after his death, it was retained by the eldest, who turned his juniors out, paying each of them their proportionate share of its assessed value or, in Perlat, the mason's charges for building it.

A difference of mothers never affected the division of the 'father's property'. If the mother of the eldest of three brothers had died or been divorced, he took his third just the same. If the mother of the third brother were a concubine, he too took his third. The inheritance came from the father, irrespective of the mother. It was otherwise with a wife's or a mother's property. This went to her son, to the exclusion of her step-son. A man who built a house with his wife's money might give his brothers houseroom until they separated, but they had no legal share in it; as husband of the heiress, he was its sole owner, and when they separated, did not pay them any part of its value. If his wife died or was divorced and he married again, the house descended to the first wife's son, to the exclusion of the second wife's. If the former son separated from his half-brother, he paid him nothing for the house; built with his mother's money, not his step-mother's, it was his exclusive property. Such cases were rare, occurring only when a woman was the sole survivor of her family and so inherited its property.

It was on the principle of father's property—or very much more rarely mother's—that big households containing several sets of cousins split up. They went back to their common ancestor, ascertained what property he had had, and divided that equally among his sons. The descendants of each son then took their portion and no more, regardless of their number. Supposing a man had had three sons who in their turn had respectively five, three and two sons. When these cousins separated the five sons of the eldest brother received only one-third of their grandfather's property, no more and no less than the amount received by the three sons of the second and the two sons of the third brother.

The question of the father's property came up again when a man died childless after separating from his brothers. For instance, if four brothers all separated they divided the dead man's property equally as having been originally their father's. If three were living together apart from the fourth who had died childless, they took his property back into the common fund, and when they separated divided it equally with their other possessions. If one of the three who lived together died childless, the two surviving took his property back into the common fund and when they separated divided it equally between themselves, but they did not give any to the fourth brother because he had separated from them before the death. Matters were usually complicated in Perlat and Mirditë when four brothers had separated into two pairs. If one died childless, any property which they had bought together was retained by the survivor of his pair, but what he had inherited went back into the stock of father's property and was divided into three portions, one for his survivor and two for the other pair. A rather better portion of land was given to his survivor in Perlat but apparently not in Mirditë.

Money a man had earned away from home—as government official, gendarme, shopkeeper or servant—had to be sent home up to the date of separation. Then it was counted family earnings and put into the common purse on the plea that although he was away working his brothers were toiling at home. If he kept any back for some months before the expected separation, it was accounted stealing, and if he was only suspected of doing so, he might be put to the oath to clear himself. If livestock was bought with his money that must be divided equally among all the brothers. If a house was built with it, that again must be divided equally. The law laid down 'What is in the house on Separation day is part of it'.

On the same principle, any debts due by the family such as government taxes or arrears of taxes were divided equally among the brothers. Each had to discharge his share independently, the others accepting and being given no responsibility for it. Any payments due to the family, such as repayment of money borrowed, were similarly divided between the brothers. Bride-price was in a class by itself, being paid to the bride's father, both while he still lived with his brothers and afterwards as well.

In a very few areas special charges on the family property were recognized. If, for instance, the youngest brother in Çermenikë did not yet have a gun, it was thought fair to give him money out of the common purse with which to buy one. In Perlat before the livestock was divided, two oxen and a few sheep were set aside for the wedding feast of an unmarried brother. In Mirditë the estimated cost of his wedding was paid to him, generally in kind, as in Perlat. Elsewhere, so far as is known, no such allowances were made.

Food and property of every description having been divided as described, accounts were balanced. Each brother paid up what money he had to pay and each received what money he had to receive. This concluded the division in most cases. It will be observed that no provision beyond 500 grosh was made for the daughters of the family. This was probably thought unnecessary by the old law-givers because a woman who had not reached extreme old age or been otherwise disabled was no burden to anybody. Her work, herding, spinning or even hoeing in the fields, was worth more to both brother and husband than the cost of her keep. An unmarried girl stayed with any of her brothers after their separation. She stood in the same relation to them all, it was thought, and was no nearer to the one than to the other. The modern civil code enacts, however, that a real and not a token provision shall be made for each daughter.

It sometimes happened that the father was alive when the brothers separated. If so, his welfare was provided for by the law. If the separation took place with his blessing he went to live with the son he liked and got on with best. This was almost invariably the youngest, who was thought nearer to him than the others, and if the youngest died, he went to the next youngest. Only one per cent of fathers chose to live with another son, and then a woman was generally to blame. If the youngest was unmarried or had a disagreeable wife who did not give much promise of looking after a troublesome old father-in-law, he went to a son with a kinder wife.

Since it was understood that he would live with his youngest son and that this son would have his house, he continued to live in his old familiar quarters. One room was allotted for his special use, but it frequently served as the general sitting-room as well because he only required one corner to sit in by day and to sleep in at night. For his support he might either keep one-eighth of his land in his own hands or arrange to be fed by his sons, either jointly or in turn. In the former case the son he lived with worked his bit of land, fed him with its produce, and eventually buried him. In consideration of the latter expense this son was allowed to keep his land and his room, though it meant getting a larger portion than his brothers. Sometimes the others contributed a little towards the old man's keep and the expenses of his funeral. In that case they had a claim at his death to an equal share of his fraction of land and his room, payable in money.

When all his sons contracted to feed him in turn, he probably continued to live with the son with whom he was happiest, and month by month asked each of the others in turn for money with which to buy food. If they contracted to feed him jointly, each sent him an agreed quantity of food and clothing per year. In Mirditë this was fixed at 6 loads of maize, 3 pairs of sandals, 25 okes of salt and 2 bushels of haricot beans. Under this arrangement there was no eighth of land to be divided on his death. His room was kept by the son with whom he had lived, but this son must pay a proportionate share of its value to his brothers.

On Separation day after a room and an eighth of land had been set aside for the father, the division of his property, both inherited and bought, proceeded as if he no longer existed, but he retained any title-deeds to all his former land which he might hold. His eighth was never enough to feed him, and the youngest son might become too impoverished to make up the deficiency, in which case his only resource was to pay lengthy visits to his other sons. With the title-deeds in his hands he was sure of his welcome; without them he might not be. So, too, if his sons had contracted to feed him, possession of the title-deeds made it more certain that they would fulfil the contract. On his death the deeds passed to his sons.

These were the general rules for his maintenance, but there were a few variants. In Çermenikë a man who had managed to buy a large amount of land during his working years had the right to keep this back when his sons separated and to leave it all to the son with whom he lived, to the exclusion of the others. More often than not, he allowed it to be divided up with the land he inherited. Sometimes he was still able to earn a little. In Lumë his sons treated his earnings as family property, taking the cost of his funeral out of them and dividing up the rest. In Çermenikë the son he lived with paid the whole cost of his funeral and kept all his earnings. In Mat, a relatively fertile district, a yoke of land was set aside for him. On his death his richest son paid for his funeral and took his piece of land in exchange. In Perlat an ox was set aside on Separation day for the public meal at his funeral; it was kept and worked till required by the son with whom he lived; its work was supposed to compensate this son for the other expenses of the funeral. In all areas the father's portion of land was often given by richer families to the poor or, among the Catholics, to the church.

A father had in the last resort the right to banish a son from his house, or a son might insist on hiving off against his father's wish. In either case he need not give him a portion, but when he died the son would take his proportionate share of the food and property, exactly as if he had never been expelled. A son who separated from his father in these conditions must restrict himself to any land his father might have given him and must refrain from interfering with the rest of the land or other property. The consequences of a premature division of property may be seen in the following story from Perlat. Two men made such scenes about their father's remarriage that he bade them leave his house. Of a just, or simple, disposition, he divided his property into three, keeping one-third for himself and giving one apiece to his sons. Afterwards he had two more sons by his second wife, then found he could not leave them more than his own portion of property, for land once divided cannot be taken back, says the law. So each of the two sons he loved best received only one-sixth, and each of the two sons he had come to dislike one-third, of his original property. An interesting variation of the above law is found in Kurbin. If a father gave a rebellious son a portion, he gave it only out of the land and livestock which he had bought since the son's birth; it was half or a third or a quarter according to the number of his sons. He kept the rest of his property, and this passed on his death to the son or sons with whom he continued to live, the expelled son getting nothing. If, however, he had built his house since this son's birth, it fell on his death to the son he lived with, but this son must pay the expelled son the usual proportionate share of its value.

When there was an old mother she, like the father, usually went to live with the son she loved best; in 99 cases out of 100 this was the youngest. The problem of her support was not so difficult as that of an old father. The relationship between the sons and their mother was so close that few quarrelled with her and refused her food and shelter. If 'wicked' enough to do so, the whole of their world cried shame and the old lady herself might react. A native of Shelcan in Shpat took his wife away and settled in Elbasan, leaving his mother in the village. She wished openly that he were dead. More important still, a mother had economic value and was seldom the useless encumbrance that most old fathers were. At her weakest she had strength enough to rock the cradle and to mind the house while her son's wife was out working in the fields. Besides, she had worked hard for the general benefit in her time, and that must not be forgotten. For all these reasons, in most places the son she lived with was content to feed and dress her. The others might or might not contribute. If they did, their contribution was generally voluntary and at their discretion. It normally took the form of small presents, such as a kerchief or a pair of sandals. It was not advisable to give such presents regularly, for that might make the son she lived with take them for granted. By exception, in Malësi e Madhe the law bade the other sons combine to send her three loads of maize every year as a contribution towards her keep. In Mat, if she stayed with one son, he must support her unaided; the others gave her no food or clothes. In this district, however, she might opt for staying a month with each son in turn, so making them share the expense of keeping her. In Godolesh, and in Shijan near Elbasan, she had the right, like the father, to take one-eighth of the general property. The son worked this land, fed her with its produce and eventually took it into his own holding in consideration of paying for her funeral. In practice she seldom exercised this right, preferring to run in and out of all her sons' houses in turn and getting a meal in any of them. She was expected to behave reasonably; in Mirditë if she were a trouble-maker her son might legally send her back to her brother, giving her three loads of grain for her support during the first year and nothing afterwards. On her death she might be buried by the son she lived with, as in Zerqan, or by all the sons in combination, as in Martanesh and the Malësi e Madhe. Here good feeling rather than the law dictated the usage.

Sometimes a minor—a small brother or the orphan of a dead brother—had to be arranged for. The essential was that he should receive his portion and not be left alone with his mother, as she might induce him to sell his land or might herself take a lover. If his grandfather were alive he remained with him. Otherwise he went to live with an older brother or an uncle. Exceptionally, in Shijan he lived by preference with his mother's brother, less probably with his father's brother, and still less probably with his own brother. His guardian worked his land or gave it to a third party to work for an agreed return and fed and clothed the minor with its produce until he came of age at fifteen. The guardian had also to feed and clothe his mother and any small brothers and sisters he might have. Sometimes a guardian brother remained in the father's house with the minor. He was its master, though not its owner, until the minor came of age. Then he must leave the house to the minor and himself move to new quarters.

Sometimes brothers who had separated joined up again. The 'remarriage' seldom lasted long; as the proverb puts it, 'a loaf once broken can't be put together again'. When they separated for the second time, their food and property were divided on the same principles as before. Due note was taken of any house they might have built or any land or livestock they might have bought during their temporary reunion; these were divided as usual, not according to the number of brothers, but according to the number of men. If one brother had died childless since the first separation, a completely new division of the property was necessary.

The division of food and property might be effected by elders, by the eldest brother, by a neighbour, or by a more distant relative, or by the father if alive. The factors governing the choice of one or other were, as usual, based on common sense. The division of property, as distinct from food, was often so complicated that only experienced men like elders could grapple with it. A father tended to favour his best loved son or daughter-in-law and was often ruled out for that reason. If the brothers were not on good terms, division by the eldest caused quarrelling, the others accusing him of robbing them and he retaliating in the usual manner. If they were on exceptionally bad terms, even distant relatives feared the unpleasantness that was bound to follow their best attempts at a fair division. For all these reasons the choice generally fell on elders. Their drawback was their need of a fee, but it was generally thought better to spend money on a fee than to quarrel with a brother. These principles were at the back of the various practices in different places. When the choice was between neighbours and relatives by marriage the latter were preferred because they were always more trusted. Each brother put in his own man.

In Perlat the father was never allowed to divide his property, elders or relatives on the male side must do so, and when they were at work, neither the father nor the sons might put in their word. In Martanesh the same fear of favouritism prevailed, and elders or the neighbours in bulk carried out the division. In south Dibër the local notables did so, their influence being thought to counteract any tendency to break the peace over the division. In Godolesh separation had always been on an official basis; it was arranged by the headman of the whole village and his two assistants, as it had been in Turkish times by the headman assisted by an elder from each of the six quarters of the village; it is to be noted that no fee was taken by these elders because separations had always been part of their official duties. In Shijan the separation might be entrusted to the husband's or wife's relatives since they were interested in preserving peace in the family, yet had no personal interest in the division. In any area, when brothers were on really bad terms, complete strangers from another village might be called in to arrange the separation.

When the brothers decided to engage elders, they engaged one between them if they were on good terms; if not, each put in his own man. In Mirditë they might engage two, four or more elders according to the amount of work to be done.

Portions were allocated to the brothers by their own choice or, more often, by lot. In the very few cases where the brothers were completely friendly, the eldest said to the youngest 'Which field will you have, this or that?' Then he took for himself what was left. If the second coveted the field chosen by the youngest, they drew lots for it or asked elders to divide it. When the brothers were a degree less friendly but the eldest nevertheless divided the property, the youngest was given first choice of the portions, the next youngest the second choice and the eldest what was left. The law ran: 'the eldest divides, the youngest chooses.' It is obvious that the risk of getting an inferior portion made the eldest divide carefully. In Mirditë by exception it was the middle brother who had first choice.

Lots varied: in Lumë they were drawn in the modern method with pieces of paper; one without holes, another with one hole, the third with two holes, and so on; and by the old-fashioned with a stone, a twig and a clod of earth. In the Malësi e Madhe grains of maize, coins and weeds as well as paper were used. Shijan preferred straw and grass, and Godolesh grains of maize and haricot beans. Maize was satisfactory when there were two brothers, as one variety has white grains and the other yellow, but when there were three brothers, haricot beans, which may be white, black or mottled, were preferred. Somewhat curiously, though stones and sticks were both plentiful, they were seldom used. In Shijan, for example, the lots were drawn with elaborate care. One of the relatives present at the division was sent some distance away and told to keep his eyes closed. Each brother selected his token and handed it to another relative. The first was recalled, given the tokens, and told to place each where he chose. Each brother was expected to accept the luck which his token had brought him, but if one objected, lots were drawn a second or even a third time, fresh tokens being chosen and a different relative asked to drop them each time. The brother who got the disputed land or other property two out of three times became its owner for good. The various positions of land and livestock, the piles of farm implements and household utensils and the rooms in the house (if this was partitioned) were drawn for in the same way. In Martanesh the procedure was shorter but there was again, for greater fairness, a man between the brothers and the person who made the decisive throw. Each brother gave his token to one of the bystanders, who carried it to the elder dividing the property. In ignorance of which token belonged to whom the elder cast them on the various portions. In Zerqan there was again an intermediary. Each brother had a secret, unpaid representative who gave a stone to a third person approved by all the brothers but ignorant of who represented each.

This third person threw the token stones on this portion or that. In Godolesh there was no intermediary. Each brother gave his token to an elder in whom they all had confidence. As they were selecting their tokens, he arranged tokens of his own on the ground, naming each aloud for the various portions of the land or house. He carefully refrained from looking at the brothers' tokens and threw them blindly one after another on his own. 'Here is the sitting-room, good luck to it. Here is the kitchen, good luck to it', he said of the house. Each brother then claimed his token and accepted his portion. With a similar phrase of good omen the elder divided the land. In Lumë there might or might not be an intermediary. The elder taking delivery of the tokens might place them himself or, if afraid he would be suspected of dishonesty, he might give them to another man to do so. Well-omened phrases were used, such as 'The luck of this stone lies there and of this twig here'. In the Malësi e Madhe the elder said which portion the bits of stick each represented, then drew them, as would be done in England. Here the procedure seems influenced by the European education of the priests.

The commonest fee for an elder dividing property between brothers was two or three napoleons, but it might be as low as one or as high as ten. Everything depended on how much the brothers quarrelled over the division, and how hard they struggled against yielding one to the other. In Perlat the elder made a distinction between rich and poor, asking a sheep from a rich family but only a kilo of coffee from a poor one. In Mirditë he had the right to a sheep and a money fee as well; the latter was as agreed. In Lumë 'it does not do to have an elder without a sheep'. Wherever, as in Godolesh, officials arranged the separation, no fees were charged.

Everywhere one meal at least of meat and rice pilaff must be given to whoever came from outside the family to separate the brothers. If these had no flocks, they must buy meat from someone who had. The expense of these meals, which was heavy for people so poor, was shared by all the brothers, the animals being taken out of the common stock before it was divided and the money for the rice, coffee and, if necessary, meat out of the common purse before the settling up of accounts. These meals were the first charge on the family property.

All stages of the division were watched by neighbours. Before the persons negotiating the separation sat down to the final meal, they reminded these onlookers how everything had been divided. Then if disputes arose later between the brothers these could bear witness to the division. No documents were drawn up, the oral testimony of the witnesses in general, and in particular the mute testimony of the boundary stones, was enough for the unwritten law. Where a dead father had held title-deeds, these were distributed appropriately among the brothers, but such cases were few.

Too often, the division was followed there and then by disputes. Most frequently they were about the land and due to greed, for each brother knew that on the portion allotted to him on that day he and perhaps unborn generations of his descendants must live, and he naturally tried to make it as large as possible. Sometimes a brother was rightly disgruntled. Dividers were human enough to make mistakes; an eldest brother sometimes tried to cheat when dividing; at times even an elder showed favouritism. In such cases the division was revised, an elder dividing instead of the eldest brother or a second elder instead of the first, on the usual 'elder after elder' basis. Or instead of having one elder between them the brothers might each put in one for himself; in this case they must all stand aside and leave the elders to fight things out.

Not infrequently one brother was simply cantankerous. Then the easiest way for the elders to make him see reason was to exercise their right to have all their meals at the family's expense until their work was done. They might go away, leaving the division incomplete and refusing to return until he bent his stubborn neck and in person fetched them back with promises to be good. This meant an extra meal, an expense that even the trouble-maker deplored in his heart, if not openly. As it was, surely unfairly, shared by the reasonable brothers these were from the first careful to do nothing to excite the other further. There was no difficulty about extracting this meal, as the commonest source of trouble, the land, was always divided before the livestock.

A story of Turkish times from Godolesh shows the elders taking cruder but no less effective steps to settle matters. A family at the top of the village refused to accept the division they proposed. 'Where is your best ram?' asked the elders the first day, and ate the animal. 'Where is the pot of *bekmès* (boiled grape juice)?' they asked the second day, and emptied this. 'Where is the butter jar?' they asked the third day, and devoured that. The brothers then came to their senses and allowed the suggested division to proceed.

The separation completed, each new household had its own master and mistress, and its members were no longer under the control of the master and mistress of the old home, who now controlled only their own establishment. It was remembered, however, that the master of this smaller home was master of the house in which they had all lived together. When he was succeeded by his son or another, his former position was still kept in mind. So when the brotherhood formed at the first separation expanded into a kin the master of this house became the 'elder of the kin'. If his kin was the most important in the ward, his name was given to the ward and so perpetuated. The names of most wards were the names of such elders.

CHAPTER VII

THE LAW OF THE DOG

The Kanùn recognized four types of dog: (*a*) chained dogs, (*b*) sheep dogs, (*c*) shooting dogs and (*d*) pet dogs. There were different rules for each.

Chained dogs were so called because they were chained up during the daytime and let loose only at night. Other dogs were, almost without exception, free day and night.

Chained dogs were house dogs with the function of guarding their master's house from thieves and enemies. The poorest man kept one and regarded it as a valuable article of property. A rich man had as many as he fancied he required. Cen Elezi of Sllovë in Dibër kept nearly thirty. They were confined during the daytime in a great pit that ran the length of his house, and at night they were released by their special attendant. This man fed them and was the only person who could safely approach them. If Cen himself or his sons had ventured out after nightfall, they would have been torn to pieces by the fierce brutes.

The natural fierceness of chained dogs was fostered by their training. As puppies they were never caressed or even addressed kindly by their master and his children. Indeed, they were often teased deliberately in order to make them lose their tempers. They were never admitted to the kitchen or other part of the house, but were restricted to the farmyard, where they had their kennel in a corner. The kennel was generally a rough structure of wattle and daub affording the dog imperfect shelter from the elements, and usually placed as far as possible from the outside gate in order to put the utmost possible distance between the dog and an incoming visitor.

Since thieves and enemies attack only by night the house dog must be free by night if it was to fulfil its function. Since honest men and friends travel during the daytime, the house dog must be chained up to keep it from doing them a mischief. So house dogs lived 'by the sun'. They must be chained an hour before sunrise and might not be loosed till an hour after sunset.

This law was rigorous, only two modifications being permitted.

If a dog was unusually fierce, it might be tied up early and loosed late. If a locality was dangerous or if the dog's master was at feud with someone, the dog might be loosed precisely at sundown and left free till exactly sunrise. As a result of the latter proviso a stranger who reached a village about sunset must ask immediately in the interest of his own safety whether his intended host is at feud with anyone. If he were, he called to his host from a safe distance —the fiercest dog did not stir unprovoked beyond the outskirts of its own farmyard. There followed an exchange of conventional questions and answers, designed to convince the host that the stranger came as a friend and not as an enemy. When convinced, the host bade the stranger stay where he was and forbade him to speak—this in case the dog charged in the direction of the voice. He then tied up the dog while some of his womenfolk went to inspect the stranger, and if satisfied that he was harmless, to bring him to the house.

When a house dog attacked a stranger the law considered three positions: (a) when the dog only threatened to bite, (b) when it succeeded in biting and (c) when it killed. In all three positions there was discrimination between attack by day and attack by night.

If during the daytime a house dog threatened to bite a stranger, the latter might kill it without incurring a penalty. The day was his time not the dog's, and he was in the right and the dog in the wrong. To attack him it must have broken its chain or pulled up the stake to which it had been tied. Its master too was at fault for not having observed that its chain and stake were insecure. Exceptionally in Martanesh the stranger was fined 100 grosh.

If again during the daytime a house dog succeeded in biting a stranger its master must indemnify the stranger, and that irrespective of whether the dog had been killed or not. In Dibër he escaped by paying the blood money due for wounding a man. In the more picturesque north he must keep the wounded man in his house free of charge until he recovered, pay any doctor's bills that might be incurred and pay the wounded man what he would have earned if well. The northerners were so poor that they found such expenses a heavy burden. In consequence they tested a dog's chain and stake from time to time and sent their womenfolk to escort a stranger to and from the house; they could not perform this task themselves because they did not enjoy a woman's immunity from attack by a lurking enemy. A poor man, desperate as he saw his dog about to bite, might even shoot the animal, regarding its loss as the lesser evil. Occasionally a man sought to disclaim responsibility, shouting that he was not a chain-making gypsy and only bought, and did not make, the faulty chain. The stranger would retort that he was not dog's meat. Then revolvers might be drawn and a blood feud begun. More probably the dog's owner sullenly invited the wounded man to partake of the hospitality demanded by the law.

If a house dog killed a stranger during the daytime, it was in most places as if its master had killed him and a blood feud sprang up between the two families. In Dibër, however, the payment of full blood money generally satisfied the bereaved family.

During the night the law was entirely on the side of the house dog and its master. No matter how the animal might threaten a stranger he might not kill it. If he did so, he must pay blood money or have a feud with its master, exactly as if it was the latter he had killed. The Kanùn says clearly that 'at night a dog is equivalent to a man'. Indeed, in some places such as Çermenikë the animal was thought more important and its murder by night was more serious. If a house dog succeeded in biting a stranger at night, the latter got nothing from its master—neither hospitality and doctor's fees nor indemnity for wages lost. From his neighbours he got mockery—'Fancy letting yourself be bitten by a dog. You're a fine man.' Even if a house dog killed a stranger at night there was no compensation, the death went unavenged. Once upon a time, in Lurë, a daughter-in-law of Demir Lleshi went out at night into her own farmyard. A neighbour's dog sprang on her and killed her, but since it was night time, the dog's time, her blood was lost. It was immaterial that the dog was trespassing and that she was on her own ground.

There was only one exception to these rules. If a house stood near a main road an aggressive dog might be killed during the night without penalty. A higher law stated that 'it is not right to cut a main road with a dog'. In the far north bajraktars and elders had been known to order fierce dogs near a main road to be kept chained at night as well as during the day.

The blood money which was payable on killing a house dog at night was generally the same as would be payable if a man had been killed. The blood money for a bitch was the same as for a dog; there was no discrimination between the sexes as there was in the case of murdered man and murdered woman. In some areas, such as Kurbin, the blood money for a house dog was assessed by the elders or government authorities.

A stranger who agreed in his simplicity to pay the owner what he demanded for his dead dog might find himself presented with a fine bill. The owner would say that the dog had saved his life on several occasions and was consequently worth six, ten or even twenty napoleons. Sometimes the owner asked the stranger, not for blood money, but for another dog of the same quality as the dead animal. The cost might exceed the conventional amount of blood money.

In the above cases a house dog had been killed in self-defence. When it was killed out of spite matters were much more serious. 'He who kills a house dog will steal your wife', says the Kanùn. Such killings usually took place at night because the aggressor would find it dangerous to approach the house in daylight. This aggravated the crime since the night was the dog's own time.

In Mirditë, Kurbin and Martanesh a man who killed a dog 'in its kennel', i.e. on its own ground and therefore spitefully, must pay its master 500 grosh, almost a fortune in these poverty-stricken areas. In north Albania his life was forfeit. When he had been killed by the dog's master, his relatives killed one of the latter's family, arguing that they could not permit their relative to be equated to a dog. In most cases the two parties being 'one for one' the dog's master then consented to make peace on condition of receiving blood money for the dead animal. He might stipulate, if he wished, that this should take the form of an ox or a horse and so cost more than the conventional blood money. Occasionally the feud was continued—it is on record that twelve men in the north once died for the sake of one dog. In any region a man who immediately pardoned the killer of his dog would be taunted as a weakling. In Lumë the man who was suspected of having killed a house dog found dead, a crime as costly as killing a man, could not clear himself unless he persuaded twenty-four elders to take oath with him.

The legal discrimination between defensive and spiteful killing made it important for a man who killed a dog during the daytime to establish his motive. He could do so simply and surely. If his bullet had struck the dog in the forehead or chest it was evident that the animal was charging him and he had fired in fear. If, on the other hand, he had shot the dog in the back he must have killed it out of spite.

Whereas house dogs remained at home and were chained up for half their lives, sheep dogs were normally free both day and night and divided their time between the mountain-side and the sheep-fold. Their function was to protect the flock from thieves and wolves. If these approached, they must bark a timely warning so as to bring the shepherds with their rifles and they must themselves attack the marauders. They must therefore be alert, courageous and fierce, true 'Molossian hounds'. In districts infested by wolves they wore iron collars set with iron spikes to prevent the wolf from tearing open their throat. In common with other sheep dogs in the Near and Middle East they did not handle the flock. That was led, or occasionally driven, by the shepherd unaided.

As fierceness was their most important asset, sheep dogs were given the same harsh upbringing as house dogs. Indeed, they were generally removed at a still earlier age from their mother so that they should not know even her caresses for long. But they were gentle enough with their flocks, from which they never parted. As puppies they were fed on ewe's or goat's milk—hence, said the peasants of Shpat, their later friendliness with the animals they guarded. In adult life they were fed on maize bread roughly baked in indigestible looking balls by the shepherds. Nevertheless, their strength and the sleekness of their coats showed that the diet was sufficient.

The law of the sheep dog varied from place to place according to the animal's position in the local economy. In the north, where men depended almost entirely on their flocks, the sheep dog was of paramount importance as the guardian of its master's whole liveli-hood and was protected by the law to the utmost. In areas such as Kurbin, where men combined agriculture with sheep-breeding, the sheep dog was of less importance to its master and some relaxation appears in the law. In fertile areas like Lumë or Krasniqë, where agriculture predominated, the sheep dog was still less important and the law less drastic. So in the north it was more serious to kill a sheep dog than a house dog and elsewhere the position was reversed.

Among the mountains of the north the law of the sheep dog was the same by day and by night. A passer-by might be bitten at any hour of the day or night, but if he killed the dog he would be killed by its master. No excuse for his crime could be tolerated. He might have lost his way or be a stranger (and so a guest to be protected). No matter! The mountain was the dog's ground day and night. Why had he gone near the sheep? Was it to steal one? There was no road through the flock. He should have stuck to the highway which was inalienably his, day and night. If he were killed by the dog, his family had no right to claim blood money or to start a feud; his 'blood was lost'. In Dibër the same harsh laws prevailed. In the partly pastoral, partly agricultural area of Kurbin a man who killed a sheep dog generally escaped with the payment of blood money; his life was not necessarily forfeit. In Martanesh, where the economy was similar, a man who killed a sheep dog in terror of his life and proved his motive was fined 100 grosh, the amount payable for a house dog in the same circumstances.

In the adjacent Çermenikë he was not even fined. In fertile Lumë the law was that 'a man can't lose his life for a dog', and on that theory a traveller on the mountain might kill a sheep dog which had refused to let him pass. For penalty he needed only to go to the dog's master and beg his pardon. He was generally afraid to go alone—the dog's master might suspect that he had killed the dog from spite and might be in an evil temper as a result. So he generally asked others to accompany him. These confessed his crime and asked for pardon. It was never refused. If he had killed a house dog during the daytime in this district, he would have had to pay blood money as for a murdered man, or would have been killed. On the rich plateau of Krasniqë sheep-rearing is relatively so unimportant that sheep dogs come under the same rules as house dogs. If, for instance, one bites a stranger on the mountain its master must pay for the wound.

Even in the gentler areas the spiteful or senseless killing of a sheep dog may start a blood feud. An extreme case occurred 'long ago' in Lumë. The sheep belonging to the Onuzi sept were sleeping in a mountain fold near the fold of the Doçi sept. The dogs began to fight among themselves and the Doçi shepherd killed an Onuzi dog. The Onuzi shepherd drew his revolver and shot the Doçi man dead. A general fight then started among the shepherds and in a few minutes six Onuzi and twelve Doçi men lay dead for the sake of a dog. The feud raged on for years, not ceasing until it was at last composed by direct order of the reigning Sultan.

Successive generations of travellers evolved practical expedients for dealing with sheep dogs. The first was to 'let sleeping dogs lie'. If a traveller were so unfortunate as to find one in his path and there was no shepherd in sight to call it in, he swerved aside, keeping well to leeward in the hope that neither sound nor scent of his presence would reach the dog. If a dog charged, the traveller might follow the example of Ulysses on his return home and sit down. The dog would probably sit down too and immobilize him until the shepherd's arrival, but it was not likely to charge again. This expedient was more favoured in central than in northern Albania. There the traveller preferred to climb a tree in the hope that the flock would soon pass, so releasing him. The dog was not really interested in him and went on with the flock. It has happened when, a flock was large and grazing, that a man has had to stay half a day up a tree, with several dogs barking under his feet; for it was customary in north Albania to leave a grazing flock in sole charge of the sheep dog for many hours. For that reason, as soon as a traveller heard sheep bells—and in that country of long narrow valleys enclosed by lofty mountains he might hear them half an hour away—he called out. If no answering shout came, he knew that there was no shepherd with the flock and laid his plans accordingly. As far south as Shpat fear of a sheep dog might send a traveller up a tree, but there rescue came swiftly because shepherds were forbidden to leave their flocks for long. Tracks in Shpat were too many and travellers too numerous to allow of lengthy hold-ups by sheep dogs. With the same motive of protecting travellers, shepherds in the few treeless areas of north Albania were required to remain with their flocks.

If, however, a flock was grazing near a main road, the sheep dog came under the law already enunciated that 'it is not right to cut a main road with a dog'. Day and night, when near such a road, the sheep dog must be kept under control by means of the shepherd's voice or a chain, preferably the latter as being surer. A traveller who found a sheep dog loose on such a road and received no answer to his call from the shepherd was entitled to kill the dog and did not have to compensate its master.

Shooting dogs had the run of the house and kitchen as well as the farmyard and were never tied up. Born gentle, they were well enough treated by their masters to remain so throughout their lives. They were not found in every house but only with the leisured or the lazy.

A stranger who was bitten by a shooting dog could neither kill it nor claim compensation for his wound. Indeed, he became a public butt for being feckless enough to let himself be bitten by so tame an animal.

If a stranger killed a shooting dog by mischance, he must compensate the master in money—two napoleons were thought adequate in most places. Alternatively, he must give him another dog as good as the one he had killed. The hour of the crime was immaterial.

If a shooting dog was killed from motives of spite, a feud followed as in the case of house and sheep dogs.

If a shooting dog put up a hare, only its master had the right to take the hare. It might be that the chase was long and that the hare was shot by a stranger before the dog's master caught it up. In that case the latter demanded the hare and offered the stranger a fresh cartridge in return for the one he had just expended. If the offer was refused a blood feud started, the first shot being fired by the stranger.

If two men went shooting with only one dog, they skinned the hares at the end of the day and divided them equally.

Pet dogs, like shooting dogs, were free of the house as well as the farmyard and ran loose day and night. Of indeterminate pedigree, they were about the size of small Aberdeens. They were not common in northern Albania, where their only purpose was to divert their master—it was thought great fun to hang a lighted cigarette round their necks. In central Albania where the average flock was small and always had a shepherd, they were much prized as watchdogs. They never failed at either house or sheepfold to bark warningly when unwelcome visitors approached. They were so brave that at sheepfolds they could dash out and tackle a marauding wolf, invariably losing their life in the unequal combat. On account of their usefulness their value was high, as much as six or seven napoleons.

The law when they killed (a virtually impossible contingency) or were killed was the same as it was for shooting dogs.

A few isolated rules remain to be mentioned. Clerics such as priests among Catholics or Orthodox or hoxhas and sheikhs among Mohammedans were forbidden to keep house dogs. Their houses must be open day and night to their parishioners or passing strangers and might not be closed by dogs. If they kept sheep dogs they must not bring them home, but must leave them at the more or less distant sheepfold. There was no ban on their keeping shooting and pet dogs.

If a house dog disappeared temporarily during the mating season so that its master could not find it at dawn to tie it up for the day, he remained responsible for its conduct. It was held that a house dog loose under such conditions during the daytime was like one that had been duly tied up but had broken loose. Happily for its master and for strangers, a dog was generally too much occupied at such seasons with its own affairs to trouble about strangers.

If any type of dog fell into a snare set by a neighbour near its master's house, the neighbour must pay its full value. He had no doubt obtained its master's consent before he set the snare, but that did not relieve him of his liability for ensuing casualties.

Damage done by dogs must be paid for in money or by the dog's death. Each case was handled with a good deal of ceremony. If a dog ate a neighbour's eggs or killed his fowls, the latter asked its master to tie it up. If he refused, the neighbour had the right to kill the dog, and its master could not exact compensation. The neighbour generally took an oath in public that the dog had developed a habit of eating his eggs or killing his fowls, and that he had asked its master to tie it up and had been told to kill it. If he killed the dog without warning, he must in most places pay its value as assessed by the local elders. But in that case its master must first take oath that it had never eaten eggs or killed fowls. If the dog was commonly considered valuable, the neighbour would probably warn its master twice before he killed it. In Çermenikë and Martanesh the law was sterner; a delinquent dog had always to be killed, but if this were done without its master's leave, a blood feud started. In such cases the culprit was generally a house dog.

In cases of sheep-worrying the culprit was invariably a sheep dog. The general verdict was that the animal must die, but there was some variation in local methods of reaching this verdict. In north Albania and in Yugoslav Kosovë the dog's master must indemnify the sheep owner for every sheep worried and must take oath that the dog acted of its own impulse and had not been specially trained to kill sheep; any proof that it had been so trained would immediately cause him to be killed by the sheep owner. He must also kill the dog or keep it chained up in perpetuity. If the sheep owner found it loose again he would kill it without more ado or, less probably, he would start a feud with its master. A sheep owner of Koplik who complained about another's dog must be able to say that he could produce two witnesses. This might cause the dog's master to pay up at once for the dead sheep. On the other hand, he might say that the witnesses, being friends of the sheep owner, were not to be believed, and that the only evidence he could accept was a public oath by the sheep owner. If the latter took the oath the dog's master must pay him the value of two sheep for every one killed. He was left to decide whether he would kill his dog or keep it chained up. In the latter event the evil soon worked its own cure. The dog would worry sheep whenever it could escape from its chain and he, tiring of paying for its ravages, would shoot it. The sheep owner does not seem to have had the right to kill it. In Mirditë a sheep dog might be shot by the sheep owner for worrying sheep, but not unless caught 'Flesh in mouth'. In Martanesh, too, this was the rule. In neither place was any compensation due to the dog's master.

If a dog harried a drove of pregnant animals, causing some to abort their young in their terror, it might be killed by the shepherd. Its blood was then equated to that of the aborted animals. If it evaded the shepherd, its master must pay in full for each abortion; he was 'keeping a tame wolf'. If a dog killed a foal or calf, whether playfully or not, its master must pay the accepted value of the dead animal.

With mad dogs the rule all over Albania was 'Kill if you can, and the sooner the better'. The owners neither expected nor received compensation. Many of them broadcast the news that their dog was mad and asked for it to be killed as speedily as possible.

CHAPTER VIII

ROADS

Very strict rules were laid down for the construction and the maintenance of roads, 'the arteries of the land' as they were called by the tribesmen.

Two main types were recognized: the public highway, 'the big road', or 'the general road' and the footpath. The former led through a village or from one village to another, and consequently was often called the 'village road'. Yet another name was 'ward road' of a village which separated two wards. A footpath lay most often across fields, but it seemed only in Zerqan that it was described as a 'field-path', 'road wide enough for a foot', or plain 'road'.

The law said that a public highway must be a horse-track, wide enough for a loaded packhorse or a pair of plough-oxen with their plough to pass along it, unimpeded by any hedges, walls or trees that might fringe it. The minimum width allowable was consequently eight spans, the equivalent of 5⅓ feet or 1·62 metres. Where more space was available, whether on mountain wastes as in Martanesh or waterless downs as in Perlat, the road was often wider, so it was eight to twelve spans wide in Çermenikë, ten to twelve in Martanesh and Godolesh, sixteen in Zerqan and twenty-four in Perlat. In spacious Krasniqë a road for plough-oxen was usually a trifle wider than a horse-track, but there were no hard and fast rules for the width of either; the only criterion was traffic needs.

Provided that a man carrying a spade on his shoulder could pass, a footpath was wide enough; rules were not so rigid for these as for highways. Consequently some were only one, and many, especially in Mirditë, only two spans wide. In other places, however, footpaths from three to six spans in breadth were found. In general a path across irrigable, cultivated land tended to be narrow and one across, say, rough pasturage broad.

These rules were for mountain roads, where there were usually so many stones that there was no mud, and the ground remained firm under the feet in all weathers. A highway across a plain,

especially near the sea, where the soil is alluvial and stoneless, had
to be thirty-two spans wide (7 yards or 6·48 metres) in order to give
a pack-horse space to dodge the mud-holes in winter, when the
road became a morass. Excellent examples of this type of road
traverse the half-drained marshes of Ngurëzë at the mouth of the
river Mat.

Mountain roads eight spans wide led to villages 'where carts had
never gone'. Certain other roads led to the rare villages 'where
carts had gone'. These crossed firm inland plains such as the floor
of the valley of Shkrel or the plain of Nangë in Lumë; in Shkrel
they had to be twelve spans wide (8 feet or 2·43 metres), and in
Lumë wide enough to take a cart. A picturesque detail from
Mirditë is that a 'flag-road', that is to say, a road along which a flag
was carried in tribal, wedding or other processions, had to be as
wide as the flagstaff was long.

Roads always followed boundaries; as a general rule, when one
passed two wards or two neighbours, exactly half of it had to be in
the territory of each. In other words, their boundary had to run
down its exact middle. Few modifications of this law are to be
noted. When fields were on a slope, the road between them was
often made on the upper one. The elders laying it out had reasoned
that it would gradually slip down the hill, increasing the area of
the upper field and diminishing that of the lower one. When there
was an irrigation channel by the road, rules varied. In Theth one
neighbour left three spans of land for the channel, and the other
the same amount for the adjacent footpath. Their agreement might
be verbal, noted only by witnesses, or it might be written down by
the priest as tribal clerk and placed in the church archives. Each
neighbour had full access to path and channel alike. In Lumë, on
the other hand, a path was left on both sides of an irrigation channel.
These were not only for men to walk on but also for maintaining
the sides of the channel, a necessary safeguard even on level ground.
Each neighbour, having his own path, was less liable to quarrel
with the other.

In Perlat a highway was twenty-four spans wide (16 feet or
4·86 metres), to enable a horse laden with firewood to pass another
without the loads touching. Elsewhere there was no provision for
two-way traffic. Road-making in our sense did not exist, and roads
were merely trodden out by man or beast in the scanty space
available between fields or across mountain slopes. On a typical

road two loaded donkeys might meet and pass, but two loaded horses could not. When these met, one or the other had to step aside from the road, turning back, if need be to find a suitable place in which to do so. This was almost invariably of nature's making; there were no artificial passing places as on narrow motor roads in England.

Load generally determined priority of passage. To use Albanian phraseology, when a riding-saddle met a riding-saddle on a horse-track the one with no saddle-bags or other load besides the rider had to turn back. The riding-saddle had to make way for the loaded pack-saddle, but had priority over an empty one. When two pack-saddles met, the one loaded and the other empty, the latter had to make way for the former. When they were both loaded or both empty, the one which was nearer a possible place at which to step off the road had to turn back. The same rules applied to carts. In the rare cases where there was plenty of room for two loaded horses or carts, there was no 'Keep right' or 'Keep left'; they could pass on whichever side they wished.

The rules about priority were apt to be honoured in the breach rather than the observance. A man who was turned back on his road felt, even if priority was not his, as much disgraced as if his gun had been taken from him. His honour was lost, and could not be redeemed unless he killed his rival. There have been many deaths for the sake of precedence. The men of Godolesh, who were satisfied when the offender was fined by the elders, were condemned by their neighbours as soft and citified. But even in Godolesh there was no more fertile cause of murder than disputes about who should have the right of way. The trouble arose because priority rules were often confused, especially on purpose by strong wilful men, with the general law of road ownership. As enunciated by Father Gjeçov, this law said that a village street or a public highway was nobody's individual perquisite, but belonged to one man as much as to another. Hence, the living and the dead—traveller and live-stock, bride and corpse—had an absolute right to use either, and no man, even if the road passed close to the door of his house, could deny this right.

A road was free to all. It was for breaking this general law that highway robbery was punished so much more severely than other forms of theft, and that a traveller who killed a dangerous dog on a highway did not have to compensate its owner.

A man could not, without the elders' consent, close an old road that, having been used by his fellow-travellers, bridal parties and funeral processions, was public property. If he did, it was reopened by the elders, sometimes by force. He was often fined too. If he had ploughed it up, so that its line was uncertain, they sought out an old trustworthy man and made him show them under oath and in the presence of witnesses where it had been. Then the offender was ordered to open it again, removing any fence he had erected and, by way of penalty, to give a meal and small fee to the old man and the witnesses. If he shut it up once more he was liable to be shot.

As always, there were exceptions to the general rule. Owing to the marshy nature of the land most of the fields near the mouth of the river Mat were enclosed by hedges of living willow and communicated with each other by stiles, not gates. If the public, having formed a shorter route, no longer used a certain field-path, the owner of the field could close the path and the stiles at either end without any compulsion to reopen them; the public had the shorter road and one was enough. If a man bought a field which had a road round it and a right-of-way through it, he had the right to close the latter and to make the public go by the road; only if a long detour was involved could he be forced to leave the right-of-way open. On the other hand, if his new-bought field was bordered not by a road but by another field, he could not block the right-of-way unless he made a new road entirely within his own boundaries. This was substantially the law which governed changes of road all over north Albania. In Lumë a distinction was drawn between permanent roads which had to remain open all the year round and winter roads which could be closed in summer. The first were known as 'roads with a boundary'; the most important led to the high pastures on Mount Gjalicë. Winter roads generally went through fields and were closed to men and animals from seed-time to harvest; as soon as the crop was in, the roads were opened to traffic. If somebody had great need to use one during the season, he might take what he could carry and go along the very edge of the sown land, taking pains not to damage the growing crop. He could not make a habit of this or take his horse and must not forget to ask leave from the owner of the land. Again, a few roads to the Alpine pastures passed through wheat fields on their way. As a necessary link with the high pastures they could not be completely closed even when the fields were under crop. An ingenious compromise reconciled the public's need to use the road and the individual's wish to protect his crop without incurring the intolerable expense of making a fence or wall. One neighbour put two hurdles across his half of the road, one where it entered and the other where it left his land; both were low enough for men to jump over and high enough to keep back animals. Each had a hole at the bottom that was too small for animals to crawl through but big enough to let logs through when they were dragged down from the mountain for fuel; logs for fuel were such a necessity of life that they could not be denied a road. The other neighbour threw across his half of the road the Christ's Thorn which grows all over the plains of Albania, thus making a formidable barrier for men and beasts. Shutting up this half of the road did not matter; animals had no right in any case to go near a sown field, and the other man's hurdle was sufficient for human traffic. After harvest the thorns were removed, leaving that half of the road clear. The hurdle remained in place, as the clear half of the road was wide enough for the traffic.

In 1935 a man from Nangë in Lumë blocked the road along an irrigation channel for the summer, half of it with a low wall and half with thorns, so that men, but not animals, could still travel on it. He had wished to sow maize in his adjoining field and been too poor and short-handed to construct a fence to keep out animals. Since irrigation was so important, there was a special law that 'a road beside an irrigation channel can't be shut up'. Consequently, his act was highly illegal. But his poverty was thought to excuse it, and he had mitigated his offence by making a new road for animals at the top of his field, where there was no maize. In so doing he had confused the right to block a road for the summer only and the need, when closing one permanently, to provide a substitute. For the law forbidding a man to block an old road permanently was not rigid. If he had good reason for the change, secured the consent of the elders (a most important point), and provided a satisfactory substitute, he could even move a very old road. It was only if he failed to satisfy these conditions that he had to leave it where it was. The poor man just mentioned transgressed by not consulting the elders; their unusual clemency lay in refraining, out of consideration for his poverty, from reopening the road.

When a man applied for leave to close an old village road, he generally pleaded damage by passers-by or a need for more land to till. In the first case he might have his house or field adjoining the road and find his dog biting strangers and shot for its pains, his children killed by passing horses or cattle, and his crops, vegetables, vines or fruit damaged or plundered. Or the road might cross his field necessitating a fence on both sides, thus preventing his sheep from passing freely from one part of the field to another, besides involving him in expense for making and maintaining it. In the second case he might wish to plough up the road, a good plea since the law said 'Agriculture can move a highway', and more pithily, 'spades can shift roads'. If the elders on investigation considered his request justifiable, they gave him leave to close the old road. They required, however, that he should provide a satisfactory substitute, not by a stream where sheep might drown or across a precipice where they might break their necks; if the precipice could not be avoided, the rock had to be blasted away with dynamite. The new road could not be far from the old one, a distance of 200 metres being the maximum allowed. It had also to be made by the man's own unaided efforts, without any help from the community, and it had to be well made. If it was poorly made, the man suffered himself when he came to grief on it and had to pay damages when another did so; he was also laughed at by his neighbours as a foolish creature who did not know how to make a road; often they went and reopened the old road. In Fulqet it did not matter if the public was inconvenienced by the change; the law said 'land must not be spoiled'. In the Breg i Matit, on the other hand, the new road had to be shorter and so more convenient. A curious point in Krasniqë was that if a man ploughed up his field he could reduce the public road to the width of a footpath; this was little more than a gesture, since oxen and horses could not in any case use the road after the field was sown and a footpath was wide enough for other traffic. In Martanesh it was never lawful to plough up a public road, perhaps because the fields were few and very scattered, and the roads few, long and often dangerous.

In case of clear necessity an old public road might be moved on the initiative of the elders. If, for example, it was inconveniently crooked or became a morass in winter, they could divert it to better ground. The old road became the property of the man whose land adjoined it. The men whose land was taken for the diversion received no compensation. They often threatened to kill the elders, but for sole reply received an exposition of the law; they might shoot as much as they pleased but could not have their way; the village could not be shut up by mud, and the public good overrode private loss. The new road was a permanency and could not be closed or moved back to the old site except by the elders. According to Vatë Marashi, the bajraktar of Shkrel, it was easier to move the bad road than to try to mend it. If it was under water, all the owners of the land through which it ran had to unite to repair it, making a ditch, repairing bridges and so on. But they had to decide unanimously to repair it; if even one hung back nothing could be done. The ditch too could only be made where there had once been one before. And men whose land was some distance from the road would object to having the water diverted from the road towards their fields.

New roads were constantly being opened, if only because brothers were constantly dividing their father's property and setting up separate establishments. For the law said 'every field must have access to a public highway' and 'every house must have its road'. Consequently, the elders supervising the separation were careful to specify the exact direction and character of the old roads which the brothers might use and the new ones which they might make to and from their houses and fields. The laws were the same everywhere. If there were two brothers, each took half the father's field. When there was no cultivated land beyond this they might make no path at all or they might make a little path along the boundary between them, only two spans in width, as this was enough for their own needs. Naturally each set aside land for half its width; as this could not be worked, it was soon grass-grown. When there was someone else's field beyond their own and there was no other way of entering this, they were bound to leave a track wide enough for a horse laden with panniers of manure or for a pair of plough-oxen. As with a field-path the land for this track came from each.

A more complicated case occurred if three brothers inherited a field which had a public highway running along its length, and was divided into three longitudinal strips with the boundaries parallel to the highway. Let it be supposed that the family home remained in the central strip. A road to the highway from the inmost strip was a prime necessity. It was most economically made by constructing a path to the old road that connected the family home with the highway. But the new owner of the central strip might object to its coming so near his house. In that case the elders directed him and the owner of the outermost strip to leave land elsewhere for it. As for the houses which the brothers in the innermost and outermost strips had to build, the former had only to see that his stood the canonical distance, the width of the eaves from his neighbour's boundary. The most convenient and economical site for the outermost brother to build on was a corner by the highway. But remembering that his dog might bite strangers and his children be trampled on by passing animals, he generally built his house with its back to the road and its yard facing his field. Alternatively, in Krasniqë, by what seems undue licence, he could ask his neighbour to remove the public highway to his land. If the latter owned waste ground or a hill close by, he was compelled by the elders to accede to the request. He could only refuse it by convincing them that in its new position the road would spoil his land.

New roads were sometimes necessitated by sales of land, and might cause trouble. Suppose a field surrounded by four others was offered for sale and the owners of the surrounding fields were unable to buy it. Someone farther away, always described as a 'stranger', then bought it and demanded a road. The natural line for this was through the field between his purchase and his house. If the owner of this field objected, the stranger bade him buy the enclosed plot. When he refused, as he inevitably did, the stranger referred the case to the elders. If these, he said, could cite any previous purchaser of a field which had no way in and out, he could not claim the road. If, on the other hand, and this was sure to be the case, they found it was good law that 'land is never sold without a road' he had to have it. There was, as usual, no need to compensate the man whose land it took up. Fear of such complications made some men, when selling a piece of land, retain the adjoining road in case they themselves or their descendants wished to use it later on.

A man was undisputed and sole master of the path that led across his field from a public thoroughfare to his house and ended there. According to the letter of the law, whatever the condition of the public road—good or bad, a sea of mud or even washed away in a winter storm—animals and wayfarers had to keep to it or to find another. They could not bypass the bad stretch by taking the path to the man's house; that was his private property, reserved for his household and his visitors. Bridal parties or funeral processions which tried to pass along his path to evade the difficulties of the highway were not so likely as habitual travellers to attempt to create a precedent, but he had the right to turn them back. If they tried to force their way past him he had the right to shoot them. Many a corpse, to quote Father Gjeçov, has found comrades in death before being buried, and many a bride has mourned the loss of a kinsman in her escort on the way to her bridegroom.

If, however, at a time when the highway was impassable, occasional travellers asked a man's leave to use his path he often granted their request. But he always made it clear that the right of passage was temporary and stipulated that his honour was not to be smirched or his property damaged. In Shkrel a man whose field adjoined a road liable to bogging in winter often left enough land in the field for a new road. This he did as alms. Any timber on either side of the new road remained his private property, and could not be cut down by anyone else though he was free to cut it as and when he pleased. He could also close the road at his pleasure; even if the public had used it for years, usage did not create a right and rob a man of his land. Sometimes a village, to suit its convenience rather than to meet its need, asked a man to allow the public to go through his land. He usually agreed, but always stipulated that if any damage was done or he needed to work the land, he should be entitled to close the right-of-way, informing his fellow-villagers that they must not come that way any more. If this became necessary, he was not required to provide an alternative, as a man who moved a public road must do. He had opened the road as a favour, and what was given as a favour could not be retained by force. The option of closing the road descended to his heirs.

The private ownership of a road is seen at its most interesting in the case of a blind alley. This was seldom wide enough to take two persons abreast and had an entrance but no exit. The commonest type led across a man's field from a public thoroughfare to his house, where it came to a dead end. In this case it was his sole property, and if he liked he could plough it up without consulting anybody. Another type served several houses, and was held jointly and equally by these. The common ownership had its drawbacks. Two out of three owners, for instance, might wish to plough up the section passing through their fields. Though this might mean his going a long way round in future, the third owner could not oppose their wish. Again the land on both sides of an alley which three families used might belong to a fourth man. If he persuaded or bribed two of the three to let him plough it up, the third man had to acquiesce. A third type of blind alley began and ended in a single field.

All types of alley were private property reserved for the sole use of their owner, joint or single, and his family and lawful visitors. If he found anyone else on it he could turn him back as an intruder, and if he refused to comply could shoot him. This was irrespective of whether he did damage or not. An honest man would not trespass. Consequently, a trespasser's intentions were felonious. In Labinot a 'foreigner' from another village was licensed to use the blind alley once. He might be unaware that he was trespassing. In Zerqan, too, if he did not trespass more than once most owners said nothing to avoid disgracing themselves. A foreigner has his rights. In truculent Lumë no allowance was made for ignorance. About 1900 three men lost their lives because a stranger from the town of Prizren rode by pure mischance along a blind alley in a field in the village of Stiqan and resisted the owner's attempt to turn him back. In all districts a fellow-villager who trespassed could not plead ignorance as a stranger could; consequently his fault was graver. Even so he was not shot in Zerqan till other measures had been tried and failed. First the owner asked him not to use the blind alley again. If he persisted the owner complained to the village and the village forbade the man to go by the path. If he still persisted the village fined him. If he still persisted the owner shot him. Such was the theory, but in practice a strong man skipped the diplomatic stages and shot the offender at his first or second offence. Sometimes a fellow-villager who had a genuine need to use a private road, for instance, to regulate his irrigation water, might be given permission to do so. But he had to go on foot and could not take his horse.

In Godolesh, exceptionally, the question of damages affected the rules for blind alleys. Such paths traversed the market gardens on which the village still depended for most of its livelihood. Usually each belonged to several owners, any of whom might use it throughout its length, though they were forbidden to introduce animals as these might damage the fruit and vegetables. A trespasser was pardoned up to three times, then one or more owners complained against him to the elders, and he was fined ten grosh in Turkish and two gold francs in modern times. In Turkish times a strong man often forced his way through and only a weak man, cowed by the guns levelled at him, turned back. The principle of private ownership was carried so far in this village that it extended even to a certain garden road which was not blind but had an exit as well as an entrance. This was reserved for the villagers of one ward, and forbidden to their animals, to the rest of the village and to 'foreigners', with one exception. If a girl from another ward or village had married into the privileged ward her kinsmen had leave to use the forbidden path when on their way to visit her. If even one man in the ward objected, however, he had the right to veto their passage. It is not known how this unusual privilege came into being. The most obvious explanation would be that the families in the ward descended from a common male ancestor, but, in fact, the families were of very mixed descent.

In the extreme north the individual's safety on certain inter-tribal thoroughfares was ensured by what was called the 'truce of sheep and shepherd', because it mainly concerned shepherds and their flocks. Actually travellers and public messengers also enjoyed its protection. Two or more tribes, meeting in full assembly of all their bajraktars, heads, and youth, swore a solemn truce to attacks on life and property on a given route or routes within their territory, and guaranteed its observance. They prescribed the limits of the road which it covered, regulated the behaviour of persons taking advantage of it, and enunciated penalties for breaking it. Thus, a shepherd could lead his flock and graze it only within a prescribed limit. A traveller or public messenger journeying from one of the contracting tribes to another had both going and coming to keep within the points fixed. As soon as he had set foot in the foreign tribe's territory he had to go straight to the bajraktar's house and not turn aside to any other. He must not venture out alone but must always be accompanied by the bajraktar or a guide of his providing. So long as shepherd, traveller or public messenger obeyed these rules and kept to the prescribed road, he was regarded as a public guest and consequently was guaranteed public protection and, what was almost more important, public vengeance in the event of being murdered or robbed. Protection came from the knowledge of the penalties which the foreign tribe would exact for any harm done him. If he were murdered the price of his blood was 22 purses instead of the usual 12. If the murderer was slow to pay up, the tribe enforced payment. In addition, they burned down three of the *kulla* (houses of two or more storeys) in the murderer's compound. If he did not possess so many, they burned his own. *kullë* and two belonging to his nearest relatives. If between them they did not have so many, the tribe searched among his more distant relatives until they found the required number, going back a hundred generations if need be. They also destroyed his property—crops, livestock and the rest—so thoroughly that nothing of it remained. The same penalties were inflicted on a thief who stole sheep travelling or grazing within the protected area. On the other hand, if a traveller, public messenger or shepherd broke the conditions of the truce, straying, for example, from the prescribed path, he was no longer counted a public guest and lost his right to public protection and vengeance. He was still a private guest however. The last man in whose house he stayed before his mishap was bound to kill his murderer or to punish the man who robbed him.

This truce of sheep and shepherd has now died out. At the end of Turkish times it was already confined to the Gjakovë group of tribes in the extreme north-east, such as Nikaj, Mertur, Gash and Krasniq. But Father Gjeçov found traditions of its existence in the Dukagjin tribes of Shalë, Shosh, Kir, Gjâj and Toplanë, and also in Puke, Mirditë, Kthellë, Kurbin and the mountains of Lesh. Father Gjeçov considers the custom to be so old that it dates from days 'before thin-necks began to vomit flame', that is to say, before firearms were invented.

CHAPTER IX

BOUNDARIES

According to the law, every tribe, village, house, field, meadow, pasturage, vegetable garden, vineyard, forest and spinney required a fixed boundary. Some boundaries were centuries old, but, ancient or modern, they could in no circumstances be moved. The stones that most often indicated their line were, in the absence or rarity of title-deeds written on paper or engraved on copper, the chief tokens of ownership of property. Consequently they were as sacred and immovable in the eyes of the law as the bones in a dead man's grave. Brothers, cousins or villages might quarrel over a boundary and keep up the shooting until it had cost a hundred lives—nevertheless, the boundary remained where it had been when the first shot was fired.

In fields of average size the boundary was marked by three stones, one at either end and the third in the middle. Each had to be planted as deep in the earth as it projected above it, and to have its centre exactly over the boundary line so that half of it stood on one neighbour's property and half on the other's. When fields were very small, there might be only two stones, one belonging to each neighbour. Instances can be seen in Shijan. Little heaps of stones marked the division between fields and pastures in Shpat and Dumre. Big cairns of rocks and boulders, each 'as big as a house' and at varying intervals from the next one with no charcoal under them, divided off the vast alpine hayfields of Martanesh one from the other and also separated its territory from that of the neighbouring villages of Shëngjerg, Bulqizë and Okshtùn. Sometimes in the lonelier regions of the Martanesh highlands deep holes were dug in place of piling up the more usual cairns. In the spacious Alps of the north only an occasional stone was used to mark off one man's forest or grazing-ground from another's.

Each boundary stone 'had two friends with it'. These were small stones which were more or less buried in the ground on either side of the big one. They were almost invariably two in number, but in Mirditë six or twelve. In most places they were picturesquely said to be there as 'witnesses', but according to a more sophisticated informant in Bytyç their business was to prop up the big stone. The association of the three, one big and two small, was so distinct that it could be seen at a glance that they were boundary stones.

In old days, in places as far apart as Kurvelesh in south-west Albania and Lumë in the north-east, some pieces of charcoal, generally three, were put under the big boundary stone; in Lumë a fragment of tile was added. Centuries might pass, but charcoal and tile remained as imperishable evidence of the true line of the boundary. In case one neighbour charged the other with moving the stones the elders dug these up; if they found no charcoal under them they knew they had been moved and dug all round until they came on charcoal and with it the original boundary. A man who went to move boundary stones always went on a dark night when the buried charcoal was as invisible as himself, and so far as was known his ingenuity never ran to taking a handful with him from home.

Boundary stones were set up with all the ceremony befitting a mark that was to last for ever. All the members of the families concerned, the village elders, as many children and youths of the village as possible, as many men from neighbouring villages as possible and all the tribal elders gathered to witness the event and to preserve its memory for their lifetime. When the entity to be divided—field, farmyard, vineyard, etc.—had been measured with a rope or by pacing into the required number of portions, the elder chosen to delimit the boundary put any chance stone and a clod of earth on his right shoulder, and after swearing upon his soul to delimit justly, moved forward along the boundary line followed by all the witnesses. It was his duty to walk in a straight line in order to iron out every possibility of future conflict—'a boundary mustn't twist' said the law—but if he deviated slightly no one could correct him; it was his responsibility. All the objector could do was to say, 'Well, lead the way and if you don't act righteously may that weight lie heavy on you in the other life'. At the two ends and in the middle the elder—no one else—dug a hole in which he set up the big stone at one end, packing the smaller ones round it. When he finished, he laid his hand on the big stone and solemnly cursed anyone who should seek to move it, saying in Mirditë, 'Whoever moves this stone, shall be weighted down with it in the life beyond'. In Lumë the curse was vaguer, 'Here are your boundaries, men', said the elder. 'Don't move them because it's bad'—in this world where quarrelling results and in the other where damnation follows. When the last big stone was in place the witnesses fired in the air to signify that the ceremony was over.

When a geographical feature was available, it was often utilized as a boundary. For instance, an irrigation channel might be recognized as such. The dividing line between the neighbours then ran down the middle. It could not be diverted or otherwise interfered with by either neighbour, since it contained running water and had been made long years before—a point that gave it the permanence indispensable in a boundary. In Mirditë a very old tree sometimes marked the division between two pieces of land. In all areas growing trees of any age might outline forest and even village boundaries. Notches were cut in each; all the ground this side of a notch belonged to one neighbour and all on that to the other. Between big units such as villages or forests, though not small ones like fields or houses, a watershed or a torrent bed often formed the boundary. 'God has separated the two; nature has decided their boundaries', said the people of such cases. Sometimes a road was the boundary between the villages; a field-path was never important enough for this purpose. Finally, in some groups of villages near Elbasan, such as Godolesh, Griqan and Labinot, there was so much buying of land in one village by natives of the others that no very definite line was drawn between their territories, though the boundaries of individual properties were as clearly marked and as fiercely defended as they were elsewhere. In the north, since no outsider could buy land in a village, there was no fluidity of boundary, whether village or private.

The delimiting elder was usually one of the recognized elders of the village. Sometimes only one was employed, more often there was one for each new neighbour, and in sprawling areas like Martanesh ten or even fifteen men might be asked to help. In Shijan elders often worked only 'for the good of their soul' and took no fee; elsewhere they charged one to two napoleons according to local rates. In Surroj they asked no less than four napoleons but seldom received them; to save this heavy fee, the older of the new neighbours set up the boundary stones, and only if he seemed to be cheating did a younger man think it necessary to call in an elder. That elder carried the earth and stone of the oath on his shoulder. In Çermenikë, however, he carried them in his hands and in Labinot he did not carry them at all, only spoke of doing so. Both these usages seem degenerations from the original. The expression 'to take on the shoulder', which is frequently heard in speech all over the country in the sense of 'to destroy' or 'to ruin', seems to derive from this obviously very ancient method of making oath. 'If I don't act justly, may I carry this weight in this world and the next', the elder swore solemnly as, irrespective of whether he was Catholic, Orthodox or Moslem, he embarked on his delimitation. In most cases he believed that if he were unfair the earth and stone would punish him literally as he said. 'Earth will rot us all one day; we can't put it lightly on our shoulders like a stone. It's a very serious thing; we stake our soul by touching it', were some of the expressions used to explain the general fear. Some men were so frightened of the dread symbols that they would not undertake to delimit a boundary, saying, 'It's a serious business to undertake such a thing; it brings you up against God's justice'. A few others, it must be confessed, were sceptical enough in consideration of a bribe to defy the consequences of perjury and to delimit unfairly.

Boundary stones then were set up by elders in the presence of witnesses as an abiding memorial to the ownership of the land they outlined. 'A fence may rot, a boundary does not', said the proverb. 'Let ever so many be killed; a field, or mountain, a vineyard cannot be seized by force; the boundary stones say who is the lawful owner', was another aphorism. In many places it was customary, generation after generation, to 'ride the marches' once a year so that the old could show the young where the stones were and so forge the next link in the endless chain of memory. Like its British counterpart, the custom gave occasion for a public holiday. Often performed, as in Nangë, at the spring festival of 'Summer Day', all men and boys in a village went round every known boundary in it. They saw that the boundary stones were still in place and not sunk out of sight, noted their position, and cleared away thorns and other concealing overgrowth. Often, as in Nangë, they were led by gypsies banging joyously on drums.

It was thought a sin to move boundary stones, since they had been set up in such solemn circumstances by elders, the highest tribal authorities. But land-hunger was so prevalent that the sin was all too common. With the lapse of time, too, boundary stones might sink out of sight in the ground and the boundary line be obliterated. Disputes over boundaries were consequently endless. To prevent them there were various deterrents. Men of weight—

tribal, religious or personal—fostered the belief that moving boundary stones made things specially hard for the sinner in the next world. In this world the elders punished the misdeed with a heavy fine—of varying amount in Mirditë, 30 rams and an ox in Bicaj of Lumë, 3000 grosh and 6 rams in Kastrat, and a Turkish pound and boycott in Godolesh. Everywhere the sinner was publicly disgraced even if he was not always boycotted as in Godolesh, and he had always to compensate his victim financially. He had in fact stolen land, a valuable article of property as representing a man's livelihood. Consequently his crime was punishable as a bad form of theft. In Mirditë a man who had not only moved the boundary stones but also killed his neighbour was fined 100 rams and an ox and publicly executed for his double crime.

Yet in Mirditë one very primitive method of moving a tribal boundary was permissible. If a man had no forest or other source of timber and he had desperate need of this, he might take his axe and go to a forest in a neighbouring tribe—naturally he did not penetrate very far from his own tribe's boundary. The noise his axe made as he felled and lopped a tree soon brought up the foresters. If he had presence of mind and strength of arm enough to drive his axe up to the shaft in the fallen tree, and if the foresters could not pull it out, the boundary of his tribe was advanced to the tree. This was the manner in which Gjokë Buca of Kaçinar won forest from Kushnen. The method may have been peculiar to Mirditë.

In the Malësi e Madhe a man who had a spinney might refuse to permit his neighbour who had none to cut timber to fence in his property. He might want to cut the timber himself next year. It was his own business whether he sold it or not. The other was getting food from his field; let him go and buy or beg wood elsewhere for his fence. Presumably what went for an individual tribesman went for his village or tribe.

When disputes arose, efforts were made to settle them before they ended in bloodshed. Two types of dispute were distinguished, public—as arising between tribe and tribe, village and village, ward of a village and ward of a village—and private, as arising between individual and individual.

Settlement in private disputes might be effected by the parties themselves, by elders or by the government. The first method was the quickest, the second tried when the first failed, and the third when the second failed. In practice recourse to the authorities was rare and seldom as effective as action by elders.

When settlement was made by the parties themselves, one of the two men quarrelling might exclaim, 'Well, take it on your shoulders' —there was no need to specify what—'and set up the stones'. 'All right', replied the other as he bent to pick up a stone or a clod of earth or both to put on his shoulders. 'May I carry it on my shoulder in this world and in that if this ground isn't mine', or 'May I carry this stone and this earth and the whole wide world', he proclaimed as he swaggered off along what he said was the boundary line. Provided four or five witnesses were present this ended the dispute. Either oath was too solemn to be gainsaid. The second in particular was convincing: who would do anything as grave as to take the world on his shoulder for the sake of an erring rope in a measurer's hand? Four or five friends of both parties attended as witnesses. Fear of being asked to take this solemn oath was a considerable deterrent against disturbing the stones. Sometimes the older disputant took an oath, with or without earth or stone, that the disputed land was his, and so proved his title to it.

When the boundary had been recently delimited the disputants might consult their other neighbours, especially if these were older than they were themselves. Or they might ask the opinion of one, two or three very old men from another village as likely to be impartial. If they consulted only one, they had both to consent formally to employing him. Sometimes, when a dispute was dragging on interminably, an old man cut in with an offer to show them where the boundary was, with earth and a stone on his shoulder.

When friends or neighbours were called in they might settle the dispute by arguing. When old men were asked, they had to point out the boundary afresh but not till after they had taken earth and a stone on their shoulders and made a solemn oath to carry these through all eternity if they delimited falsely. When the old men were from the same villages as the disputants, they were unpaid; when from another village they were each given a Turkish pound.

By the second method of settlement the elders in Munë took two or three napoleons from each disputant as a pledge of his future behaviour, and arranged for five or six elders as well as some ordinary householders to meet at an early date at the boundary. In presence of the assembled company the claimant swore with earth and a stone on his shoulders that the boundary was where he said. The elders then dug to see if they could find the stones. If they did they gave judgement in the claimant's favour and vice versa. If the losing disputant did not accept their ruling they kept his pledge. In Martanesh, according to Mr Lef Nosi, the case was entrusted to a single elder. First he tried to decide it by questioning the neighbours of the disputants. If he doubted what they said he put them to the ordeal of an oath on bread and the Koran. If he still thought one or more of them was lying he bade them set up the boundary stones where they wished. If they dared to do so he could say no more, but sometimes they jibbed at this final perjury and then his judgement prevailed. If the loser objected to his allowing the neighbours to mark the boundary, he hushed him by bidding him let them perjure themselves and then offering to indemnify him out of his own pocket for his loss, but here the elder was on safe ground. Shame prevented the loser from accepting this offer.

When the elders failed to effect a settlement the injured party in Shijan complained to the government—not always unsuccessfully. Shijan was so near Elbasan that the government's writ ran there even in Turkish times. In many other places, in modern as in Turkish times, it was thought that if elders had failed it was useless to apply to the government, and a shooting match began. In Lumë the man who had taken the oath with earth and a stone took the initiative. In a fury at finding he had risked his soul with an oath for nothing he apostrophized his absent enemy, 'I put the stone on my shoulder. You could have done it, but you wouldn't. Now I'll kill you.' When he succeeded the bitterest of feuds started. Sometimes for greater ignominy they beat each other with sticks. This too started a bitter feud.

When bigger units disputed a boundary each party generally engaged an elder, paying him a fee of 250–500 grosh in Martanesh in Mr Lef Nosi's time, against 50 for a quarrel between individuals. Elders, disputants and witnesses crowded to the boundary, where the elders questioned and argued interminably. If they failed to come to an agreement, murder soon followed. When both sides were sickened by the shuttlecock of the feud they called in famous elders from another unit who could not possibly have an interest in the matter and asked them to set up the boundary stones where they thought right. But sometimes many lives had been lost in the interval. Once the elders of Bytyç found, when summoned to intervene in a boundary dispute between Gash and Krasniqë, that in two days it had cost the lives of 124 men.

Characteristic processes often marked the arbitration. For example, when two village wards quarrelled in Çermenikë, the chief elders of the village summoned two of the oldest men in each and questioned them separately in the presence of witnesses. If their answers tallied, there could be no more question where the boundary lay. For ratification the old men were asked to walk along it, earth and stone on their shoulder, or to swear formally to its being the correct line. If there were discrepancies in their answers, the dispute was referred to the government authorities in Elbasan or, more probably, to elders from another village. If two villages of Kthellë quarrelled the three bajraktars went with the leading men and a sufficient number of hangers-on to the boundary. One village said where the line was, the other contradicted this. Finally, the most important of the bajraktars, lifting a stone set it on the shoulder of an old, wise, upright man and bade him set it down exactly on the boundary. When he had done so the line was established beyond controversy and no more murder could be done for it.[1]

To begin with the bloodshed method, if different villages or tribes were involved, when men quarrelling over a boundary or shepherds jostling over a grazing ground killed each other at the very time that the boundary was being delimited, there was no more need for elders. The tribal or village boundary was where heaps of stones marked the graves of the murdered men. If it was from a distance that they killed each other, the boundary of each village or tribe was by his grave and the ground in between became the common property of both. If one was only seriously wounded and was able to stagger or roll himself along into the foreign territory before he died, a cairn of stones was piled over him where he died, and though in foreign territory, became the boundary of his village or tribe. Boundaries so established were the most permanent; the

[1] In Mirditë boundary disputes between villages and tribes were sometimes decided with bloodshed or a rock, obviously very primitive methods. Indeed the latter, a glorification of physical strength, seems to antedate the discovery of gunpowder.

greediest man would not venture to disturb the cairn or to steal land for which another had lost his life.

Near boundaries of villages and tribes might be won with a boulder and distant boundaries with a slab of rock. In the former event what was a contest in throwing the heavy weight took place; in so poor a country the weight could only be a stone. When the two tribes had quarrelled over a boundary each selected a champion athlete to throw the weight. Whichever threw it farthest won the land in dispute for the tribe. Father Gjeçov does not make it clear where the men stood for the throw. When more distant boundaries were in question, each champion carried a slab of stone or a rock on his back until he dropped under it. The one who held out longest won all the ground he had covered for his tribe.

The relations between a boundary and adjoining structures, such as a fence, wall or house, and natural features like hedges, trees and ditches, were as carefully regulated as the site of the boundary.

A fence or a wall generally enclosed a farmyard and sometimes a field, a vineyard or the like. Fences were made of hurdles or, much oftener, withered Christ's Thorn, depending on what grew in the locality. In the marshes at the mouth of the river Mat withies were interlaced between living willow trees planted like posts in the ditches surrounding the fields. In well-watered areas inland hedges of living Christ's Thorn were common. Walls were usually dry, like Scottish dykes; the more pretentious had their stones bedded in mud. Dry or mud, they were rare round fields, because fences were easier to make and less trouble to maintain. In upland pastures there were neither fences nor walls, presumably because the boundaries were too long. The rules for both fences and walls were pretty much the same.

When an old farmyard was divided between two brothers or cousins who were on friendly terms, their respective portions were separated only by boundary stones. When they were not on friendly terms what they did depended on the degree of their enmity. If not embittered, they built a wall three spans wide (60 cm.) or a fence, centred exactly over the boundary line and possibly broken by a door that led from one yard to the other. Each built half of the barrier and became the recognized proprietor of what he built. When it was a wall he made a square niche on his own side to mark his ownership. When it was a fence he had no such material way of safeguarding his rights but could always rely on public memory. If only one of the two wanted a barrier, he had to build it unaided and entirely on his own ground, leaving the boundary stones on his neighbour's side. In this case its position relative to these stones was enough to show whose it was, but he nevertheless constructed the usual niche on his own side. He could not, however, build the wall right against the boundary stones but had to leave its width free between them and its outer base. For the law said that any rain that fell on a man's house or wall must run off on his own ground and not damage his neighbour's property. It needed no legal compulsion, of course, to make him construct the various buildings in his own yard in such a position that their drips did not damage his fence. Incidentally the 60 cm. of free space served at need for a footpath. When two brothers were embittered, each built a partition wall, naturally without a communicating door.

If a man wilfully damaged a tree or other property on his neighbour's land he had to answer for his crime by paying damages. If a stranger who did not know he was trespassing on another's property and was not warned off by a shout from the owner did similar damage, he, too, had to appear before the elders. But if he could prove ignorance of trespass, he had no damage to pay. To keep animals under control so that they should not stray to another's property, a wall or at least a fence round the yard was an essential concomitant of a house. This too had to be its own thickness inside its owner's boundary to guarantee that rain drips did not damage the ground next door. In the Malësi e Madhe the man building the wall could claim any timber that during building operations fell not more than half-way down on his neighbour's side. But whatever fell more than half-way or reached the ground—even the scrap of land he had left himself between the wall and the boundary—became his neighbour's. This discrimination applied to every form of wall.

Sometimes when one of two brothers was enclosing his yard he was permitted to utilize his neighbour's wall for one side of his enclosure. There was no risk of this confusing the ownership of the wall, for the neighbour, when building it, had not only put a proprietor's niche on his own side but had also left the boundary stones outside so that they fell within the new yard. A more distant relative could not utilize an existing wall, but had to build one of his own, parallel to the neighbour's and distant by the regulation width from the boundary. If this involved him in more expense it also saved him and his descendants from ever quarrelling about the wall. It also gave his dog room enough to run round his house at night, a not unimportant point. But even a brother could not be allowed to erect a building against his neighbour's wall. The risk from the drips of rain from it was too serious.

If one neighbour wished to fence or wall in his field he did no wrong, strictly speaking, by building the barrier along the middle of the grass-grown footpath along the boundary between fields, and so on the very boundary line. But this caused so many quarrels that in Mirditë and the Malësi e Madhe the law bade him leave the width of his barrier free between its outer base and the boundary, just as he must do when building a wall across his courtyard. In its wisdom the law was providing for the future.

Theoretically, a man could not only build his fence or wall along a boundary line, but could also ask his neighbour to make half of it. In practice, however, the neighbour might be too lazy or might say he was too poor or too ill to do his bit. In Kastrat[1] he could be fined 250 grosh and three rams for his unneighbourliness, and this possibility sometimes drove him to action. In the ingenious Malësi e Madhe the first man might in malice run up a fence parallel to the boundary but with an opening sixteen spans (3·20 metres) wide at either end. This ensured that his animals strayed through the opening on to his bad neighbour's field and ate it up. To give the neighbour no chance to make him move his fence he ran it up four spans, half the width of the horse-track, from the boundary. Most men, however, preferred to make the whole fence themselves, constructing it at least half the width of a footpath from the boundary. If two neighbours made half the fence each, but one made his half badly, this man was at fault—whether his sheep strayed into the good fencer's field or the good fencer's into his. The loss always fell on him; in the first case he had to compensate his neighbour, and in the second he had no right to be compensated for the damage done by the animals.

Sometimes a man wished to fence in a field which was bounded by a road. In Krasniqë and some other hilly districts he had to leave a strip of his land as well to allow for the fence slipping down on to the road, an ever likely possibility.

Most hedges of dead thorn were directly over the boundary line,

[1] See Appendix, Document V, § 11, p. 264.

and if properly placed to begin with, caused no trouble. The same was true of living hedges inland. On the other hand, living hedges in the marshy areas near the mouth of the river Mat sometimes grew so tall that they damaged the neighbouring land with their shade. To prevent this, the owner had to lop overgrown trees once every three years. Failing this, his neighbour could complain to the headman; inevitably they gave him leave to cut the trees down to the root on the owner's ground, an intrusion that was in itself a punishment, and fined the owner 250–450 grosh for breaking the law about lopping.

Similar rules regulated the planting of fruit and other trees, olives being included among the former. In Mirditë a fruit tree might be planted only 5 'feet' (1 metre) from the boundary; another kind had to be at least 10 feet away. In Godolesh, a great fruit-growing area, a fruit tree could be planted on the very boundary, but in adjacent Labinot it had to be a span away. In Shkrel it could be planted anywhere on one's own ground, as it never caused trouble by itself. As with living hedges, care had to be taken that a tree did not cast harmful shade over a neighbour's land. If one did so in Shkrel the owner agreed amicably to lop it, raising no objections unless he had already quarrelled with his neighbour over something else. In Mirditë he was bound to lop the offending branches; if he failed to do so his neighbour could lop them as high as he could reach with a hook, the handle of which did not exceed $3\frac{1}{2}$ spans in length. In the mountains of Lesh the owner had to uproot the tree or to pay annual damages to his neighbour. In Godolesh the neighbour was entitled to stretch as far as he could and cut the too luxuriant branches with his short-handled axe. If a tree was doing no damage to neighbouring ground, it could not be lopped except by its owner. A man who transgressed this law in Mirditë had to pay its owner 500 grosh.

Sometimes an open drain adjoined a boundary. When it was first cut, each of the two neighbours provided half the ground required, did half the work and retained the earth excavated from his own side. Three stones, one big and two small, were left at the head to mark the boundary; the two other sets, normally placed in the middle and at the foot, were removed to make room for the water; as the drain discharged into a bigger channel, they could not possibly be left at the foot. The boundary naturally ran exactly down the middle. In most places the drain had to be cleared out annually. In Godolesh the two neighbours did it in alternate years, having exclusive right to the earth with its valuable fertilizing properties for the year when they did the clean up. In Lumë two neighbours cleared the drain together year after year and flung half the earth on one side and half on the other.

In other places one ditch seldom drained two neighbouring fields on the principle that 'you can't walk on my path or use my drain'. In Gurrëzë the man who wanted a drain had to cut it on his own ground with a 'footprint' (20 cm.) of land between the boundary and its edge for the protection of his neighbour's land. Without this buttress the drain might overflow or burst its bank to the detriment of his neighbour. In either contingency its owner had to pay compensation to his neighbour, but prevention of damage was always better for both parties. His neighbour might also accuse him of encroaching on his land, an insulting remark that provoked instant retaliation. If, later on, the neighbour wanted a drain he had to make one for himself, also a 'footprint' away from the boundary. In Lumë and Elbasan there was little risk that open drains would flood, but there too a space had to be left between their edge and the boundary. The avowed purpose of this space was to support the boundary stones. In all cases of single ownership the owner, on clearing the ditch, threw the earth on his own side, where it testified to his ownership if this was ever questioned.

Sometimes a man of Shkrel wanted both a drain and a fence. In that event the ditch was cut along the boundary and a strip of ground of the same width was set aside on the other side of the boundary. All the earth excavated from the ditch was thrown on this strip and so the neighbours became quits, one had a 'hole' on his land and the other a 'hill'. The fence was erected on the 'hill'.

We come now to one of the most important considerations in boundary making. North Albania is one of the wettest regions in Europe, and when the land was waterlogged it inevitably tended to slip downhill. The tropical intensity of many rainstorms increased the mischief. Terracing the fields would have helped to check it, but such manual labour is contrary to the habits and dignity of the north Albanian. His law, however, gave him every possible protection. When there were two fields on a slope, one above the other, they might be separated by a field-path, a road, an irrigation channel or a fence. (The term 'field-path' includes the little 'headland' which formed along the top of the lower field as the plough-oxen turned in their ploughing.) It was vital to save the upper field from being undermined by the tillage of the lower one. So the field-path (or headland) was always assigned to the upper field, with the boundary and the fence, if any, along its lower edge. The upper man was strictly forbidden to work the path, generally grass-grown, and so fairly cohesive. The lower man was even more strictly forbidden to cultivate right up to the path for fear he brought it down; since his own land slipped a little lower every year as he tilled it, the field-path soared higher above it. Only if the lower field was in grass did the law revert to its usual form. If the upper field was planted with maize and the lower one a grass meadow, all the land under the boundary stones belonged to the lower field because grass is in itself binding enough to stop landslides.

If a road or an irrigation channel divided the two fields, the upper bank belonged in most places to the upper man, and the lower to the other, since there seemed no risk that cultivation of the lower field would undermine the upper one. In Greater Dibër, however, no risks were taken. Both banks of an irrigation channel were given to the upper man in case the lower one worked too close to it. In any area, the owner of a lower field who made a drain for it had to make it four finger-breadths from his own boundary to make sure it did not damage the upper field.

If building a new house, the owner of the lower field had to keep it far enough away from the boundary to do no damage to the fence, as any such damage would make the upper field slip. On the other hand, the owner of the upper field had licence to build his house as close to the fence as if the site were flat, that is to say, with only half the width of a footpath intervening, but he was never foolhardy enough to do so.

Sometimes it was the lower man who received protection from the law. In Martanesh, for example, when the upper one built a fence or wall round his field, he had to leave the boundary stones as well clear of it as if the field were flat. This was in case it moved and encroached on the boundary.

Sometimes a fence was misplaced. Even if it was only one cm. inside the neighbour's land, it had to be moved. In Bicaj the neighbour sent a mutual friend to say so to the owner; if the latter ignored the message the neighbour took down the fence and saw that when next it was erected it was correctly sited, otherwise shooting began. In the Martanesh area the village headman, with two official and two unofficial assistants, was usually called in to set the fence up on the exact boundary line. If the offender moved it forward again, the elders sent word to his relatives that if he touched it again, there would be shooting. So restrained, he usually settled down.

An opening was never to be made in a fence by force or without the owner's leave. Only a foolish and 'lawless' man would do such a thing; it could only be the preliminary to using the field as a road, or to stealing something.

Fines were imposed as a deterrent. These amounted to 50 grosh in Turkish times and 100 koronë in the 1920's in the Malësi e Madhe, with 150 grosh and 3 rams in Kastrat in 1892; even if the offender closed the gap again, he had no right to make it in the first instance. If he destroyed a fence altogether in the marshes at the mouth of the Mat he was fined 250 grosh, five times the amount imposed for opening a way through it. If he did not pay the fine he was killed by the owner. As many as three lives have often been lost for one opening.

So with a wall in the marshland of the Mat. If it was holed, the owner asked the offender furiously if he was agreeable to having elders assess the damage. If the offender objected to assessment or refused payment, the owner shot him; at best he was sharply fined by the village. A breach in a fence or wall had always to be repaired by the owner.

Elsewhere manners were milder. In Martanesh there was no punishment at all for making a hole in a fence. In Perlat permission to make one was readily given either as a favour or in exchange for a passage through the other man's. In Fulqet a traveller could make one without leave if the highway was deep in mud and the only dry ground within reach was the field behind the fence. Often enough the owner of fence and field shot at him, but this was illegal; there was only one legitimate way of keeping the traveller to the muddy road. This was for the owner of field and fence to fill up the holes in the road with stones. If he took this trouble and the traveller still trespassed on his field he had full right to shoot him.

CHAPTER X

PASTURAGE

Mountainous northern Albania is largely a pastoral country with large flocks of sheep and goats and considerable numbers of plough-oxen, cows and horses.

To a great extent the nature of a village's pasturage depended on its position, whether it was in the shrub zone, the oak zone or higher up among the pine and beech forests of the alpine slopes. In the low-lying belt of shrublands the poorest type of grazing was found, and here the pastoral life was seen at its lowest level. A poor man might have only one to five sheep, a cow or, where foliage was more plentiful, a few goats. Most villages had little or no pasturage proper and the animals grazed on the verges of paths and fields, in small spinneys and in the waste spaces overgrown with shrubs. Each family would do its own herding, the animals being tended by the old people and by small boys and girls. For security against thieves and wolves the animals were brought home at night to the little farmyard with its low stone wall, or to a stable under the living rooms of the farmhouse. The low altitude of such holdings, where the climate was neither too hot in summer nor too inclement in winter, ensured fairly constant grazing all the year round. During the winter, however, when the daylight hours were fewer, a meagre sheaf of maize and, less frequently, wheat straw or chaff, was fed by hand to each animal on its return from the open. When wheat chaff was fed to a horse it had to be well damped with water or the horse would not touch it. As for the goats, they would be given an armful of dried leaves which had been cut and stacked by the men in autumn and carried into the house by the women. No grain feed and no roots were fed to the animals; the former was needed for human consumption and no root crops are grown in Albania. Occasionally, however, when oats of a very poor quality were grown, the grain as well as the straw was fed to the animals. Albanians were astounded to learn that the British eat porridge. 'Food for animals' they would exclaim at the sight of a packet of porridge oats.

Poor and insignificant as they were, these small owners were

so numerous that their livestock amounted to a considerable
percentage of the total in Albania. They were found mostly in the
shrub areas, though a few very poor men lived also in the oak zone.
But the vast majority of this leafy belt herded their flocks on
a larger scale. Above each village there was always the overhanging
mountain with its forests of beech and pine to hold the waters and
keep the pastures green and sweet. Under the higher beech trees
no grass grew, but in the sloping clearings the animals could graze
at will. In winter, however, these clearings were too high to
permit of habitation; besides, such tilling of the soil as did take
place occurred at roughly the same level as the village, and it was
there that the flocks found most of their feeding. In summer the
fields and meadows, whether open or enclosed, provided hay for
the animals; in the autumn the stubble served for a few weeks;
while in winter they wandered over the grass. In spring the winter-
sown wheat was improved by being eaten down a few inches by
the sheep. Dried leaves from the numerous oak trees supplemented
this winter feeding.

Sometimes the number of animals was such that all these sources
did not suffice during the lean months, or sometimes a village had
no suitable winter pastures or had lost them for political reasons.
Many animals would then be slaughtered at the commencement of
winter and the meat smoked or salted down, while the remainder
lived to fare as best they could. The many owners who could not
afford meat, fresh or salted, had to try to maintain their livestock
until the spring. By that time the poor creatures were no better
than living skeletons hardly able to walk out to the pastures.

On the long coastal plains and marshy river banks the owners of
large flocks and herds were scorched out of their pastures in
summer or plagued by the mosquitoes from the marshy swamps.
This necessitated a wholesale migration at the beginning of summer
to the cooler alpine slopes, a feature of Albanian life as characteristic as picturesque.

A few of the purely winter pastures belonged to the State, a few
to private persons, and the immense majority to some community,
either a tribe, a village or a village ward. State-owned pastures
dated from Turkish times and were consequently found only on the
plains near big centres, as Turkish control had little reality elsewhere. Examples of these were the forested swamps of Mamuras
and the Highland village of Gurrëzë on the left bank of the river

Mat. They were extensive, if not numerous, and must be distinguished from the other state-owned pastures which, also in Turkish times, were added piecemeal to the community's possessions from the confiscated property of tribesmen who had transgressed an important law.

There were both alpine and winter pasturages in private hands in the 1930's, but the former were few and small; examples of these were some meadows on Mt Dragû between Bulqizë and Zerqan, and an upland plateau east of Sllovë in Dibër. The former, carrying 1500 sheep, was owned by Dervish Ali of Fulqet, and the latter, carrying not more than 1000 sheep, by Cen Elezi of Sllovë. Up till 1920, when Prenk Bib Doda Pasha bequeathed all his property to the tribe of Mirditë because he disliked his heir, the Mal i Shenjt (Holy Mountain) above Orosh was the private property of each Hereditary Captain. As for winter pasturages, much of the marshy land from Mamuras to below Durrës was in private hands. Thus the estate known as Cakalë belonged to Abas Kupi of Krujë, and several others near Shijak to members of the Toptan family. Some scandal was caused in the 1920's when three of these were leased for 99 years to Italians. A few meadows, some coppices and all the fields of stubble (for arable land was never owned by the community), complete the tale of winter pasturages which were private property.

Everything else, big and little, on the mountains and the plains, by the river bank and the wayside, belonged to some community. This was usually the nearest. For example, the plateau on the mountain overhanging Zerqan was owned by that village, the upland meadows round Okol in north Shalë by the various wards of Theth, one by each, and the swamps between Gurrëzë and Mamuras by the village of Laç near Milot. A major exception was the summer grazing which belonged to the village of Kuturman in Çermenikë. This pasturage lay twelve hours away on Mount Shebenik, more popularly known as the Mal i Kuq (the Red Mountain) on the eastern frontier between Albania and Yugoslavia. But its acquisition has been accidental. Most of it came as the dowry of a girl of Ricë who was her father's sole surviving heir and who married a man from Kuturman. The rest was subsequently purchased by the village; the copper plate on which its title to this portion was engraved in Turkish, a great curiosity in view of the rarity of title deeds, remained in the possession of Beqir Ali of

Kuturman until his family died out and the plate disappeared. The summer grazing which belonged to the village of Bërshenj near Fulqet was three days away on Mt Dragû. The Highlanders, living at the mouth of the river Mat, had their summer pasturages on Mt Vermosh five days away from their winter homes.

A clear distinction was drawn between the laws governing private and public pasturages. In broad outline what was private could be fenced or sold or built on at its owner's sole pleasure, and was divided up between his sons at his death. What was public was marked off by boundary stones from neighbouring properties but had neither outside fence nor internal boundaries. Though all the households in the tribe or village had equal rights in it and could each graze as many animals, cut as much firewood or timber, build as many huts or folds and shoot as much game on it as they pleased, these rights came to them only as members of the community and were not transferable to strangers. They could not sell their grazing rights to an outsider, share a hut with him or graze his animals along with their own; if they wanted to give an outsider friend pasturage, they must do so on their private ground. They could not sell part of the common or dispose of firewood, timber or game for their individual gain; only the community could negotiate such sales, and all the profit or loss from them was community profit or loss. They could not build a permanent house on the common. When the head of a family died, his rights were not divided among his sons like his private property but descended to them jointly. Gypsies, it may be added, were allowed to pitch their tents, graze their animals and gather firewood on the common. Being as resourceful in Albania as elsewhere, they needed no permission and snared what game they could; as they did not carry firearms they could not shoot it.

Those communities which did not possess their own private summer pasturage, hired or rented it from near and far. Breg i Matit rented theirs partly from Shkrel and partly from Theth, and the latter was a full week's journey away. Modernity having come to Albania, they paid cash down. Fulqet rented a neighbour's mountain every summer and paid for it in the old-fashioned way with half an oke of butter, the same of sour-milk cheese and 2½ oke of sweet cheese for every forty sheep. Perlat again gave their own winter pasturage in return for leave to summer on the mountains of Lurë and Selitë. In Turkish times, Lurë asked neither money nor produce nor an exchange for summering the flocks brought to the Crown (Kunora) by tribesmen living north of Shkodër, but welcomed them because their sheep manured the fields. Comparatively recently, Lurë gave a Selitë man leave to summer his flocks gratis on Mt Murije, which, lacking their manure, would hardly have been worth the labour of tilling. Dervish Ali of Fulqet too was glad to let hundreds of sheep graze free in his meadows on Mt Dragû. Surroj and Arrn pastured sheep belonging to the Hereditary Captain of Mirditë without payment, because they also had so little arable land.

Except where the soil was so poor that the manure was welcome, as in Lurë, or where grazing was very plentiful, as in Theth, outsiders were rigidly excluded from alps which were owned or rented by a community. Nangë said it had not enough feed for its own flocks. Martenesh, Gurrëzë and Breg i Matit said they did not want their pastures disturbed by strangers. All infringements of the ban, both petty and grave, were punished by fines.

CHAPTER XI

BAJRAKTARS

It is an Albanian tradition that when the Turks began to raise Albanian levies for their army they chose specially brave tribesmen to lead the levies and called them by the Turkish name of *deli*, meaning 'madman' or 'desperado'. At a later date they called them *spahis* (cavalrymen), and at a still later date *bajraktars* (standard-bearers), from the Turk *bajrak*, standard. So the word bajraktar conveys the business of the man so-called, and the origin of his title. He was the military leader of his tribe and owed his appointment to the Turks, not to his fellow-Albanians.

Neither delis nor spahis seem to have been blood ancestors of the bajraktars. Each tribe knows how its first bajraktar won his flag but never says that he was either a deli or a spahi. In the folk-tales which purport to recount their deeds, the spahis figure not as heroes but as ordinary cavalrymen of the type we still find in Algeria. Certain families, notably in Lumë and Yugoslav Losovë, are surnamed Spahi. These claim descent not from medieval bravos but from relatively modern cavalrymen, and they are not bajraktars. The memory of the delis and their deeds survives only in folk-tales and an occasional personal name. The bajraktar of Hot at the beginning of the century was Deli Metë Çuni. In the folk-tales the delis, more fortunate than the spahis, preserve their reputation as doughty fighters.

Tribal traditions agree that most *bajraks* were bestowed on the original holder like a Victoria Cross, for valour in battle. The combats were generally against the Serbs and Montenegrins, natural enemies of the Albanians as they were their nearest neighbours, and had not ceased ever since they appeared in the Balkans to steal ancient Albanian territory. Some bajraks are said to have been gained hundreds of years ago, and others only a few generations since. The historical details in the traditions are generally meagre and the chronology vague, but these defects make on the whole for greater credibility, assuring us that no lively imagination has been at work. To minds running as Albanian minds do on courage as the highest of virtues, the traditions are a great inspiration.[1]

The following traditions are samples. The bajrak of Hot was won four hundred years ago by an ancestor of Deli Metë Çuni who distinguished himself by cutting off Montenegrin heads, a pastime in which the family has ever since indulged with gusto. Sul Alija, the great-grandfather of Adem Bajrami, who lived four generations ago, was made bajraktar of Krasniqe in reward for the bravery he displayed during a war between Turkey and Montenegro. Sefer Ahmeti was given his bajrak at Moraç near Belgrade after a battle against the Serbs. The first bajraktar of Nikaj also won his standard at Moraç, possibly in the same battle. Kolë Voci, who lived six generations ago, became the first bajraktar of Shalë-Gimaj in consequence of killing a Serbian bajraktar and carrying his head and standard to the officer commanding the Turkish forces. In the same battle the bajraktar of Plan was killed, but Voci caught up and saved his bajrak from capture by the enemy. Avdi Kola, a later bajraktar of Gimaj, was proud to boast that since Voci won the flag no male of his house had died in his bed.

Certain tribes had more than one bajraktar, some as many as five. Where there were two or more bajraktars the senior took precedence over the junior. If a senior bajraktar was killed in battle it was the junior's duty to take his flag.

The office of the tribal bajraktar was hereditary, going from father to son. If a bajraktar died without leaving a son he was succeeded by his brother, his brother's son, or in default of these, a cousin in the male line. If he was too old or too ill before his death to act, these relatives deputised for him. If the natural heir was a minor at his father's death, his father's brother or nephew took office until he came of full age and powers when twenty, twenty-five, or even thirty years of age, the date varying according to his capabilities. In 1933 Kolë Ndue was senior bajraktar of

[1] The bajrak was not, however, always granted for military valour but was sometimes conferred for less martial reasons. For instance, Pec Peci of Pecnikaj, Shalë, was summoned to the presence of the head of the Begolli family to explain why he, a peasant, had seven wives, while the great Begolli contented himself with only three. Pec's explanation, that only one of the women was really his wife and the others servants who looked after his land and flocks as menservants might have done, though known to be untrue, so fascinated Begolli by its astuteness that he forthwith made Pec bajraktar not only of Shalë, but also of all Dukagjin.

Shalë but only as trustee for the small son of Lush Prela, his predecessor, killed some years before.

Succession from father to son depended on merit, and was determined in the lifetime of the reigning bajraktar. A son who was obviously unfit was passed over in favour of his younger brother. Both, if unfit, might be superseded by their paternal uncle or cousin in the male line.

If the natural precedence between brothers was once lost, the bajrak generally passed from the elder's heirs for good. Only when the son of a dispossessed elder brother turned out much more competent than the other heirs of his generation could he regain the glory which his father's weakness had lost. For example, Muharrem Bajraktar, the standard-bearer of Ujmishtë, Lumë, was the son of Nezir Bajraktar, a younger son. His cousin, Liman, son of the elder brother to whom Nezir was preferred, was almost as capable as he was but had no right to compete with him for the succession.

For grave cause the claims of heredity were sometimes disregarded. If a bajraktar's family produced no competent male for several generations, another family might wrest the standard from its feeble hands. The transfer had naturally to be approved by the tribe. Muharrem Bajraktar of Ujmishtë, Lumë, descended not from the original bajraktar who lived at Shkavec, Lumë, but from the family which superseded the feckless descendants of the original man some generations ago. The first bajraktar of Nikç was Gilë Prëntashi, but eventually the family degenerated to such an extent that the bajrak was taken over by Turk Vuksani, a very distant cousin who lived in the same quarter as the natural heir. A more remarkable transfer took place early in this century in Perlat. For three generations there had not been a good male in the family of its bajraktar. Then Prenk Pasha, consulted as the head of the Gjomarkaj family of Mirditë and therefore the source of all wisdom, advised Perlat to desert its inadequate leader for his sister's son, the bajraktar of the neighbouring tribe of Rrshen. Perlat took the advice and followed this man and after him his son Zef Bardhoku, thus going right outside the tribe in the quest for a better leader.

With the exception of the bajraktar of Lumë, all bajraktars hitherto discussed were military leaders of tribes which were wholly or predominantly Catholic. Mirditë, Bogë, Vukël, Shalë, Nikaj,

Mertur and some others were wholly Catholic. Nikç, Selcë, Hot, Kthellë and Lurë were more or less mixed Catholic and Moham- medan. Certain tribes such as Has, Bytyç and Krasniq are at the time of writing completely Mohammedan but were partly Catholic until three or four generations ago, as their genealogies testify. Lumë asserts that it has been completely Mohammedan since the coming of the Turks five centuries ago. It was also not fully tribal, since each bajraktar's following consisted not of a single kin or agglomeration of kins with the same ancestors, but of a number of little kins of varying ancestry.

There were also bajraktars in certain non-tribal areas, such as Shpat and Martanesh in central Albania. Here the dignity was not hereditary and localized, but moved with successive holders from family to family, from quarter to quarter or even from village to village. Fitness for military leadership of the local levies was always demanded, and that quality did not necessarily remain from one generation to another, in the same family, quarter or village. Hysejn Zavolina of the village of Shelcan was a famous bajraktar in Shpat in the last years of Turkish rule, but it was at Fushë e Kuqe in the more central village of Gjinar that he set up his standard. Hysejn Ramaj became bajraktar of Martanesh because he was as popular as he was competent. After having carried his standard to victory in Montenegro he 'got religion' and turned dervish. As Baba Hysejn (Abbot Hysejn) he presided first over the Bektashi monastery (tege) at Krujë and then over that at Martanesh and was buried in the monastery of Zerqan. When he took to the cloister the bajrak passed to Murat Xhabolli, who was from the Gjoni quarter and quite a different family. The great lawgiver, Mus Ballgjini, of the village of Gurakuq was bajraktar of the district of Çermenikë when Turkish rule over Albania ended, but his son did not inherit the office. When Albania developed a conscript army of European type, there could be no more bajraktars in central Albania. Officers led the conscripts, and there was no hereditary principle to preserve the ancient title as there was among the tribes of the north.

In certain areas of the north there were no bajraktars. Since beys were feudal lords of the soil it fell to them to lead their henchmen in war. So wherever there were beys of any importance there were no bajraktars. Mat was the classic instance. There were bajraktars to the north of it in tribal Kthellë and Lurë; there were bajraktars to the south of it in non-tribal Martanesh; but there was none within its own boundaries. There factions, not tribes, were the social units, and all power, military and otherwise, was concentrated in the hands of four powerful bey families.

From first to last the primary function of a bajraktar was military. When one learned that war was imminent and troops were required, he had immediately to inform the tribe in the first instance by firing eight shots in quick succession into the air, and in the second by sending out the official runner called *kasnec* with news and a statement of how many men were wanted. One from each house was the usual number. The muster was soon complete, for it was thought shameful to hang back or to hide at home and no time was wasted hunting for deserters. When all had gathered, the march began. Two tribesmen in some cases, and in others four, led off singing. Next came a man closely connected with the bajraktar, preferably his eldest son, carrying the flag. The rank and file followed, firing constantly into the air to show their joy at the call to arms. Any sign of depression at leaving their homes would have been thought disgraceful and unmanly. The best warriors among them had the bajraktar in their midst and would guard him and the flag with their lives till they all came marching home again. No equipment was issued to bajraktars or 'soldiers'; each brought his own rifle and pistols and came in his ordinary clothes. Nor was any military training given them. Their value as soldiers depended upon the rifle practice which they had had at home. It was usually sufficient to make them all good shots. After a few months the war ended and they came home again, still in their peasant clothes and again firing into the air for joy.

In time of peace the bajraktar performed civilian duties. One of the chief was caring for the poor. If they got into trouble or needed work he intervened with the authorities. If they were benighted he gave them free board and lodging. On high occasions he sent them a ram on which to feast. So that they could buy on credit what they needed for their weddings and funerals he went guarantee for them at the village shops; perhaps he even paid for the goods when the following harvest failed and left them unable themselves to clear the debt. At times he lent them money without interest. In return he asked only that if required they would put their rifles at his disposal, joining him in attacking an enemy, spending some weeks annually in his house as unpaid or poorly paid guards, escorting him to town, guarding him during his stay there and escorting him home again. If they refused without justifiable cause to give him such service, he withdrew his support from them at least for a time.

The bajraktar was also much occupied with local administration Here he was assisted by one or more headmen, hereditary officials like himself. Independently or together, he and they checked quarrelling, judged and formulated new laws. He was admittedly their superior, and when their views diverged his prevailed. If pressure of work made him think an increase in their number desirable, he had power to make extra appointments provided only that he first submitted the names of his nominees to the Turkish government for approval. In short, he was the acknowledged head of the local administration.

As supreme administrative head the bajraktar had power to summon a general meeting for administrative as well as military purposes. If the matter at issue was important and affected the whole tribe, he sent the *kasnec* (tribal messenger) to command the presence of one man per house. If narrower issues were involved he summoned only one or more headmen and the local *gjobtarë* (fine-collectors) or other elders. Plenary meetings dealt with anti-social acts grave enough to involve the death penalty or expulsion, judged cases of sacrilege against the church, tightened up tribal discipline by enacting new or re-enacting old laws, decided whether to revolt or not against the Turkish government, and heard important messages from the government. In 1908 a plenary meeting[1] was held by each tribe to decide whether or not it should accept the Young Turk Constitution. Smaller meetings handled business where fines were sufficient punishment for transgression. Notably they regulated grazing rights, fixing the day for a general move to summer pastures, stipulating how many animals each family might feed on a common. They also regulated wood-cutting rights and controlled the supply of water for irrigation. The bajraktar presided at all such meetings, took an active part in the deliberations, and signed or set his seal on any minutes that were kept. He and the elders, as being socially superior, sat apart from the commoners. In the Malësi e Madhe he sat on the ground while the tribesmen stood respectfully on their feet.

[1] See M. E. Durham, *Some Tribal Origins, Laws and Customs of the Balkans*, p. 74.

In certain cases the bajraktar and the local headman could act alone. For example, in case of sacrilege against the church they had power to pronounce even a death sentence. In practice, however, they preferred to consult the tribe and the ecclesiastical authorities. After the Young Turks introduced their constitution in 1908 they tried to make everything in Albania very legal and proper. If land was bought, for example, they required a deed of conveyance where the word of witnesses had formerly sufficed. The best lawyer in the land might write out the document and great men witness it, but it had no legal validity until the bajraktar and local headmen had affixed their seals.

As a legal figure the bajraktar had special weight. If called to serve on a jury of twenty-four men, his single person was counted equal to the twelve jurors left unnamed by the elders. A peace made in his presence was particularly binding. If at all distinguished he was often called in by another tribe to settle a dispute that had baffled its own elders. In his own tribe, besides acting as judge in many ordinary cases, he was ultimate referee in all difficult cases. Boundary disputes, the most fertile source of trouble among these land-starved tribes, were often referred straight to him for settlement. Disobedience to his ruling might entail the worst penalties. Particularly in the Malësi e Madhe, he and the local headman had power to appoint elders to settle a quarrel. If these failed to do so, or were found to have based their decision on a false oath by one of the litigants, it fell to the bajraktar and the local headman to reopen the case and to pronounce a final judgement. If a headman judged a case and gave a verdict the bajraktar disliked, he could upset this verdict and substitute one of his own. But neither headman nor elders could upset his judgements; these were always final and unalterable.

All the above applies to the non-tribal areas of central Albania as much as to the northern tribes. Mus Ballgjini of Çermenikë, for instance, was almost more famous as a law-giver than as a military leader. By a seeming exception the bajraktar of the Perlat tribe of Kthellë did not judge but left such matters to the elders. The explanation of the anomaly probably lies in his notorious incompetence. It was every bajraktar's province to judge in peace as well as to lead in war.

In all areas the jurisdiction of the bajraktar was subject to certain limitations. If the commoners did not like one of his decisions, even if made in concert with the headmen and elders, they were not bound to abide by it and could compel him to re-examine the case. Neither he nor a headman could, singly or in combination, fine a tribesman without first securing authority from the tribe. After all, he and the headman might have a personal grudge against the man and might fine him for no other reason. To take an example from the non-tribal valley of Bulqizë, Miftar Meta the bajraktar and Lam Isaku his assistant were much respected and admired but they had no power, on their sole responsibility, to fine a man from Fushaj, their own village. Still less had they power to fine a man from another village in Bulqizë. They could not act in either case until they had secured the backing of the culprit's village at a general meeting. Nothing less, it was felt, guaranteed the impartiality of the sentence.

If a bajraktar misconducted himself, all the headmen and commoners of his tribe, or possibly the commoners alone, sat in judgement on him. They could not ostracize, expel or burn him out like an ordinary criminal; he was too inherently a tribal institution for that. But they could, and did fine him. In 1907,[1] the Kryezi tribe assembled in plenary session, one man from each house, and fined its bajraktar and headmen 100 rams and an ox for some judgements they could prove to have been unjustifiable and prejudiced. The commoners could also ask an erring bajraktar to give a rifle or other valuable as security for his good behaviour in the future.

The misconduct for which a bajraktar was fined was seldom more heinous than sending his sheep to pasture on another's ground or pronouncing a biased judgement. On the whole, each was so carefully selected and trained by his predecessor in office that he rarely committed the graver crimes. When one did, he was sure to be so 'strong', i.e. influential, that the tribesmen thought it more prudent to close their eyes to his iniquity. There was much grumbling at the venality of bajraktars, but neither the tribal law nor the Turkish government took cognizance of this offence. If a bajraktar, serving as judge or arbitrator, took a bribe, the only remedy lay in the individual tribesman's freedom to choose another law-giver next time. If a bajraktar accepted a 'present' for doing a favour, there was no remedy at all. His victim could only comfort himself by noting how God, or Allah, punished such greed. It was

[1] See Appendix, Document XII, p. 271.

popularly believed in Shkrel that the three sons of Vatë Marashi, the bajraktar, and the three daughters of the Voivode Preng Mirashi, had turned out badly because the deeds of Vatë and Preng had been evil.

In time of war a bajraktar from the north-west group received triple pay and triple rations. A bajraktar of Shalë received double pay and double rations, one portion as a person and the other as standard-bearer. He also received pay and rations for three servants, two of whom followed him to the war both to guard and to serve him, while the third, a specially trusted man, remained behind in his house in Shalë as guardian of his property, women-folk and children. The allowances for these servants were only what ordinary soldiers received, food and *katik* (pocket-money: in Turkish, any relish eaten with bread) at the rate of one grosh per day, which was barely sufficient for their tobacco.

As an administrator a bajraktar was unpaid in so far as he had no fixed salary. He earned something, however, by his judgements, for which he was paid at the same rate as an elder. In the Malësi e Madhe, as often as he appointed elders, he too received a fee, although they did all the work and he did not stir from home. If they could not agree on a verdict, the litigants appealed to him. He then received a double fee, one the same as the elders' and the other in respect of his own journey to the scene of the quarrel. In other tribes or groups of tribes he did not get off so lightly; he had always to judge the case himself before he received any payment. The fees varied with the importance of the case and the rapacity of the bajraktar. In the tribal, but not in the non-tribal, areas any fines imposed were divided between the bajraktar and the headmen or 'good families' of his tribe. In the Malësi e Madhe a bajraktar who was summoned to Shkodër received ten grosh (50 koronë) per day from the Turkish government for his expenses. But everywhere a bajraktar's best source of income was bribes.

The bajraktar was both the military and administrative head of his tribe. His military and administrative precedence came 'from the staff in his hand', the flag stick of Turkish donation, but descent was the test for social precedence, and priority of descent was not always his. In many tribes there were 'good families' who descended from an older brother or a social superior of his ancestor, and on that account had, generation after generation, taken social precedence of his family.

Modern civilization with its army and dense array of gendarmes and officials swept away the military and administrative functions of the bajraktar, but his social position remained untouched. So in Krasniqë, Sali Mena, the bajraktar in 1939, had the precedence because he descended from the eldest son of Gjô Vata of the village of Bunjaj; but Hakik Meta, the bajraktar of Lurë, remained inferior to Doçi, Nezhë and Vlad families in that tribe because their ancestors were from better families than his.

Social precedence was marked in several characteristically Albanian ways. For instance, if the bajraktar of Perlat in Kthellë met a Simonaj and a Gjet-Kolaj at a feast, his seat would be third from the corner and his portion of meat only the leg. The Simonaj would sit in the corner and get the head and the Gjet-Kolaj would sit next to him and get the shoulder. Even in wartime a bajraktar was kept in his civilian place except during the actual fighting. On the way to and from the battlefield he sat in the seat and ate the portion of meat that appertained to him by descent. In 1935 Lurë was mustered to check a revolt at Fier in central Albania. The bajraktar's men carried the flag out of Lurë into Mat, and by arrangement met Zef Doçi's men at Burrel in Mat. There, though both were on a warlike errand, Zef Doçi sat in the chief seat and the bajraktar and his flag in the fourth. The revolt was suppressed before the tribesmen advanced beyond Burrel. If they had gone on, rifles would have cracked at Fier before Zef Doçi had to yield the first place to the bajraktar. If one of the bajraktars of Kthellë found it necessary to discuss something with one of the six 'good families', he could not ask its head to come and see him as he would an ordinary tribesman. Instead, he must gird up his own loins and go and see the other. If they disagreed during the discussion, he could not persist in his own view but had to fall in with the other's. Trivial though this insistence on correct precedence and its manifestations may seem, it had its value in maintaining tribal discipline. Slackening of the social framework in communities so backward as these tribesmen would only have ended in anarchy.

The 'first families' excepted, the bajraktar was unquestioned first among the tribesmen, this being signified in the usual manner of corner seat and choicest portion of meat. Any male of his family old enough to walk enjoyed the same precedence and was, by the courteous and diplomatic, addressed as 'bajraktar'.

A 'bajraktar' of tender years could evict a greybeard commoner from the corner seat, and the greybeard would be distressed if left in it. A worthless and ignorant 'bajraktar' got the head of the roast lamb while successful and learned commoners had no precedence by right—they belonged to their father's tribe and were counted aliens in the bajraktar's. Sometimes, however, the tribesmen gave them precedence as a courtesy.

When a bajraktar or any male in his family, infants excepted, died in his bed, a black flag was stuck at the head of his grave to mark his rank during life. Otherwise he and his were treated in death like ordinary mortals. If he himself was murdered, the ensuing blood feud was no worse than it would have been for a commoner—Lek had laid down that in death one man was as good as another. Besides, another bajraktar succeeded him and with the office continuing, the personality of the holder had no special significance. His family alone had to show a sense of his unusual importance; it could not stain its honour by accepting blood money instead of killing the assassin. If a bajraktar was killed by somebody in another tribe, his tribe undertook to hunt down the assassin, but this was no more than it would have done for any tribesman dead in comparable circumstances. Conversely, when a bajraktar killed anyone, his victim's family sought his blood precisely as they would have sought a commoner's.

As between bajraktars, seniority of the ancestor's appointment determined precedence. Gjejaj of Dukaj, the first bajraktar in Perlat, lived long before there was a bajraktar of Rrshen. His modern representative was, as already said above, so weak that Perlat had abandoned him to follow the Rrshen man's leadership. Yet in everything social, by virtue of his ancestor's seniority, he walked ahead of his supplanter. Once, however, a Kthellë tribesman entertained all three bajraktars of his tribe together. There is no record of how he seated them, but when the roast lamb appeared, he split the head in two, gave the two halves to two of the bajraktars and a shoulder to the third. Half a head being reasonably equated to a shoulder, he thus gave equal honour to all three men and did justice both to descent and to strength.

When a bajraktar encountered a beg, as a bey is called in north Albania, the latter sat in the corner because a beg is bigger than a bajraktar. When bajraktar and agha met, the bajraktar sat in the corner. Such a meeting was rare in the north owing to the paucity of aghas. The title of agha was a courtesy title bestowed by the populace. By special provision of the Turkish Government there had been hereditary aghas since the Turkish conquest at Botush in Yugoslav Kosovë; these, says their representative in Albania, took precedence of all bajraktars in Albania and Kosovë.

Given the pride of a bajraktar in his standard and of a 'first family' in its descent, a clash between the two was not uncommon. When this took the form of an ordinary isolated quarrel, elders were called in from another tribe to judge between the disputants. Their own tribe did not venture to try the issue, knowing that it might suffer, as outside elders could not do, for an unwelcome judgement. If the elders failed to effect a settlement, shooting began between the parties, both bajraktar and 'first family' being followed by his own kin. A man related to both followed the one to whom he was more nearly related; this at least in theory. In practice they often showed a naive sense of which side their bread was buttered and joined the disputant with the stronger following.

Sometimes a long struggle for precedence developed between a 'first family' tenacious of its ancient privileges and an ambitious bajraktar. In Lurë, for instance, both the Catholic Zef Doçi of Lurë e Vjetër (Old Lurë) and the Mohammedan Ibrahim Gjoçi of Kreje had long been rivals of the Mohammedan bajraktar Hakik Aliu Meta. In 1926 Gjoçi had the largest following, because he maintained the tribe with surpassing generosity. Within a decade he ate himself out of house and home, and then lost nearly all his power, retaining only the tribesmen's affection and respect for his past benefits. He therefore ceased to hamper the ambitions of the bajraktar. Zef Doçi, the 'first family' in the whole tribe, was a more obstinate rival, as his power rested less on his lavish doles than on his descent and personal wisdom. Ancestor after ancestor had been 'captains' in Turkish times, whereas Gjoçi and Meta had never been 'captains' till created by King Zog. The bajraktar began by undermining Doçi's position with traditional doles. He sent sheep to the poor at every festival and went guarantee for them in the shops during crises such as weddings and burials. 'So they all follow me now', he told the visitor with disarming simplicity. He had resorted to direct action, seizing every chance to kill off the guns in Doçi's family. In 1933 some brigands, who had killed one of Llesh Doçi's men, were harboured in a mountain sheepfold by the bajraktar's shepherds. Together with Zef and other relatives,

Llesh ambushed the brigands and wounded one. As one of his men was killed, the two sides were 'one and one', equalized, and could have made peace. But the opportunity was too good for the bajraktar to miss. By the law of the mountains Llesh should not have attacked the sheepfold until he had asked the bajraktar to withdraw his protection from the brigands and had met with a refusal. So the bajraktar vowed he would not make peace but would have Doçi's blood for the 'injury'. Soon he learned that Zef Doçi and all his male relatives were at a wedding in a poor man's house. Under cover of darkness his followers crept up to the house and shooting through the windows killed two and wounded four of the wedding guests. A year later the bajraktar managed to have a third man from Zef's family killed, leaving Zef almost alone.

In his charities this bajraktar of Lurë took no account of the recipient's religion, helping a Catholic as readily as one of his fellow Mohammedans. If he discriminated between the two he would gain nothing from the Albanian government, which ignored religious differences. In Turkish times discrimination in favour of Mohammedans would have furthered his designs by winning approval from the Turkish government. He found, however, that the proved loyalty of his family to King Zog's stood him in even better stead. A marriage had also proved a useful asset. Metë Hoti, the best shot in Lurë, would have been expected to join Zef Doçi, because his mortal enemy, Dalip Kaci, followed Zef's enemy, the bajraktar. Unfortunately for Zef, Metë had a sister married to one of the bajraktar's household. Since joining Zef meant shooting at the bajraktar's men, Metë feared to have the blood of his nephews on his hands and continued reluctantly, side by side with his mortal enemy, to follow the bajraktar.

The result of the struggle can be shown by the numbers of the levies raised by the three captains for the Albanian government in 1926, 1933 and 1935 respectively. They were as follows:

	1926	1933	1935
Zef Doçi	150	50	23
Ibrahim Gjoçi	300	40	32
Bajraktar	4	300	400

It would have been interesting to revisit Lurë to see the effect on the position established by the Italian occupation. The bajraktar,

as King Zog's man and therefore anathema to the Italians, must
have lost much ground. Zef Doçi as his enemy and as a good
Catholic may have regained some.

According to Albanian tradition there were no bajraktars before
the Turks came, and headmen were literally the head men of their
tribe. This would seem to be confirmed by a document dated 1403
which cited Alexius Kastrati, as headman of the tribe of that name,
in a list of Albanian chiefs who were rewarded by the Venetians
with gifts of cloth. Albanian tradition further alleges that the
Turks aimed deliberately at weakening Albanian chieftains. So,
on the one hand, Sultan Mahmut destroyed thirty-six kins, root
and branch, and his son Mexhi a further number. On the other
hand, Sultan after Sultan appointed bajraktars, ostensibly as
military leaders but really as pillars of Turkish rule. By recognizing
their nominees as administrative heads as well as military leaders
they reduced the old headmen to a subordinate position, and thereby
lessened their chances of engineering a successful revolt. This
policy would explain why some bajraktars were social as well as
administrative and military leaders, and others were not. The
former presumably descended from headmen who were com-
plaisant enough to accept Turkish rule, and the latter from strong
men of lower position in tribes where the headmen were recalcitrant.
The Turks must have trusted that pleasure in their official rank,
and the increased possibilities of money-making would keep the
bajraktars quiet in their turn. Recognizing the hereditary character
of the bajraktar was another shrewd step on their part. As the
non-hereditary delis and spahis aged or died, a hiatus unfavourable
to their rule might arise. When it was a case of 'the bajraktar is old
or dead, long live the bajraktar', they never lacked an agent. When
King Zog, as Minister Ahmed Zogu, began to unify Albania he
saw the danger from the numerous bajraktars. Accustomed to lead
their tribes to war, unaccustomed to any restraint by a central
authority, ignorant and untravelled for the most part and generally
of autocratic temper, all of them might not have been willing to
submit to the new government in Tirana. Methods of bringing
them into line with or without their own wish had, therefore, to be
devised. If one was willing to serve loyally, the government
treated him as the Turks had long before treated a pliant headman.
It made him an officer in the reserve, the modern equivalent of the
ancient bajraktar, gave him the half-pay of his rank, and provided

for his sons and nephews, granting them state scholarships on which to complete their education or military training abroad, and finding them employment as officials or officers when they came home. The most notable example of this 'pliant headman' type of bajraktar was Hakik Meta of Lurë, who was himself a captain and had several relatives who were officers in the Albanian army. If a bajraktar was likely to be recalcitrant, King Zog's government tried two methods. The first was a duplication of the system applied to the pliant headman type with reserve rank, half-pay and provision for relatives all included. Thus Gjon Markagjoni, the Hereditary Captain of Mirditë, who rebelled openly in 1921 against the central government, was rewarded for his subsequent submission by being made a lieutenant-colonel in the reserve. Cen Elezi of Dibër, whose father was killed in battle against King Zog's men in 1924, was later made a major. But fewer of the relatives of such men were educated at state expense, and the education given to those few was not so advanced—it seems to have been dangerous to put too much knowledge into their heads. And when they were ready for office they were kept in outlying unimportant districts, 'safe' areas.

The second and far more important method employed by King Zog with possible recalcitrants was the Turks' very own. The usual favours of rank in the reserve, half-pay and the provision for dependants were bestowed on a number of tribesmen who had given proof in the past of their loyalty to the régime and were 'strong' enough in the military sense to combat the influence of the obstinate bajraktars. Captain Mark Miri of Gurrëzë, who was a counterpoise to the Gjetë Coku family of Breg i Matit as well as to the bajraktar, was one example of this type. So was Major Miftar Selmani of Lumë, who was supposed to balance his fellow-villager, Muharrem Bajraktar. The transfer of the administrative powers of the bajraktars to state officials completed their weakening. The unity and stability which characterized King Zog's Albania to an extent surprising in a Balkan country were the best commentary on the policy.

CHAPTER XII

ELDERS

It is impossible to understand the laws and customs of the Albanian mountains without a knowledge of the varieties and responsibilities of the elders. A man could be an elder not only in the literal sense but as a legal personage. Seven types developed in sequence one from another among the southern tribes.

Everywhere the word for 'elder' is (sing.) *plak* (plur. *pleq*), which is pure Albanian and means literally 'old man'. There is a corresponding feminine (sing.) *plaka*, 'old woman'. In households of any size there might be several men and women who were really old in years and were 'elders' in the literal sense. These were the first type. The majority were ordinary people and had no legal importance.

The idea of age disappears with the second type, found in every household irrespective of its size. Here there were always one man and one woman who bore the special title of 'old man (or elder) of the house' and 'old woman (or elder) of the house'. These under their more usual Albanian titles of master of the household and mistress of the household were not necessarily elders in the sense of 'older people'. They might have attained their position when under forty and have found themselves in authority at that comparatively early age over older men and women.

The third category of elders appeared as soon as a household split up and each brother or male cousin in it acquired his own house. Then, a 'brotherhood' (*vllazni*) was formed. In this community each new house was as much a separate entity as the parent one, and was no longer under the control of the master and mistress, the 'elders' of the old joint home. It had its own 'elders' of both sexes who managed all its affairs, external and internal. The 'old man' of the joint home, now administering a much smaller household, thus lost a proportionate share of his importance. But the new masters also lost some of theirs. So long as the family lived together any competent adult among them might deputise for the master in village or tribal affairs or in the administration of the communal home, but from the day they separated, the old master reserved such business for himself and his sons, leaving only their own concerns to the masters of the new houses. As he remained the eldest or the most capable of the brothers, his help and advice tended to be sought by the others, particularly in external business, and his opinion was more regarded by outsiders such as tribal or government authorities. So he developed into the 'old man (or elder) of the brotherhood'. As the generations passed and the houses of the original brotherhood split up in their turn, the dignity of brotherhood elder remained in his family, handed down inalienably from master to master. The term 'brotherhood elder' was little used, however; 'first (or head) of the brotherhood' was preferred. There was no woman elder of the brotherhood or any larger unit. The mistress of the household of a brotherhood elder had neither authority nor influence outside his house, as he had. She was a foreign importation into the brotherhood, a stranger to it in blood, her only duties being to bear her husband's children and to work in the house, her only rights proceeding from her fulfilment of those duties.

In course of time so many households split up that a number of new brotherhoods were formed. In some the sense of brotherhood or even cousinship with the others faded, and only a remoter feeling of kinship due to descent from a common ancestor persisted. The agglomeration of brotherhoods then constituted a 'kin' (*fis*). In this, the fourth type, each brotherhood retained its own elder, and at the same time looked up to the elder of the original brotherhood as leader, calling him 'elder of the kin' or 'head of the kin'.

In the next, fifth stage of development several kins united to form a village. They might be distantly related to each other as in the village of Vuksanaj in Shalë, or of quite different stock as in the village of Nangë in Lumë. If related, they remembered which kin descended from the eldest brother in the ancestral home and regarded the elder of that kin as the village elder. If not related, they selected one of the kin elders, preferably the head of the strongest kin, for that position. Alternative names for him were 'senior elder', 'senior headman' and 'head elder'. According to the usual pattern of development each kin and each brotherhood in the village retained its own elder. Already it is possible to understand such data as the following. In the tribe of Lurë there were twelve elders, two for each kin. In the village of Perlat there were two men called village elders or senior elders; in the last days of Turkish rule these were the famous law-givers Dedë Lleshi and Likë Gjegjaj. Again, when Per Dedë Ndoj was senior headman of the village of Gojan in Mirditë, he took the lead in publicly executing a man of his own kin, Buçaj, for murdering a guest who belonged to the Martinaj kin in the same village. The story is related by Father Gjeçov.

This fifth type was the recognized superior of the sixth, the body of men who were unitedly called 'village elders'. These consisted of all the brotherhood and kin elders in the village as well as the village elder himself. For instance, in the district of Kurbin there were sixteen villages, each of which had its 'head (or village) elder'. But according to a document published on p. 129 of Father Gjeçov's book, there were altogether forty-five elders in Kurbin. Besides the sixteen 'head elders' there were twenty-nine ordinary 'village elders', some of them kin elders and some brotherhood elders. In Mirditë these village elders were known as 'canon elders', because it was their business to see that the law was respected and applied. To avoid confusion between the single village elder and the body of village elders these will henceforth be alluded to as canon elders.

The document mentioned by Father Gjeçov introduces us to the seventh type, a personage styled 'chief elder'. In the document he was chief of the 'forty-five elders of the region of Krujë' (i.e. Kurbin). There is no explicit information of how his position came to this man or whether it was hereditary in his family. It can only be inferred that as he was a Përvizi of Skuraj, and this family led Kurbin, the position was hereditary and a tribute to the outstanding strength of his family. In so large an area as Kurbin there could not be any question of all the villages being related by blood and owning allegiance to Përvizi as the descendant, master after master, of the master of the ancestral household. In other districts where a chief elder existed, it may be assumed similarly that he owed his position to the personal qualities of his family rather than to its descent.

Some other kinds of elder were found, both among the southern tribes and elsewhere, but it will be easier to understand their position after the characteristics and functions which were common to the elders have been elucidated.

Viewed as a human being, an elder was an ordinary man without privileges other than the corner seat, head of the roasted animal and first cup of coffee, which were offered to any man of standing. He lived in the same style as the rest of his social unit and was their equal in the eyes of the law. The latter point was clearer in the old days. If he were killed an ordinary blood feud ensued; if this was compounded, the price of his blood was no higher than an ordinary man's. If he killed someone, his life was forfeit in the usual manner to his victim's family. If he committed a crime against the community, he was liable to the usual punishments for such a crime and could be asked to give the community a rifle or other recognized article as security for his good behaviour in future. He had also the same social obligations as humbler tribesmen. These included serving in the tribal 'army', feeding the tribal 'youth', doing forced labour for the government, sharing communal labour for the village, and subscribing to public objects like buying an extra piece of communal pasturage or forest. He had also, like common men, to do military service and work annually without payment for a short period on the roads.

As a legal personage, however, an elder was on a higher footing than ordinary tribesmen. If, for instance, a village elder were to witness an oath in a case grave enough to require twenty-four jurors, his single person counted as the twelve jurors who were left unspecified by the judging elder. Another elder did not count as high, for a village elder ranked higher than a kin elder, and the latter higher than a brotherhood elder. An elder's duties were twofold, administrative and legal. The former were an expansion of the master's, for he had to take the same fatherly care of his brotherhood, kin or village that a master took of his household and had to run it on much the same system. On the external side he had to present its case skilfully to higher authorities and defend it from oppression. Internally he must maintain law and order by checking the chief evils, assassination and damage to property. He had to try to nip quarrels in the bud by persuasive reasoning, arbitrate when they menaced and judge when they developed. He had to lend the weight of his presence not only to the giving of an oath but also to the bequeathing of a legacy to church or mosque, the planting of boundary stones, and (generally) the separation of brothers. The embodiment of the tribal law, he was at once advocate, judge and law-giver.

An elder's age and wealth did not matter to the ordinary members of his social unit, who drew no invidious comparisons between him and themselves on those grounds. Provided he was correctly descended from the master of the ancestral household through a succession of what were conventionally called 'eldest' brothers, and were really the most competent, they accepted him as their elder as unquestioningly as the English nation accepts its king. Sometimes a new elder seemed unfit for his duties. Then the others took him with them when they went to work, and told him how his dead father judged or arbitrated: the most telling and least offensive method of training him.

When a dispute occurred it was the duty of the aggrieved party to inform his brotherhood elder first of all. When he did so and the matter was trifling and lay between two members of his brotherhood, this elder judged the case out of hand. If the disputants belonged to different brotherhoods, he consulted with the elder of the second brotherhood. When the case was graver he carried it to his kin elder, who might judge it straight away or carry it to the village elder. The village elder might in his turn pronounce judgement forthwith or call a General Assembly of the village in order to thrash the matter out in public and get a backing for any decision taken. Often the aggrieved party went straight to the village elder who was accessible to all tribesmen. In that event neither his kin nor his brotherhood had the right to resent the man's going over their heads. Moreover, the village elder's superiority was so well established that no resentment was likely to be felt. In no case was it lawful for an aggrieved man to seek advice from an elder in an outside village before he had consulted one of his own. If a kin elder or the brotherhood elders in the kin oppressed others in the village it was the duty of the village elder to repress them; and he had the right to summon the elders of the other kins in the village, if necessary, to his support. Article 10 in the Convention of Kurbin[1] betrays a strong feeling that there must be no shooting until the village elder has been informed of the dispute and given a chance to settle it by quieter means.

Elders could also act collectively. In the old days no new law could be passed, nor any judgement affecting their social unit be pronounced, unless they were present and gave their approval. When the bajraktar summoned a General Assembly for such important purposes as concluding a truce, trying a serious case or enacting new laws of tribal behaviour, their attendance was

[1] See Appendix, Document XI, p. 271.

compulsory. Any who failed to attend and could not justify their absence were fined. Together with the general public, they had to investigate complaints against a senior elder or a bajraktar, and if they found him guilty, they had to fine or ostracize him. In their attempts to prevent breaches of the peace they were entitled to try any method from peaceful persuasion to forcible restraint by the whole village. When, for instance, a tribesman refused to accept a judgement that was demonstrably lawful and unbiased, they could call a General Assembly to discuss the case. A public fine generally ended the man's obduracy. If not, the village elders could ask all the headmen and 'soldiers' of the tribe to come and bring him to his senses by threatening to destroy his house and property. They continued to apply the old law, the public preferring these methods to those of modern officials.

Canon elders were subordinate to the bajraktar and the voivodes of their tribe, acting as their assistants at General Assemblies.

In non-tribal districts like Shpat and Martanesh the canon elders of Mirditë were represented by a body of men called 'local elders'. These were hereditary, found in every village and restricted in their law-giving to their own village.

Another type were called 'specialist elders' in the southern tribal areas, 'regional elders' or 'mountain elders' in Martanesh, and plain 'elders' in Theth. The great majority owed nothing to heredity and everything to themselves, being ordinary men who had gradually built up a reputation for good sense, conciliatory temper and especially knowledge of the mountain law. A few were hereditary elders who had displayed the same qualities. Except in a few unusual cases they did not hand on their gifts or their position. As it required time to build up their reputation, the generality were older than herditary elders when they attained this position. They began by settling petty troubles within their brotherhood and gradually as their reputation grew, they extended their sphere of action to their kin, village and district in succession. A brotherhood elder must not interfere in another brotherhood, a kin elder in another kin or a 'local elder' of Martanesh in another village. But the specialists might travel far and wide outside their own social unit judging and arbitrating wherever required. Provided that they judged according to the law, their judgements were binding and overrode any delivered previously by a local man. As gifted men do not arise at will, they were never common but were found only here and there. After the introduction of modern codes of justice they had little chance to emerge.

Above all elders, in both Mirditë and the adjacent tribes, came the Gjomarkaj family. This family was regarded as the source of all knowledge of the mountain law and represented the final court of appeal. The villagers of Martanesh carried many of their graver troubles to its head, but at the same time had often a 'special elder' whom they consulted in such cases. Selim Peshku, who died about 1910, was the latest example. The tree under which he sat dispensing justice in Martanesh is still shown. In the north the bishop or a specially gifted priest was the ultimate referee. They were consulted not so much for their knowledge of the law but because of their reputation for probity.

Functionally the brotherhood elders of Mirditë were represented in the Malësi e Madhe by the 'ward elders', who ruled and judged in their own small community, the village ward in which they lived. They were more commonly called *gjobtarë* ('fine-collectors') from their primary function of collecting fines. As legal functionaries they resembled specialist elders rather than brotherhood elders because they were ordinary tribesmen and owed their position as elders, not to hereditary right, but to special appointment. They were selected, however, not by the public like the specialists, but by the local bajraktar or voivode. On taking up an appointment to judge or arbitrate they were known as 'soul elders', on account of the solemn phrases with which they were commissioned. The commissioning bajraktar or voivode first asked, 'Do you pledge your souls, elders, that it was so?' On receiving their assent he laid a stone on the ground before them, saying, 'With body and soul, with a stone in front of you and with God's justice set these two people straight in any way that you can see'. It goes without saying that only upright men were willing or were asked to accept a charge laden with such danger to their soul after death. These northern ward elders had no connexion with the ward elders of Godolesh near Elbasan, who were seven in number for the six wards (mëhallë), all subordinate to the paid non-hereditary headman and his two assistants.

Another functional type, which was most important for the repression of crime and was found everywhere, was constituted by 'juror elders'. When trying a case, the judging elders might decide to make one of the disputants take an oath that he was not guilty.

Then, to guard against the man's forswearing himself they stipulated that a certain number of men must swear at the same time to his innocence. These might or might not be more than men of standing and reputed probity. Whether or not, they were called 'juror elders' for the period covered by the oath.

A subsection of juror elders was known as 'murder elders'. Men of unusually high repute who never shot without cause or stole or burned a neighbour's property, but not necessarily drawn from the ranks of canon elders, these were qualified by their character for swearing to the innocence of a man accused of murder. This crime being the most serious of all, twenty-four of them had to be found on each occasion. As usual, half were nominated by the judging elders and half found by the accused. When the first half had given their oath the accused was virtually cleared and the oath he then gave was only a formality. In Lumë the more important 'murder elders' refused to waste time on giving their oath in cases of petty crime but always came forward in murder cases if they thought the accused innocent. The mere fact of their coming forward in a case sometimes ended it, the rest of the proceedings seeming farcical by comparison.

In the more organized north there were, besides the Gjomarkaj family, recognized substitutes for elders. The Hereditary Captain of Mirditë represented the family which had ruled over the Alpine region of Orosh and its kindred of Dibër, Fan, Kushnen and Spaç for several hundred years and was said by some to be descended from the Albanian national hero, Skanderbeg. It had remained Catholic, and its long pedigree may be found in the church registers of Orosh. This family was the 'foundation of law'. Specially difficult cases in Mirditë were referred straight to its head for solution. Any case which three pairs of elders had failed to settle was taken to the chieftains of the subtribes and finally to the head of the Gjomarkaj family. Beyond this there was no appeal. Outsiders, even Mohammedan outsiders, were often glad to refer knotty problems to the family. In view of his exalted position the head had many legal rights. He took precedence in every assembly wherever and whenever met. He had the right to summon chieftains and populace to a General Assembly. Whenever necessary he could summon one man per family to a General Assembly in Shën Pal. At every trial or arbitration he could intervene. He had the right to uproot a family and expel it from Mirditë. He could even pass a sentence of death, for the 'quarters of the body are a matter for the tribes but the head belongs to Gjomarkaj', says the law. In virtue of these rights, if a village rebelled against the authorities of its tribe, word had to be sent to the Gjomarkaj family, which then summoned the other subtribes and led them against the insurgent villagers and reduced them to reason by fining some, banishing others and destroying others root and branch.

But there were limitations to the head's power. Laws made in concert for themselves by the elders and commonalty of a village about such matters as instigation to crime, breaking one's pledged word, murder and robbery could not be upset by either the tribal authorities or the Gjomarkaj family, provided that these new laws were not innovations contrary to the spirit of the ancient law of the mountains.

CHAPTER XIII

THE ADMINISTRATION OF JUSTICE

It was the law that every injustice done by Albanian to Albanian must be righted by means of elders and pledges, not by killing. This was crystallized in the adage, 'Killing for a fault is not permissible'. If, for instance, a man caught his neighbour stealing his sheep he had no right to kill him. He should bring him before an elder who would set the proper legal machinery in motion against him, even sending him if necessary before a General Assembly.

Associated with the elders in the administration of justice were the bajraktar and voivodes with, in Mirditë, the Gjomarkaj family. They were not judges in the Western European sense of public officers appointed to administer the law. They were men who judged by right of birth or weighty personality within their native area and they were permanent officers, irremovable so long as their physical powers lasted. They were always illiterate, trained only in the school of experience; practical men and not theorists. It was their special function to preserve the peace in their area by wise and just judging. They were in the literal sense of the words Justices of the Peace. But they could only interpret and apply the law. To make it was the prerogative of a General Assembly of the tribe.

As administrators elders received no fees, nor did they receive any when serving as juror or murder elders. But they were almost invariably paid for judging or arbitrating. In the Dibër area their fee was simply called 'pay', but it was camouflaged as 'sandals' in the north and Mirditë, and as 'coffee' in the south. In north Albania, where the formula was 'fee by the jobs', the fee was fixed and varied with the case. In Lumë, for instance, it was six Turkish pounds in a murder case and a watch worth one napoleon in a water dispute. In Mirditë it was five grosh for a case slight enough to finish in one morning and ten grosh for more serious cases in which the elder, stone on shoulder, had to give his oath. Ten grosh was the canonical fee in Kastrat after the Convention of 1892.[1] In Perlat the fee was adjusted to the client's means, an oke

[1] See Appendix, Document V, § 17, p. 264.

of coffee if he were poor, a sheep if he were rich. Farther south, the fee varied with the elder's importance and the bargain he made beforehand. In Martanesh it was ordinarily one Turkish pound, but Selim Peshku accepted this only in easy cases; he asked, and was gladly given, three or even five in more complicated cases. Cen Elezi of Dibër asked in 1938 twelve napoleons from each of two cousins who were quarrelling about a boundary. Two elders employed in a dispute were usually paid alike, each disputant paying half the total. But when each disputant bargained separately with his elder, one elder might be paid more than the other. Even where fees were conventionally fixed as in Lumë, an elder often bargained for a larger one. An elder who came from a distance was naturally paid more, as he had to spend at least one night and two days away from home. An average fee in Shkrel for such cases was one napoleon, whereas for cases near at hand it was a silver Turkish dollar in Turkish times or 10–20 koronë in 1932. Almost always an elder was given a sheep in addition; 'an elder without a sheep doesn't do', it was said. Elders could not exact prepayment; it was evidently felt by the old law-givers that if prepaid they might be tempted to default on the work. At the same time they had to be protected from the litigant who tried to default on their fee. A litigant had, therefore, to deposit a rifle or a silver watch or a silver tobacco box or the like at the outset of the case as a pledge that he would pay the fee at the end of the case. Judgement pronounced, he paid the fee and was given back his pledge. Because of this arrangement elders were called 'pledge elders' when they undertook work involving a fee.

In addition to his fee and sheep an elder also expected at least one meal for himself and his party. It had to be of the highest class, with meat and rice pilaff, and the meat had to be goat, ewe or ram, more rarely beef and never that inferior thing, chicken. When the elder's party was small, the sheep-breeders of the north gave *mazë*, a delicious dish compounded of butter, cheese and maize flour. In Kosovë the meal was generally taken from the richer disputant so as to save the poorer litigant expense, or from the one who had insisted on calling in elders. In Martanesh it was taken from the one who had caused the trouble. In Shalë, on the contrary, each elder ate at his own client's expense except in road cases, where both elders and their suites ate at the expense of the litigant in fault. In Zerqan, if the case dragged on so long that the elders required two meals, each disputant had to provide one; if the case was shorter and only one meal was required, the two disputants halved the expense and both sat down at the table with the elders, not always with too good a grace on the loser's part. If dinner-time found the party up on the mountain, far away from either disputant's house, the food had to be sent up to them there. If supper-time found the party still at work or only just finished, they all ate and slept in the house of one disputant. The expenses of feeding the elders and their party had, despite its burden, to be faced by the poorest man when wronged, for without an elder's intervention he would be trampled on by his fellows. The thought of its cost sometimes acted as a deterrent to the litigiously minded.

Litigants themselves chose the elder who was to judge between them, much as Englishmen choose their lawyer. In non-tribal areas litigants were completely free to select whichever elder they trusted most, irrespective of where he lived. In tribal areas they were obliged to choose one from their own village, at least to begin with. It is obvious that such an elder was likely to have some independent knowledge of the case and its rights and wrongs. In Mirditë and Kthellë a litigant who insisted on going outside his own village had to engage the bajraktar or a voivode of his tribe, not a smaller man, and must not go outside his tribe. The higher fee required by the bajraktar and voivode was usually enough to make the man stick to his own village. If a quarrel was not bitter, the two parties often agreed to entrust the case to a single elder and to divide the cost of his fee and meals. They then said to each other, 'Whom shall we have?' and mentioned various names. After debating—usually at some length—the merits of the owners of the names they fixed on one. Each then asked the other ceremoniously, 'Have you confidence in this elder?' 'I have', the other replied. Great importance was attached to this unanimity; it made the elder's decision more binding on both disputants, procuring in fact judgement by consent.

The preliminaries over, the two litigants contacted the elder, generally by going to his house, and told him their trouble. 'Are you willing to leave it to me?' he would ask. On their consenting formally to do so he stated his fee. This depended in Mirditë on the importance of the case and elsewhere on the importance of the elder, the distance he had to travel, and the astuteness of the litigants. In Martanesh a gold Turkish pound was commonly paid, for which reason both elders and litigants thought bargaining about it superfluous.

The litigants having formally consented to pay his fee, the elder next asked each of them to bring him a pledge. This served a threefold purpose. Once given, it could not be taken back till the case was settled and the fee paid. The litigants might repent of going to law or of engaging this particular elder, but unless they forfeited their pledges, they could neither stop the case nor change the elder. The pledge was, secondly, the elder's security for payment of his fee. As soon as he had delivered judgement he was entitled to his fee, and until it was paid he was entitled to retain the litigant's pledge. Occasionally in Zerqan an elder trusted a client enough to dispense with a pledge, and some in Martanesh asked only a token one, such as a cigarette, thus paying the integrity of their clients a high compliment. The normal pledge was of greater value than the fee, or share of the fee, payable by each litigant. Since pledges had been instituted in days so distant that money was hardly—if at all—known, a material article such as a gun, a revolver, a watch or a silver tobacco-box was generally handed over. It was for the elder to choose which it should be.

In Mirditë the article deposited was known as the 'pledge of acceptance or agreement', because its third purpose was to bind the litigants to accept the elder's decision. If one was refractory the elder had the right to retain his pledge. In a certain boundary case Cen Elezi of Dibër, having stipulated for a fee of twelve napoleons from each litigant, asked each to bring his tobacco-box as a pledge. As his son put it, this did not nearly cover his fee but was rather a preliminary 'symbol of acceptance' of his decision. Indiscipline in such matters naturally weakened the social fabric by destroying one of its most unifying factors, the authority of elders. Various steps were taken to reinforce decisions. Selim Peshku of Martanesh charged fees that ranged from five gold Turkish pounds to one, but he never took up a case until the larger sum had been deposited in pledge of submission to his judgement, and in case of recalcitrancy he showed no scruples about pocketing the pledge money. The disparity between his lowest fee and his unvarying pledge shows that he was trying, not so much to safeguard his own fee, as to maintain social discipline. Mirditë sought the same end by enacting that a judgement delivered without pledge being taken was invalid before the law and that a verbal pledge was valueless; something concrete and tangible must be given.

The pledges deposited, the elder set to work on the case in earnest, questioning any villager who had information, visiting the scene of trouble, interviewing any private informant who volunteered to give evidence, and so arriving at the rights and wrongs of the simpler cases. In more difficult cases he put one of the litigants to the oath, dictating his terms and stipulating the number of 'good men and true' who were to be persuaded by the litigant to take it with him. This rarely failed to show which litigant was in the wrong, and the elder came forthwith to his decision with confidence.

When the litigants were friendly, they might agree to engage two elders. In that case they selected them one after the other by the same method of mutual consent as they would have selected one. They also agreed to divide the cost in elders' fees and meals. That done, they laid the case before the elders, one after the other, and bargained with each about his fee and the number of meals he was to be given. These rewards were not necessarily the same for both elders. Sometimes they visited the elders together; more often each visited one only. In the usual way each was required to deposit a pledge with the elders.

When the litigants were not friendly, and this was the most common contingency, each found an elder for himself, without consulting the other or considering his views on the man. Each brought his own elder whatever pledge he desired; this meant that one litigant might have to deposit a gun and the other a tobacco-box. Each also bore the sole responsibility for his elder's fee and meals and made for himself the best bargain about them that he could.

A pair of elders worked on these same lines; singly perhaps during the period of investigation, certainly meeting at its conclusion to argue out the pros and cons of the case. If each represented a separate litigant, each tended to favour his own client, so introducing a new principle. The elder was no longer only a judge as he was when he was engaged by the two litigants; he was also the advocate of his own litigant, trying to do the best for him by arguing against the advocate of the other litigant. The loser was more likely to contest the decision under such circumstances.

When the two elders had hammered out an agreement they sent for the two disputants, said they had come to an agreement, and asked if they were willing to accept this. In the most fortunate event the disputants consented and the elders communicated their decision. Each then said to his own man, 'Now bring me my dues and I'll return your pledge'. As soon as his fee was paid he gave back his pledge to his client. If the disputant had no ready money for the fee, a common enough occurrence, he said he would wait a month or two, provided that the disputant could find someone to go bail for him. When the term he had fixed was up without bringing payment of his fee, he sold the pledge and so recouped himself. If he got rather more for the pledge than the amount of his fee the disputant had no right to claim the extra money. The elder never sold the pledge before the date he had fixed. If within the term he fixed the disputant found enough money for his fee, he was no longer allowed to pay it directly but had to transmit it through his guarantor, who in return brought back his pledge from the elder. Sometimes the guarantor saw that the disputant would never be able to redeem his pledge and paid the elder's fee for him. Unfortunately, elders had no power behind them with which to enforce their judgement. Their work was in fact arbitration rather than judging in the English sense. It was, therefore, common for elders in central Albania to communicate their findings to the disputants and then to add, 'Now settle the matter as you like. We have decided that this one of you is in the right.' Too often the loser shot his successful rival, so starting a bad blood feud. Pjetër Gjoni of Theth had his house burgled, and the thief bribed the elders into putting too low a value on the stolen property, assessing it at two napoleons. Pjetër, who had already spent one napoleon on finding out who had been the thief, declared immediately that he would not abide by this judgement and killed the thief. In revenge the thief's family burned down Pjetër's house and carried off all his cattle.

Naturally many attempts were made to prevent such sequels to judgements. In Martanesh, Selim Peshku kept the pledges of both disputants for a time. This was against the rules, but Peshku had the peace of the community at heart and made 'anything for peace' his motto. In Zerqan all the elders in the village would meet and would fine a recusant before he could shoot the successful litigant. Sometimes in the same village the two elders refused to deliver judgement until the disputants had promised to abide by it and had each found a guarantor who undertook to see that they kept their promise—if they did, there would be no shooting. Each had to give this guarantor a pledge of the usual type—rifle, revolver, watch—which was laid before the elders. The elders then delivered their judgement, the two disputants accepted it and had their pledges returned. If a disputant broke his promise and shot his rival, the village Council of Elders would fine the guarantor, asking him why he had let the man break his word. In this way, through the medium of the guarantor a good deal of pressure was brought to bear on the loser to make him keep the peace. In the Elbasan area it was agreed that a disputant who gave a meal to the elders thereby accepted their judgement, so that the strong instincts of hospitality came into play. In Mirditë the elders whose decision was flouted bade the disputants 'go to Shupal (St Paul's Church) or the Grykë e Oroshit (Defile of Orosh)', i.e. bring the matter up before the next General Assembly for the tribe at one or other of these famous meeting-places. If the loser would not abide by the decision of the General Assembly he could be fined by the tribe, ostracized or even banished for a period. Occasionally a strong man subjected to such sanctions killed the offending elder; by so doing he involved himself in yet another blood feud. In Mirditë and adjacent areas emphasis was laid on the fact that the recusant loser had himself chosen and approved the offending elder, and had signified the same by giving him a pledge. By these acts he had stripped himself of the right to take back the pledge or to express active disapproval of the judgement given. Only in the event of the judgement's being demonstrably biased or unfair were the disputants allowed to challenge it. 'A crooked judgement can be annulled', the law stated. Often the crookedness was established by the loser going secretly to ask another elder for his opinion. In that event the disputant had everywhere the right to appeal against the judgement and to call for a new examination of the case by another elder or pair of elders. In some parts, the law ruled that 'the law does not admit of elder on elder, and trial on trial', and that a man who had 'chosen and approved' elders had no right to call in others.

Frivolous changing of elders was restrained by the extra expense this entailed. In Lumë, for instance, if two brothers were displeased by the manner in which their chosen elders were dividing their property, they could call in one more elder, a *staraplak* (ancient), whose decision was final. But his regulation fee was five napoleons. In cases other than those of division of property he received only two napoleons. He took over the two pledges from the original elders, and as these were redeemed from him at a price by the two disputants, the first pair lost their time and trouble and received nothing. If a disputant in Martanesh was disgruntled he could call in a regional elder, but he had to pay, not only the fee of the elder whose judgement he questioned, but also that of the regional elder. One of Selim Peshku's devices for making a recalcitrant litigant keep the peace was to bid him bring another elder and he, Selim, would pay the fee as well as return the litigant's pledge. The man, knowing no elder would reverse a decision by Selim Peshku and somewhat stunned by the latter's generous offers, invariably submitted.

Another check on frivolous lawsuits was the arrangement under which the litigants were not allowed to tell their stories to the second pair of elders. These were briefed by the first pair, apart from the litigants, who were also required to stay with their comrades among the general public while the new elders argued out the case. There was, in theory at least, no possibility of the new elders being 'got at'. In Mirditë, the head and fount of the law, rules were more stringent. The disputants were not allowed to choose the second pair of elders; this was done by the first pair. They had also to hand over to the second pair the pledges they had taken from the disputants. If the second pair found the first pair's judgements sound, the disputants had to pay a fee to both the first and the second pairs. If, however, they found the first pair's judgement unsound, they, by this time the holders of the pledges of the litigants, were paid their fees by the first pair, who in addition got no fee at all for their previous trouble. A third pair of elders might be chosen in Mirditë but no more. After that it was a matter for the expensive chieftains or the Gjomarkaj family to settle. In Kurbin, too, it was the rule that when elders failed to come to an agreement, it was they and not the litigants who chose the second pair. In disputes about water, land, boundaries and the like up to sixteen elders might be chosen, two by two. If any pair came to an agreement, their predecessors and the litigants had to accept their decision. Each of the successful pair received a napoleon as his fee; the unsuccessful elders received nothing. When the sixteen possibilities within the tribe had been exhausted without result, elders were called in from an outside tribe, naturally at an enhanced fee. These outside elders were generally taken from old, important tribes like Mirditë, Beshkash, Kthellë and Lesh, or from Krujë town.

Here then we have the working basis of their judgements. The elder or elders originally judging the case had an interest in settling the matter because they received a fee for their judgement. They had a further interest in settling it quickly because their fee was fixed at the outset, and by contrast with lawyers in a western law court they received no more if the case dragged on. Delay over one case also entailed a risk of being unable to undertake other cases that might arise. They had an interest in not splitting hairs with each other, for that might preclude their coming to an agreement and cause their supersession by others, with consequent loss of fees. They had an interest in not giving a crooked judgement because that might lawfully be upset, again causing them to lose their fees. They had, lastly, an interest in not taking bribes, for an elder who was detected in that was detected only once; he was never again asked to be an elder.

CHAPTER XIV

GENERAL ASSEMBLIES

Turkish suzerainty affected the life of the remoter areas so little that each tribe, and in non-tribal areas each region, was virtually a self-governing unit. The governing bodies in tribal areas were the General Assemblies and the Partial Assemblies. In Turkish times these meetings were often called *mexhlis* (from Arabic *'majlis'* meaning council, assembly, parliament). *Kuvend* is the Latin *'conventio'* (gathering) in Albanian dress. In non-tribal areas regional or village assemblies corresponded to the general and partial assemblies of the tribes.

The General Assembly was usually a tribal gathering, but the word *Kuvend* was used by the Albanians to indicate the national parliament during the German occupation in 1943–4 when Albanian nationalism expressed itself in rejecting the use of words of foreign origin.

In the fifteenth century there was a *Kuvend* of great historical importance when the men of the region of north Albania met to hear Lek Dukagjini, the lord of the extreme north, debate points of law with Skanderbeg, the lord of north central Albania.

Tribal assemblies brought together one or more tribes. These were plenary, attended by the whole tribe (or region) on the basis of 'one man from each house'. They were convened and presided over by the highest authority available. This was the bajraktar in most tribes, but one of the Gjomarkaj family or a bajraktar in Mirditë. In Dibër, Mat and Kurbin it was the head of the leading family, and in Çermenikë the regional elder. Miss Durham found the president elected in Theth, and stated that this innovation was spreading. Where a General Assembly of two or more tribes took place the meeting resulted from a conference of the chief men of each tribe, convened by the highest dignitary in each tribe and presided over by the highest of these high dignitaries.

Partial Assemblies too were plenary and were convened and presided over by the head of the unit concerned. The more important were formed by a village or a kin. In a document preserved for us by Father Gjeçov,[1] the last clause announces that though the Pecnikaj kin of Shalë laid down the law enunciated in clause 2, it had the support of the Lotaj, Abati (Abat) and Bobi (Bob) kins in doing so. Its first and its fourth clauses consider the adhesion of the brotherhood of Theth as well. Occasionally there was a partial meeting of a brotherhood, and at the bottom of the scale there were household meetings at which the master set some common problem before all the men in the family.

Generally speaking, assemblies of all types took place at irregular intervals, to meet some special need, though the demand that they should be called regularly once a year was not unknown.[2]

When a kin or smaller meeting was in question, the convener sent anyone he could find to call it. Bigger meetings were summoned by word of mouth by the public messenger. In Mat a gipsy beat out the summons on his drum and in Shpat church bells were rung.

Attendance at a plenary meeting was compulsory, non-attendance punishable by a fine. For instance, an elder of Kurbin who failed to turn up and could not satisfy the other elders that his absence was justified was fined five rams. An ordinary tribesman in the same area was fined one ram and in Kastrat 250 piastres. The strength and solidarity of the tribes were closely connected with the plenary character of their assemblies.

Most public meetings took place in the open air, as church houses were usually too small and schoolrooms and village halls did not exist. Meeting places had to be central and free from cultivation, rock, scrub and forest so as to provide adequate seating space In Catholic areas the yard of the church was commonly used for General Assemblies and in Moslem areas that of the mosque. Assemblies of a village or kin could be held in the most central of the smaller clearings of the area, and a house was big enough for a brotherhood or household assembly.

Some meeting-places were specially famous. At Lesh, a thriving seaport at the mouth of the river Drin, and not the malarial inland townlet into which it has been converted by the advance of the Drin towards Italy, Lek Dukagjini and Skanderbeg met by preference, as it was centrally situated for both their domains. The place of meeting was probably the grassy sward near the ruined church on the right bank of the Drin, opposite the modern town.

[1] See Appendix, Document XII, p. 272
[2] See Appendix, Document V, § 16, p. 264.

In Lower Martanesh Selim Lashku dispensed justice to the village of Martanesh under a branching tree by the *Gur i Kuvendit* (Stone of Assembly). At the spring called Gurrë Gega, which is at the confluence of the Shëmil and Gurakuq torrents in Çermenikë, he used to meet his famous contemporary of Gurakuq village, Mus Ballgjini, at plenary meetings of the twelve villages of Çermenikë. A list of the usual meeting-places of his day is to be found in Father Gjeçov's book.

The convener fixed the time and place of meeting. The favourite time was the early morning, as this left the whole day free for arguing.

The bajraktar presided over the General Assembly and sat cross-legged on the ground in the most honourable place. Near him sat other dignitaries—voivodes, village elders, clan elders, village ancients and clan ancients in due order of social precedence. Facing them and well apart sat the rest of the tribe, the youth, the commoners, the public messengers and the fine-collectors (*gjobtarë*), in a half-circle in Mirditë, and elsewhere in a roughly shaped rectangle or circle. The essential thing was that each man present should see and be seen by everybody else, and should have room to advance, if required, to the dignitaries. Since neither youth nor voivodes and fine-collectors existed in southerly districts like Martanesh, General Assemblies there consisted only of the bajraktar, elders, commoners, and public messengers.

Every effort was made to keep a meeting orderly. When a presiding dignitary, a judging elder or a witness was speaking no interruption was allowed. Insulting remarks and abuse were prohibited under pain of a fine that might amount to as many as five rams. Calling another a liar meant a fine of 500 piastres. For the better observance of these rules when a case was being tried, the disputants were not allowed to address the court. Each had to go some distance away with his elder in order to tell him his story quietly, and had to return to his place at the meeting to await judgement in silence. The elders drew apart from the meeting after their briefing, argued the case out with each other, and returned to the meeting to announce their decision in the hearing of all present. In this way only two or three men talked, the rest sat quiet and listened. In Mirditë a stranger might not take part in a general meeting, but in Lumë and Çermenikë, in the belief that a stranger could have 'nothing in his bosom or his pocket', that is to say, no interested motive for his opinion, he was actually encouraged to express his views. Among the Catholics of the far north the priest was permitted to speak, as though he were one of the tribesmen, but his views did not necessarily prevail.

It was unthinkable, of course, that the tribesmen should come without their arms in view of possible dangers on the way. So the law said explicitly that they might bring them. But as soon as they took their places cross-legged on the ground they had to lay their guns on the grass in front of them or on their laps and had to keep them so until the meeting ended. The Catholics sometimes let the priest coax them into depositing their arms in the church house for the duration of the meeting. If anyone raised his gun in anger, it was promptly taken from him by his neighbours. If anyone fired his gun the rest of the meeting immediately formed itself into a firing squad and killed him, and then went in a body to his house and burned it down. Even at the smallest meeting there were four or five important men present who kept a sharp look-out ready to prevent trouble. The priests too kept good watch, and a Franciscan found in Theth by Miss Durham in 1908 told the following story: 'We nearly had a row at the *mexhlis*[1] a little while ago....I heard a fearful noise and as I ran out a lot of them got up into a bunch like bees and raised their rifles. They were just going to fire. They would not listen to me. I rushed into the church and rang the bell as hard as I could. It had a splendid effect. As soon as they heard the bell, from habit they all shoved their pistols into their belts and took their guns in their left hands and began to cross themselves. No one knew what had happened. They poured into the church to see. By the time we came out again...they were quieted.'

Proceedings usually began with a statement by the president that the tribe had assembled to consider certain matters in the manner required by God and the canon, that is to say, with justice and without innovations or departures from the established law. Great importance was attached to the latter point. The decisions of specialist elders were accepted only on condition that they conformed to the accepted law and did not constitute innovations. This proviso was thought unnecessary in the case of elders who had been bred to the law as the specialists had not, and were therefore trusted to stick to it. This conservatism maintained the strength of the law, the main factor in keeping the tribe together.

[1] General Assembly.

The following story told by Miss Durham[1] throws light upon the mind of a tribe on this point:

In the spring of 1908 a tribesman of Gjan, quarrelling with a tribesman of neighbouring Shosh, snatched a firebrand from the hearth and flung it in his face. It would have been bad enough to kill the man of Shosh, but it was worse to insult him with such a blow. The Gjan man, fearing the wrath to come, fled with all speed. The Shosh man was so enraged that, unable to catch the actual culprit and clear his honour by shooting him, he went to Gjan and shot 'an unhappy little boy, unarmed and but eight years old'... 'whose only crime was that he belonged to the same tribe as the offender'.... 'Gjan was filled with rage. That Shosh had the right to take blood of any man of the tribe they freely admitted, but to kill a child was dishonourable.' On the following Whit Sunday a General Assembly of Shosh met to debate the case. 'Shosh was violently indignant over the affair and public opinion ran so high that the murderer had not dared to remain in the tribe but had fled. The *Mexhlis* now was held to decide whether his house should be burnt as punishment. Many were in favour of this. The difficulty was that there was no law under which this could be done. The blood had been taken *outside* the tribe; it was therefore not a crime against the tribe and not punishable by it. The duty of vengeance lay with the dead boy's family. All agreed that if they liked to come and fire the house Shosh would not oppose it. But as the near relatives were a crippled father and a child they were incapable of executing justice in the face of the opposition which would certainly be put up by the murderer's family. The question caused great excitement. The burning of the house would entail passing a new law to punish a man for a crime against another tribe. This would mean an entire reconstruction of the code and nothing less than considering themselves as a nation, and not as detached tribes.' Miss Durham asked 'whether it were not possible at least to pass a law to punish any man killing a child not of age to bear arms'. It was pointed out that if Shosh did so and neighbour tribes did not, Shosh would be at a disadvantage.... The question was discussed for two days, and was undecided when Miss Durham left.

Proceedings at a General Assembly terminated in Catholic areas with the drawing up of minutes by the priest, the only man present

[1] See *Some Tribal Origins* etc., p. 165.

who could write. Though strictly speaking a stranger, he was expected by every tribe, Mirditë included, to attend all its meetings and to act as clerk. Sometimes each man present, sometimes only the president, appended his mark, generally a Turkish seal, to the document. The priest signed as witness, added the date and place, and placed it in the church archives for safe keeping and future reference.

CHAPTER XV

ASSEMBLIES AND THEIR WORK

Assemblies sometimes dealt with internal matters such as criminal trials, formulation of laws, local administration, and sometimes with the external relations of the community. Internal affairs were dealt with, according to their gravity, by the tribe, village or kin, but a plenary assembly had to be called to consider foreign affairs.

During the nineteenth and early part of the twentieth century the northern tribes of Albania were singly or collectively in constant opposition to Turkish sovereignty, and plenary assemblies were summoned by tribes whenever they planned to break out into open revolt. Earlier in 1855 and 1862 there had been attacks on the Montenegrins by the Mirditë, which had followed on plenary assemblies of the Mirditë tribes.

In 1881 the Albanians of Kosovë formed the League of Prizren in order to struggle more effectively for independence of Turkey. All over Kosovë and what afterwards became the kingdom of Albania plenary meetings were held by tribes, and, where these did not exist as in south Albania, by districts, to decide on whether to join this League or not. Again in 1908, as Miss Durham relates,[1] the northern tribes held plenary meetings about accepting the new Turkish constitution. The Albanian attack on the Turkish garrisons in Skoplje and adjacent towns, that began the Balkan war of 1912, was prefaced by general assemblies of every tribe in Kosovë and north Albania. In the summer of 1914, when Esad Pashë Toptani revolted against Prince William of Wied, then *Mbret* (king) of Albania, his supporters raised central Albania in his favour by carrying the Koran in one hand and a crucifix in the other to plenary meetings of the villages and bidding the Assembly, generally consisting of Moslems only, choose between the Moslem Esad and the Christian 'Mbret'. In 1942 a plenary meeting of all Mat was convened by the subprefect of Mat in the hope of enforcing obedience to the Italian government of the day. The decisions reached at the meeting were embodied in a document

[1] *Some Tribal Origins* etc., p. 120, n. 1.

published in the Albanian newspaper *Tomori* on 7 November 1942,[1] a curious mixture of Fascist ideology and ancient mountain law. But the decisions were honoured only in the breach. A few months later, many hundreds of families represented at the meeting were homeless, victims of Italian reprisals for their persistent revolts.

Sometimes a tribe met in plenary session to deal with inter-tribal matters. It might have quarrelled with a neighbour over a grazing or forest boundary between their territories, or the neighbour might be harbouring one of its dangerous criminals. In either case the tribe had to meet in plenary session, first of all to discover by public argument the best way of enforcing its boundary rights or procuring the surrender of the criminal, and secondly to secure public sanction for the steps it decided on. These might even include war. Miss Durham describes a General Assembly of Shalë which she witnessed in 1908.[2] The Moslem tribes to the north and east, surreptitiously armed by the Turkish government, had threatened to massacre Shalë and its Catholic associates if they did not embrace Islam by the next Ramazan. Shalë met in General Assembly, and amid scenes of wild enthusiasm passed a resolution to warn its Moslem neighbours that within seven days of their receiving notice Shalë and its fellow-Catholics would be at war with them.

Sometimes a pair of tribes met in plenary assembly for mutual aid. Several examples of contracts made on such occasions are given by Father Gjeçov; translations of three appear as Documents IV, VII and VIII.[3] In the first the tribes of Nikaj and Mertur pledge the safety of man and beast at certain times of the year. The second is between the tribes of Nikaj and Shalë in 1894, and the third, dated 1895, is between Nikaj and Curraj, a 'brother-hood' of Nikaj. In these latter, each contracting party guarantees the safety of the other's tribesmen when travelling along certain specified roads in its territory; in the first Shalë's guarantee is extended to tribesmen of Shosh, its western neighbour, and Nikaj's guarantee to tribesmen of Mertur, its eastern neighbour. In this way they facilitated a considerable amount of movement from tribe to tribe. Such documents were really an early form of passport, allowing the tribesmen of one tribe 'to pass freely without let or hindrance' in the territory of the other.

---

[1] See Appendix, Document XIII, p. 272.
[2] Op. cit., pp. 71, 72.   [3] See Appendix, pp. 263, 265, 267.

Like tribes, villages sometimes met together to try to agree about matters of common interest. Villages often quarrelled over irrigation water, and a forest or pasture boundary. They quarrelled even oftener perhaps because the tracks of stolen animals led from one to the other; cattle-lifting and sheep-stealing were common. The most satisfactory way of dealing with troubles was for the two villages to meet in full assembly. After thrashing the matter out in public they generally reached a settlement, failing which they could only go to war. In the early years of the twentieth century cattle thieving was listed as one of the thirteen most important matters brought before General Assemblies in Martanesh. In 1942 it was still so active a disturber of the public peace that the pro-Fascist subprefect of Mat legislated for it among the questions which were the real occasion of his calling together the 5000 families of Mat.[1]

Law-giving was also an important function of General Assemblies. This activity came to an end with centralization and western legal codes, and its nature can be studied in the documents quoted by Father Gjeçov and reproduced as an appendix to this book, pp. 261 sqq. These documents show the variety of matters with which the law-giving of the Assembly was concerned. For instance, Document I, coming from Malësi e Madhe and dated 1864, is wholly devoted to such subjects as betrothal, bride-price, divorce and abduction or elopement. Document XI, which comes from Kurbin in 1906, is much occupied with stealing and with tightening up the social fabric by making attendance at General Assemblies imperative and the authority of elders supreme. With the proclamation of Albanian independence of Turkey only six years ahead, it contains an interesting political note; no Kurbin man is to become a gendarme in Turkish service or to give one food and shelter; and no Moslem of Kurbin is to curry favour with the Turkish authorities by denouncing a Christian fellow-tribesman. Document XIII, which comes from Mat in 1942, is also dated by its politics enjoining support of the Italian régime in Albania.

In the midst of the variety of subjects in the documents, crimes against life and property are continually appearing as the fundamental threats to the security of the community. A study of the documents shows them as reaffirming and modifying old and recognized laws, rather than formulating new ones. Assemblies

[1] See Appendix, Document XIII, § 4, p. 273.

were called together to deal with specific problems and their findings emphasize aspects of the law relevant to these problems. The agenda of the assemblies therefore, reveal a good deal of social history. For example, in Document III from Kastrat dated 1891, six of its eleven provisions deal with the use of mills, fountains and springs. Document V, also from Kastrat dated 1892, restates what must have been established law about the constant threat of murder and theft, but it also includes provision for dealing with the owner of a dog entering a field or vineyard without a wooden collar, and the person who washes clothes at the place where the district gets its water.

In 1894 again Kastrat decrees penalties against the man who takes a woman to live with him without marrying her; against anyone tearing his face in mourning for the dead; against persons obstructing chiefs and fine-collectors in carrying out the tribal law.

The documents from Nikaj and Shalë also throw light on the social order to which they refer and its special problems at the time of their formulation. Document VII, dated 1894, is concerned mainly with safety from attack on the roads and the 'pledge of safety' for certain classes of people—mowers and reapers, shooters, women, etc. It was found necessary to reiterate many of the same provisions with the penalties attached to their breach in the following year in Document VIII.

A letter from Shalë to Theth, dated 1907 (XII), asks that the latter shall subscribe to a number of rules about murder and the position of the murderer laid down by Shalë, and after discussing this important subject, states that the rules are under the authority of the Youth.

Document XI (1906) is particularly interesting from an historical point of view, as it combines concern with the usual domestic issue of stealing with anxiety about the machinery of government, and reflects the opposition of the tribe to the Turkish sovereign. There are clauses about non-attendance at General Assemblies and about the use of elders to settle disputes. Heavy penalties are laid down for men joining the Turkish government police, complaining to the government about a Christian, or for anyone giving food or entry to his house to any policeman whether Christian or Mohammedan.

The most recent of the documents (XIII) is the so-called Covenant of Mat which appeared in the Albanian newspaper

Tomori on 7 November 1942. The greater part of this document
deals with an entirely new situation and the methods by which the
people of Mat undertake to adapt themselves to it. But even in this
document there appears the familiar restatement of old laws against
the familiar crimes of murder, theft and the abduction of women.

Differences in the penalties laid down for the same offence may
possibly point to social and economic differences among the tribes.
For example, in Nikaj, Shalë and Curraj (Documents VII and VIII)
a defaulting debtor is to be deprived of civil rights and may be
killed or robbed unless he meets his obligations. In Kastrat (V) he
is fined twenty-three grosh as a defaulter, but much more heavily
fined if his sureties have to pay his debt. Nikaj was a poorer area
than Kastrat, and that fact may explain to some extent the difference
in penalty. The treatment of stealing also differs as between
Kastrat and Shalë which was the poorer of the two. In Kastrat the
robber of another's house or sheepfold is to be fined 500 grosh and
five rams, but in Shalë (X) the thief who steals a single animal—
a ewe, a goat, a cow—is to have 'his harvest burnt, his fields
plucked bare and his grain panniers smashed'.

Some stories related by Father Gjeçov illustrate the application
and development of the law. About 1860 a villager of Fregënë in
the Mirditë tribe of Dibër told a neighbour to kill a certain man
and promised that when the time came to pay the blood money he
would see to it. On the faith of this promise, the neighbour
ambushed the man on the high road and shot him dead. A little
later, Captain Bibë Doda, the Gjomarkaj of the day, went on tour
for the purpose of composing current blood feuds. The Fregënë
feud came up, among others, and the murderer was ordered to
rebuild his victim's house by way of paying blood money. He
asked his evil counsellor for the money he had promised, but the
latter declined to pay. Captain Bibë and the heads of the tribe
summoned this man, and asked him if he had told his neighbour
to commit the murder and promised to pay the blood money. The
man dared not deny doing so. Then Captain Bibë, together with the
bajraktar of Dibër and other heads, reasoning that 'lips can't land
a man in a blood feud' and 'words don't make a funeral', made it
law that 'Murder depends on the finger'; that is to say, the
murderer who must pay with his life or money for the crime is
the man whose finger pulled the trigger. They then sentenced the
Fregënë murderer to pay blood money for his crime, saying that

while he had gone to the ambush by another's instructions he had walked there on his own legs. As the instigator of the crime had broken his promise about paying the blood money, they sentenced him to have his house burned down by the tribe.

On one occasion Lek Dukagjini had come at Skanderbeg's invitation to discuss some blood feuds at a General Assembly of all the tribes in the land. Skanderbeg opposed the principle of 'a life for a life' on the grounds that all men were *not* equal; the blood of a physically fine man was different from that of a poor type. At Lek's suggestion, however, he inquired of his mother, upon oath, what sort of a man his father had been. On learning that he had been a poor type, Skanderbeg at the next Assembly agreed to the principle of equality!

About 1870, when Kolë Prenga the Great was Captain of Mirditë, a jar of butter was stolen from the church house in Orosh during the priest's absence. On his return his servant, who had also been away at the time, informed him of the theft. The priest, a Franciscan, informed the bajraktar of Orosh. The latter convened the tribe (*bajrak*) but no one confessed to the theft. The bajraktar then informed Captain Kola. The captain undertook to track down the culprit, and one day ordered the tribe to assemble on the open space in front of the church at Orosh. In spite of Captain Kola's questions no one came forward to confess to the crime. Then Captain Kola, together with the chiefs of the tribe, sentenced the unknown thief to death and banishment from the tribe; his house, too, was to be destroyed and his land left uncultivated. Not long afterwards the thieves were discovered. They were two young men of Orosh, Prengë Kolë Marku and another whose name has been forgotten. Captain Kolë Prenga the Great again ordered the tribe to assemble, one man from every house, at the church at Orosh. The two young men also came by order to the meeting. Captain Kola read out the sentence that had previously been pronounced. The two thieves were stood in the middle of an open space, unarmed and with their hands folded at the waist. The tribe stood up awaiting the captain's order to fire. But the priest, filled with pity for the culprits, begged the captain, the chiefs and the commoners to grant them their lives. This was done, they paid money to the church for their sacrilege, returned twice the quantity of what they had stolen, paid the usual fine and were expelled from the tribe.

It was not the theft but the sacrilege that on this occasion called the tribe of Orosh to a General Assembly and made them pronounce even the death sentence; without the sacrilege the fine would have been penalty enough. Murder of a priest, again heinous sacrilege, raised the same issues, but without hope of any reprieve from death save what secret flight might provide. Murder of a guest or of a man with whom the murderer had previously sworn an oath of peace, that is to say, of persons who had a right to protection, also came before a General Assembly and was punished by the severest penalties, including death. Yet theft in the ordinary way was handled by elders and punished by a fine, and murder of the ordinary type was left to the victim's family and punished by blood vengeance. These were crimes against the individual and matter for individual handling. Sacrilege, however, and the murder of protected persons, were crimes against society, the former threatening the authority of the Church and the latter the tribal fabric.

When a man's general behaviour was a public menace or nuisance, he usually found himself before a General Assembly. To begin with, the elders of his social unit took the matter up as was their duty, attempting first to reason him into a better frame of mind. If this failed, they had to call a plenary meeting of the village to try the culprit and to carry out whatever sentence was pronounced. This was usually burning down his house and leaving his land untilled for a specific number of years. If he still persisted in his evil-doing, and this was serious socially speaking, the elders could call the whole tribe to their assistance. For public pests incited public extermination, and this required the sanction and the whole force of the tribe. Miss Durham relates what she calls 'an amazing case of wholesale justice' which occurred in the Mirditë tribe, Fan, in February 1912. A certain family in this tribe had become notorious for evil-doing, robbing, shooting and general misconduct. A 'gathering of the whole tribe' condemned all the males of the family to death. Men were appointed to lie in wait for them on a certain day and pick them off. And on that day the whole seventeen of them were shot. One was only five and another only twelve years old. It was even proposed to kill an unfortunate woman who was pregnant in case she should bear a male and so renew the evil.[1]

[1] Durham, op. cit. p. 75.

Disobedience to accepted authority was not permitted to an individual tribesman, a villager or even a tribe if that formed part, like the Mirditë tribes, of a group of tribes. Several of the Documents end by indicating the penalties that await tribesmen who defy the authority of the General Assembly that had laid down the preceding laws for the public good.

Examples of penalties prescribed are a fine of 3000 grosh, a choice between being burnt out or paying an ox to the tribe and 300 grosh and a ram to the government's representative, and a sentence of having one's house burned down and oneself expelled. Number XIII, the Fascist document from Mat, simply declares that any delinquent will be called a traitor. In each case the whole tribe was to meet again in General Assembly and go in a body to carry out the sentence. According to Document XI the breaker of a pledge guaranteed by the General Assembly of the Elders and Commoners of Kurbin was warned that the said Elders and Commoners would be obliged to burn his house and expel him.'

Elders were seldom tried before a General Assembly. They were kept in check by the fact that if their judgements were found unfair they lost not only face but also fees, for they were seldom asked to judge again. If there were complaints against one he was first asked, like an erring bajraktar or voivode, for a pledge; if he refused to give it he was haled before the General Assembly.

If a disputant flouted an elder's just and carefully considered judgement, he found himself before a General Assembly. For an elder represented a lawful authority. 'If you don't like the decision, go to St Paul's church or the Defile of Orosh (*Grykë e Oroshit*)' was the formula in Mirditë in such cases, church and defile being the favourite meeting-places for the General Assemblies of all its five tribes. If the Assembly upheld the elder's judgement, the penalty usually imposed was banishment for three years for the culprit and his family, the burning down of his house, the destruction of his crops and trees, and leaving his land untilled until he returned.

Sometimes a village was a public nuisance, harrying travellers, stealing its neighbours' beasts, cutting off their irrigation or mill water, trespassing on their forest or grazing, and so on. The bajraktar, voivodes, elders, and all the commoners in the rest of the tribe then gathered in General Assembly, one man from each house, and brought the village to its senses, fining the more harmless offenders, banishing others, and executing the ringleaders if these had committed any crime entailing the death penalty.

Sometimes a village went to actual war with the rest of the tribe. As it never did so unless it knew itself to be very strong, the rest of the tribe was sometimes unable to reduce it. If the tribe was alone, the war went on until both sides were exhausted enough to cry halt. If the tribe was one of a group its heads could call in all the men of the other tribes to reduce the belligerent. In Mirditë a Gjomarkaj called the General Assembly which decided on this step, and led its members against the belligerent.

Sometimes, like a pestilent village, a tribe that formed part of a group made itself a nuisance to its neighbours. In that case the General Assembly of the other tribes in the group sentenced it wholesale to the usual penalties—fines for mild offenders, burning out for medium offenders and death for bad offenders. A whole tribe, however, could not be banished. It could only be ostracized, cut off from all intercourse with its neighbours; this penalty lasted until it consented to furnish the usual pledges for its future behaviour.

Village Assemblies dealt with matters of exclusively village interest. They regulated wood-cutting and irrigation rights, for example. They fixed the date at which beasts might be sent up to their summer pasturage on the high mountains. They stipulated the number of beasts that might be sent up by each family. They took steps to see that no one appropriated more than his fair share of forest, irrigation water or grazing. In so doing they made a valuable contribution to the public peace. Some aspects of murder also engaged their attention. The actual crime and revenge for it were the concern only of the families of the murderer and his victim. But it was the concern of the village that the range of revenge should not spread, increasing the number of avenging assassinations and so disturbing the village peace. So the law having laid down that the avenger must allow the murderer a day or two's grace to settle up his affairs before he was besieged in his house, the village had to extract a promise of this grace from the avenger. In cases where the grace lasted for thirty days, the village had to see that the murderer did not abuse his privilege and harry the victim's family. If he showed any such tendency, the village in General Assembly had to fine him and bring his period of grace to an untimely end.

Assemblies of tribe or village watched above all over their
honour. Sometimes their interpretation of honour took strange
lines. Father Gjeçov gives the following story from the Mirditë
tribe of Spaç. The sister of a villager of Gomsiqe was married to
a villager of Dush in the same tribe. It happened that on one
occasion when she came to pay a visit to her brother she took ill and
died. He and his friends laid her on a bier and carried her, not
to their own cemetery, but to her husband's house in Dush,
presumably to avoid the expense of burying her. When the village
heard what they had done, they met in General Assembly, and
after carefully appraising the dishonour brought on Gomsiqe by
such a public exhibition of meanness, fined the man a cow. This
they divided into fifteen portions, which they distributed among
the fifteen houses of the village. The fine was justice at its most
precise. If the man had buried his sister as he should have done,
the funeral feast would have cost him a cow. The event took place
about 1903.

Another type of meanness had a similar end. About 1872
a villager of Urë e Shtrejtë in the tribe of Drisht happened to call
on a neighbour about midday and was kept for dinner. As they
finished, his host scraped his plate. The visitor afterwards complained to the village of the disgrace brought on his own dinner-
table by the host. The village met in General Assembly and fined
the host 500 grosh for his meanness. According to the law
'a dinner-table is disgraced in a guest's eyes when the host wipes
or licks the porringer or scrapes his plate'.

The smallest General Assemblies—those of brotherhoods and
households—dealt with what were essentially family matters. They
met perhaps to decide on expelling or even killing any hopeless
member if his misdeeds were serious enough to threaten the whole
brotherhood or household with wholesale punishment by the tribe.
They considered the pros and cons of buying an extra bit of land.

Tribal government was entirely democratic—of the people, by
the people and for the people, but it differed from tribe to tribe and
from time to time, enough to prevent unity. As the tribes in
general would not have accepted the law of any one of them as
supreme, it was ultimately necessary for Albanian unity that tribal
government should be superseded by a modern system evolved in,
and exercised from, a capital.

CHAPTER XVI

THE OATH

I. OATH-TAKER AND COMPURGATORS

Elders faced with a knotty case concerning property might put one of the disputants to the oath. The victim of the crime, suspecting who had committed it, might test his suspicions by asking that the man should make oath in public that he was innocent. It was only by oath too that a suspect could clear himself; mere protestations of innocence were not enough. 'Denial means an oath', said the law. The oath (*be*, oath; *beja*, the oath) was in fact a most efficient instrument of tribal justice, cutting gordian knots for elders, settling the ownership of property, clearing the innocent and convicting the guilty. It was equally efficient as an instrument of social cohesion, binding the tribe when occasion arose to concerted action against crime within and danger without.

The subject is difficult to understand, because of its remoteness from English practice. The following example from life gives the general scheme of the ordeal, for such it was. The story comes from Labinot, a village well south of the tribal area; but with one or two small exceptions each item might have come from anywhere in the tribal north. It is a criminal case, but if the words 'claimant' and 'oath-taker' be substituted for 'accuser' and 'suspect' it can be read as a property dispute. The general procedure was the same in both cases.

A Moslem of Labinot called Qazim who had lost a plough-ox suspected Asllan, a fellow-villager, of having stolen it, and through the headman demanded an oath from the suspect. The latter, though protesting his innocence, agreed. A few days later when the accusation was formally laid at the Village Assembly, Qazim, as was his right, immediately began to name half the number of twelve compurgators insisted on by the headman. These were chosen on account of their connexion with the accused—had this not existed he could have refused to accept them. Asllan was then told to find six other compurgators and attend the Assembly with them again a week later.

The week was spent by the compurgators in investigating the case, by the accuser and accused in visits to the compurgators, each seeking their support. Had four refused at this stage to take the oath Asllan would at once have been publicly convicted—if less than four, two substitutes would have had to be produced for every one that refused; two for one, four for two, and six for three, and there would have been no extension of the time limit. In this case, however, all the compurgators agreed to swear to Asllan's innocence, and he himself, towards the end of the week, swore on the Koran that he had nothing to do with the theft. Later the compurgators, led by Qazim's nominees, took the oath of Asllan's innocence before the whole village. Actually, Qazim cut short the proceedings after six or seven had sworn, as by then the compurgators most likely to know the truth had sworn to the suspect's innocence.

Having celebrated his acquittal with a banquet to the compurgators, Asllan two days later yoked the stolen ox, hidden during the case in a lonely sheepfold, to his plough. Now, although the mistake—either designed or accidental—of the compurgators was obvious, there was no legal machinery for annulling the verdict. In the opinion of the village, however, Asllan received his punishment when shortly afterwards his son was born lame.[1]

Qazim in Labinot put his case into the hands of the headman of his village. In the tribal north he would have entrusted it to the elder of his brotherhood, ward or village or perhaps to the bajraktar of his tribe.

Tribal officials, being hereditary, had more authority to act for their community than had the temporary headman in non-tribal districts such as Labinot. In Milot, the most northerly village of Kurbin, the victim tackled the suspect himself, asking him first if he had committed the outrage and then if he would take oath that he had not. In view of the fieriness of Albanian tempers this information is surprising—one would expect shooting to put an abrupt end to such an interview—but it is confirmed by information from the neighbouring village of Laç. When one of its inhabitants denied having received a loan, the lender asked him directly to swear in the presence of two or three witnesses that he had never been lent the money.

Only men of military age and capacity had standing enough to

[1] A very similar system of compurgators exists among the Naga tribes of Assam. There, however, though in some tribes there is no means of modifying the verdict if an oath prove to be false, in others a compurgator who discovers that his principal is lying can 'withdraw his life', otherwise in danger from the false oath, and so reopen the case *ab initio*. (Ed.)

be put to the oath; such an ordeal was not for boys under twenty, old men over sixty, women, gipsies or lunatics. All of these were considered so irresponsible that even their sworn word carried no weight. One exception comes from Zerqan, where a woman accused of a petty theft like stealing a dress might take an oath in the semi-privacy of her home that she was innocent. If her fault was more serious, her oath was not accepted. A man—her husband or son or, failing these, her brother—had to take one for her, as he would have done for his senile father or his infant son. Another exception occurred in family oaths, as described later. But this exception was apparent rather than real. The infant boys who were present did not themselves take the oath. The master alone repeated the words dictated; the boys and other males were present solely to be implicated to the maximum extent possible in the dread consequences of perjury.

In criminal cases it was the suspect, the man who denied an accusation, who had to take the oath. In such cases its sole purpose was to clear him of suspicion; if he could take it, he was acquitted, and if he could not, he was convicted. The accuser was never allowed to support his accusation by an oath; even if he insisted that with his own eyes he had seen the crime being committed, he could not swear upon oath that what he said was true. For motives of spite might have induced him first to accuse his neighbour falsely, and then to swear a false oath. So the law said firmly 'It's for the denier to take the oath'.

Occasionally a suspect refused to take the oath. Then his accuser was at least tempted to shoot him. If it was a case of stealing he had to think twice; shooting the suspect would start a blood feud because 'murder for a fault (like stealing) isn't allowed', and perhaps the lost property was not worth the nuisance which the blood feud would cause. If it was a murder case, it did not much matter if he did shoot the suspect; he was already at feud with the murderer. In property cases refusals to take the oath seem to have been unknown when the dispute was in the hands of elders; if they ordered a disputant to take an oath, he dared not disobey for he knew that the whole community would gather to enforce the order. If one disputant, before the case had reached the elders, asked the other to take an oath that the property was his, his request was refused as often as not, and then shooting became inevitable.

More often a suspect volunteered unasked to take an oath. For example, about 1931 a man in Zerqan shot his wife for some reason unknown and was then, very properly by local standards, hunted by her relatives. In desperation he offered to take an oath with twelve compurgators, the statutory number for a murdered woman, that he had not killed her. He managed to persuade all twelve to take the oath, and so, though the public still believed him guilty, he secured a formal acquittal and escaped further molestation by her relatives.

Here is another example. In the early 1930's a villager of Nangë in Lumë killed a neighbour, in order to marry the widow. The victim's cousin, as required by ancient custom, shot the woman and tried to shoot the man. He missed him again and again, but made his life such a misery that the man volunteered to take an oath with twenty-four compurgators, the statutory number for a man, that he had not killed his neighbour. Less lucky than the scamp of Zerqan, he was left to the cousin's vengeance. One compurgator failed to come to take the oath, so convicting him. It transpired later that the cousin had bribed this compurgator with two napoleons not to come, but the verdict of the oath could not be quashed and the case retried.

In property disputes the choice of the oath-taker depended almost universally on the wishes of the elders. When they decided that a dispute about land, or irrigation water was to be settled by an oath, they generally said that one of the disputants must swear that the property was his. Most often they preferred the man in possession, but sometimes they chose the one with the weaker claim in the hope that he would shrink from the ordeal, and so bring the dispute to a speedy end. In Çermenikë, and no doubt elsewhere, when there was some disparity of age they selected the older disputant, on the assumption that his greater age would mean greater knowledge of the facts. Very occasionally, before the dispute was laid before the elders one disputant bade the other take the very serious oath on the head of his son. Sometimes, particularly in boundary disputes, the elders put neither disputant to the oath. Instead, they chose an old man who had no direct interest in the dispute, but had learned the facts from his father and was trusted.

There were various names for the two principals. In all types of case and in all areas the oath-taker was called 'the master of the oath', but in theft cases he was often called the 'thief', and this from the outset of the case until he was cleared. Father Gjeçov also calls the oath-taker in criminal cases 'the accused', but this seems a literary term chosen by himself rather than a popular usage in Mirditë. In theft cases, the accuser was most often described by a periphrasis—being called in Godolesh the 'plaintiff', in Mirditë 'the owner of the lost property', in Martanesh 'the owner of the stolen property', 'the injured party' or 'the man robbed', in Fulqet 'the injured party', and in Zerqan 'the owner of the property'.

In murder cases, save for Father Gjeçov's occasional 'loader', the accuser was always called 'the man with the feud', the 'avenger' (lit. 'the owner of the blood'), and in disputes about property 'the plaintiff'.

When an oath has been sworn by a suspect or a claimant to property, the innocence of the one or the claim of the other had generally to be established by the oath of a predetermined number of compurgators.

It was legally impossible for a suspect to clear himself by his unsupported oath. In the words of a proverb 'A wolf licks his own flesh and eats a stranger's'. An oath-taker might not flinch from perjury in order to establish his own innocence or his claim to a property, but as compurgator he was likely to be more scrupulous. So the law said there could be no complete oath without a jury. But as usual it made exceptions. When a suspect or claimant was ordered to swear one of the very solemn oaths in which perjury involved the extinction of his whole family, his personal stake was so great that a jury was dispensed with. The best example comes from Martanesh, where a jury was necessary in oaths sworn on the Koran or bread, but not in family oaths sworn at Balim Sulltan's grave.

It was both the right and the duty of the members of the jury to gather all available evidence about the case and to make up their minds about its rights and wrongs before they came finally to court to record their verdict. An interval was therefore left between the nominations of jurors and the final oath-taking, in order to give them time to investigate the case. As a last step in their collection of evidence they then gathered to hear the oath-taker take the prescribed oath. They brought in their verdict by exercising their right to decide whether or not to take the oath. To return a verdict in the oath-taker's favour they turned up on the appointed day to repeat his oath themselves in public. They returned one against him in either of two ways; either they refused during the period of investigation to take the oath, or they did not turn up to do so on the appointed day. In the case of early refusals some modifications were allowed, but at the final oath-taking the law was rigid. If even one compurgator failed to turn up the suspect or claimant lost his case; there was no question of majority vote. They took no oath until the end of the case. They were not sworn, as elders were, to investigate fairly and to bring in a true verdict.

The general rule for selections was that half the compurgators in criminal cases were chosen by the oath-taker and half by the accuser or by the elders: the latter in Mirditë, Godolesh and Fulqet, the former in the Malësi e Madhe, Lumë, Martanesh, Zerqan and Labinot. In disputes about property the elders almost everywhere named the jurors. Whether they did or not seems to have depended mainly on whether they were local or from a distance. When local, they knew the character of each potential juror and could safely make their selection. When from a distance they did not have enough knowledge to choose, and preferred to leave the choice in the hands of the claimant. In Kurbin when house quarrelled with house or village with village about irrigation water, the claimant named twelve of the twenty-four compurgators required.

It did not much matter who were chosen as compurgators by a suspect. The practical certainty that they were his partisans and would clear him made their oath comparatively unimportant. For that reason they were not allowed to take it until the accuser's nominees had done so. In Mirditë the suspect was expected to announce their names to the elders before the ceremony, but elsewhere, as in Zerqan and the Malësi e Madhe, he had only to bring them along to the oath-taking. The only person he was forbidden to include was himself; 'though 100 compurgators are needed the suspect can't be one', said the law. If he liked he could even include a gipsy. He seldom or never did so, of course; regard for his own prestige prevented him from choosing so low a creature. On the other hand, it mattered very much who were named by the accuser. His quota took the oath first and so gave the others their cue. Their oath was weighty for several reasons. As the accuser's nominees they were supposedly free from bias in the suspect's favour. Then they were very carefully selected.

Since the truth or falsity of the result of the ordeal depended in the first place on their probity, and since it had to be certain that one or more of them would refuse to sell his soul by swearing falsely to a criminal's innocence, their personal honour had to be beyond question—they must never have been caught, for instance, swearing a false oath or taking bribes. They had further to be free from ill-will against either party—they must not be malicious. It was also important that they should have some knowledge of the case at either first or second hand. Hence the accuser liked to name the suspect's relatives and neighbours, as in the case of Qazim of Labinot, men who came from the suspect's village if not his brotherhood. In the case of a stolen animal, for example, the relatives in particular might have seen the meat being eaten by the suspect's family or the bones being gnawed by his dog. In all cases of theft a near relative would know that the suspect was not at home at the time. But if any of the suspect's relatives were unscrupulous the accuser naturally preferred to nominate others. Better an ignorant but upright compurgator.

Certain members of a tribe could not be compurgators. A gipsy, we have said, might serve on a suspect's behalf, though he might not be put to the oath to discharge himself of an accusation or to make good his claim to a property. Old men, boys and lunatics were never allowed to take oath either as suspects or as compurgators; nor were women except in very rare cases.

A Moslem hoxha or sheikh counted as only one compurgator, but, being regarded as a man of weight, tended to come high on the accuser's list. A Catholic priest was theoretically exempted by his office from being put to the oath as either suspect or compurgator, but if named as compurgator, he counted in his single person as equal to twenty-four. If a bajraktar of Mirditë or one of the Gjomarkaj family was chosen as compurgator in a case involving twenty-four, the court named twelve others and declared the bajraktar or Gjomarkaj equivalent to the remainder.

The suspect had the right to object to the accuser's nominees if they were not in a position to know the truth of the case, or to risk taking an oath to clear him. If his objection was obviously well founded, the accuser had to change his nominees. The suspect was also protected from ill-will on the part of a compurgator. As

soon as they were named, the presiding authorities were legally
bound to ask if he thought any of them would leave him in the
lurch out of jealousy or spite. If he could produce reasonable
evidence that any of them would, those he mentioned had to be
changed. But only up to a maximum of three where twenty-four
had been prescribed, and of two where twelve or eight had been.
In Zerqan, however, the suspect could not raise objections to the
accuser's nominees; in compensation the replacement rules were
somewhat relaxed.

Men sometimes declined nomination. Those proud of their high
reputation for uprightness disdained to be mixed up in a case
where the suspect was notorious for evil-doing, even if it was known
that for once he was wrongfully accused. Others would not lend
their weight to a petty case and consented to take the oath only in
serious matters, such as murder.

In most of the tribal areas, a man whose wife was pregnant could
ask to be excused. It was believed that it would be a crime for him
to take the oath. If he swore falsely, through inadvertence or not,
his sin would be visited on the unborn child, bringing it into the
world lame or with such deformity as six fingers instead of five.
Sometimes he agreed to take the oath if it were postponed until
after the child was born, but more often his brother or cousin took
it in his stead.

Refusals for such personal reasons as the above almost always
took place as soon as the nominations were made. No difficulty was
made about accepting them and before the Assembly dispersed
another compurgator was named in each recusant's place. Later
refusals were never prompted by anything but disbelief, real or
feigned, in the suspect, and were treated differently. At the same
time as the compurgators were named, the authorities informed the
suspect of the precise terms of the oath which he and his compurgators must take to vindicate him, and of the time of the ceremony.
It then became his duty, not only to find his own quota of compurgators, but also to inform the accuser's compurgators that they
had been nominated. His own never caused much difficulty. One
or more of the others might decline. A compurgator who could
not believe the suspect's oath dared not repeat it himself. Possibly
the suspect was likeable enough but 'an oath can't be taken out of
favouritism'. Other nominees did not refuse out of hand but
waited until they had made some inquiries into the case and

cross-questioned the suspect. Anyone who discovered that the man was guilty sent in his refusal to go on the jury. Sometimes, too, a nominee was bribed or persuaded by the accuser into refusing. Or one might have a grudge against the suspect, and, though knowing him to be innocent, might seek to gratify his grudge by declining to take the oath.

On every occasion when a named compurgator eventually declined to serve, the suspect had to find two substitutes for him, and these had to satisfy the accuser. If the first pair suggested did not please him, the suspect had to search until he found two who did. In Çermenikë he was allowed twenty-four hours in which to find them. But if more than three out of a total of twelve or eight, or one out of a smaller number, declined, this provision did not apply. It was concluded that the oath could not be taken, and without more ado the suspect was pronounced guilty; he had in criminal cases to pay the legal penalty for the crime, and in disputes to forfeit the property he claimed. Occasionally, as in Zerqan, when the recusants were strongly suspected of refusing from motives of spite, an accuser might overlook their refusal and inform the suspect that he need not even find one at all. More often, however, a Zerqan accuser followed the usual practice and exacted two compurgators for every one that drew back. In Fulqet it was the Village Assembly, not the suspect, who selected substitutes for recusants.

The number of compurgators depended on the nature of the case. For such trifling matters as the theft of a pig, sheep or goat a 'little jury' of one man sufficed. Otherwise a jury consisted of anything from two to twenty-four men, according to the importance of the case. In murder cases there was a universal rule that twenty-four compurgators were necessary when the victim was a man and only twelve when she was a woman. In most other cases the number required varied with the locality. Although it might have been expected that economic factors would explain these variations, that where horses, for instance, were scarce, the case would be thought more important and the number of compurgators increased in proportion, this does not appear to have been so.

If a dog was killed in the farmyard in Lumë, twenty-four compurgators, the customary number for a murdered man, were required. The murder of a dog was as serious in Lumë as the murder of a man, as is further indicated by the fact that the same blood money had to be paid. Possibly, too, there was a feeling here as in other areas that the dog's owner might have emerged into the farmyard and been killed by its assassin. In all cases of damage to property the number of compurgators depended, not only on the value of the property, but also on the risk to the owner's life which the crime entailed. This risk depended largely on the site of the crime. If, for example, a house was set on fire, it was reckoned that one of the men in it might have lost his life; if not burned to death he might have been shot by the incendiary when trying to escape from the burning building. The oath in such a case was on that account with twenty-four compurgators. But if a haystack was fired six were enough. The risk to life was infinitesimal, and the value of the haystack much inferior to that of a house. Similar considerations graded thefts. If a house was burgled by a thief who went upstairs and stole bedding or kitchen utensils there were again twenty-four compurgators. For a thief wicked and desperate enough to enter another's house was an obvious killer. A thief who bored a hole in the wall of the farmyard and stole something from the yard was certainly 'a big thief', but so much less of a menace to his victim's life that he was put to the oath in Kurbin, Fulqet and Zerqan with only twelve compurgators. A thief who stole at a distance from the farm buildings needed only six in Fulqet. In Zerqan, however, even this form of theft was considered heinous enough to demand twelve compurgators.

Some of the same principles operated in thefts of sheep and goats. In Martanesh, the Malësi e Madhe and Shalë only one compurgator was required when a single sheep or goat was stolen at a distance from the farm buildings. The animal's value was small and the risk to a man's life infinitesimal. The number of compurgators increased, up to a maximum of twenty-four in Martanesh and twelve in Shalë, with the number of animals stolen. In Fulqet the grading was more detailed. If a single sheep or goat was stolen at a distance, the suspect, most exceptionally, required no compurgators to back him up; it was enough if he swore himself that he was innocent. If, however, the stolen animal was a bell-wether, the most valuable animal in the flock because it led it, he had to take the oath with six compurgators.[1] If an ordinary sheep or goat was stolen from the farmyard he had to find four compurgators, and if several animals were so stolen, twelve. In Labinot the law was

[1] Vide infra, p. 208.

more severe, three to six compurgators being needed when only one goat had been stolen in the most innocuous circumstances, while grazing in the forest. In Kurbin the law was still more drastic. Whether the stolen animal was an ordinary sheep or a bell-wether, an ordinary goat or a bell-goat, and whether the theft took place in the lonely forest or in the fold at the farm, the suspect had to take the oath with all his family, the gravest oath of all.

In disputes about property the number of compurgators mainly depended on its value. In Kurbin as many as twenty-four might be prescribed in irrigation disputes, this number probably reflecting the frequency with which such quarrels ended in murder. In Fulqet there were twenty-four compurgators in land disputes but in neighbouring Dibër twelve were enough. In Fulqet all the land is under water, but in Dibër very little can be irrigated. A rod of land in Fulqet is consequently more valuable—better worth fighting for—than a rod in Dibër.

The number of compurgators was not absolutely fixed by law and so might vary with the case. In all areas it was settled by the elders in disputes about property, but in criminal cases the usage differed. In Mirditë, Labinot and Godolesh the elders again said how many there should be, but in Malësi e Madhe, Fulqet and Martanesh the accuser had this privilege. Too often the number then depended on the degree of ill-feeling between the parties. The angrier the accuser was, the more compurgators he demanded. For the more they were, the more trouble the suspect had in persuading them to take the oath that would acquit him.

The compurgators, it should be mentioned, received no payment for their trouble except for the meal given them in most places by the suspect.

CHAPTER XVII

THE OATH

II. THE OATH-TAKING

When the elders first sat on the case in small or large Assembly, either they or the accuser issued full directions for taking the oath, prescribing the time, the place, the sacred formula, the sacred object and the terms in which it had to be taken.

In the case from Labinot the Assembly—or rather the presiding elders—decreed that the suspect should take the oath about a week later. The case being one of simple theft, they considered this interval long enough for the suspect to find the compurgators and for these to make the necessary inquiries. In Mirditë, the Malësi e Madhe and Dibër too, the elders fixed the date for taking the oath at their first Assembly; it was near or remote according to the clarity or obscurity of the case. A month was the average allowance in the Malësi e Madhe, but in graver cases a year might be allowed. In Zerqan the day was not fixed until after the suspect had found his compurgators. This done, he informed the accuser that whenever the latter chose, he was ready to take the oath. The accuser then appointed the day without consulting the elders.

After fixing the date, the elders warned the suspect that if the oath was not taken by that date, he would lose his case. At the same time they informed the accuser that he must have patience for the appointed term. If the oath was not taken when stated, he would gain his case by default. Sometimes, however, the final oath-taking was postponed. In Labinot and Zerqan postponements were not favoured; it was considered that legal business should not be allowed to drag on; obviously the longer the period of uncertainty the greater the danger of gun-work. In Mirditë, however, if the case was so complicated that the compurgators could not complete their investigations or make up their minds, they had the right to postpone taking the oath for as much as six months or even longer; it was only the named compurgators who sought to exercise this right. In the Malësi e Madhe the right of postponement lay with the accuser, not the compurgators. Any compurgator who was still dubious about the case could ask the accuser to extend the time limit. The request was always granted. But a second could not be made by the same compurgator. If the final day slipped by unnoticed, as sometimes happened when it was distant, an extension was generally arranged by mutual agreement.

In Catholic areas the incidence of Lent might delay matters, as Catholics did not take oaths during holy seasons.

In most districts it was the elders who said where the oath was to be taken, but in Kurbin and Lumë it was the accuser. A spiteful accuser of north Lumë, for instance, could send a suspect, with all his compurgators, to take the oath in south Dibër, a four days' journey there and back, with all expenses falling on the suspect. It was probably to prevent such displays of malice that the choice of place generally rested with the elders.

There was often a close connexion between the place at which, and the sacred object on which, the oath had to be taken. The chief sacred objects on which Catholics were called to swear were the Gospel, the crucifix and the local church or its altar. Among Moslems, there were the Koran, the local mosque and a saint's grave. The Gospel in the one case and the Koran in the other was usually chosen. Dibër, a purely Sunni Moslem district, and somewhat fanatical, claimed to take the oath only on the Koran.

North Albanians went to church to swear on the Gospel or crucifix, but to their scandal the Catholics of Kurbin, Mirditë and Lurë had these sacred emblems carried to the suspect's house. Indeed, in Kurbin and Lurë an oath was never taken on the Gospel except outside the precincts of the church; the same was presumably true in Mirditë. No reason for the taboo is known; perhaps the combined sanctity of Gospel and church was thought to involve too much risk. When swearing on an altar, the oath-takers had naturally to enter the church, but when swearing on the church itself they remained outside, touching only a stone in the south door, possibly the threshold, perhaps a door-jamb. Sometimes they repeated the prescribed oath in the neighbourhood of the church. Oaths were most commonly taken on the church in cases of petty theft; graver cases demanded an oath on the Gospel or crucifix.

Moslem procedure was in general so similar to Catholic that it seems to have been inherited from the days when all the area under study was Catholic. To swear on a mosque, as the Moslems of Çermenikë sometimes did, it was enough to touch its door-jamb or threshold, precisely in the Catholic manner. To swear on the Koran, some preferred to go to the mosque, as the Catholics in the north went to church. But more often the Moslems, like the Catholics of Kurbin, went to the suspect's house. Since no possible sanctity could attach to a private house, it seems to have been the sacred book rather than the building which gave such oaths their value. In Zdrâjshë and Zerqan, indeed, it was openly said that provided an oath was taken on the Koran, the place where it was taken did not matter. It is probable that the same view was held in Krasniqë in the north-east, where oaths were taken in either the mosque or one of the shady spots called *ulicë*. It seems possible that these groves might be sacred because growing on the sites of former churches, but the local Moslems said that there had never been churches there and that no sanctity attached to the spots.[1] When taking oath by a sacred grave, Moslems usually entered the mausoleum; for such oaths there was no Catholic parallel.

In Zerqan a suspect must never be asked to take an oath in or near his own house, for if he swore falsely the house might collapse or otherwise come to grief. This fear was not acknowledged in the many other areas where such oaths were common, but it may have been implicit. If a suspect staked his own house by taking the oath in it, he would naturally try harder than ever to avoid perjury.

In mixed districts the suspect and the accuser might be of different faiths. In that event when the decision lay with the elders, the suspect's religion decided whether it was in the church or mosque, on the Gospel or the Koran, that the oath should be taken. When the decision lay with the accuser his wishes prevailed. In such districts the jury too was often mixed. They had all to take the same oath as the suspect. So Catholics had to make oath in a mosque and on the Koran if the suspect was a Moslem; and in the opposite case Moslems had to make it in a church and on the Gospel. In Vinjollë, lying some six miles north of Krujë, after it became Moslem an oath could still be taken on the Gospel as well as on the Koran. In Lurë, when it was abandoning Catholicism, a man could swear, at least in conversation, by the mosque or church, according to which came into his head first, irrespective of his own or his hearer's religion.

Moslems but not Catholics might take oath at a sacred grave. This might stand in a single mausoleum or form part of a monastery. The most important of these graves were Sulejman Pasha's at

---

[1] But doubtless a pagan survival of the sacred grove (*lucus*). (Ed.)

Tirana, Sheikh Hasan's at Nangë in Lumë, Sheikh Ibrahim's at Surroj across the river Drin from Nangë, Sheikh Fejza's at Bulqizë, Balim Sulltan's at Martanesh, and those of two abbots at Krujë. Sulejman Pasha and Sheikh Ibrahim lie in an isolated mausoleum, Balim Sulltan in a cave, and the others in monasteries. These saints belonged to different sects; Sulejman Pasha, the soldier who founded Tirana in the seventeenth century, was a Sunni; Sheikh Hasan, founder of the monastery at Nangë, and his brother, Sheikh Ibrahim of Surroj, were Khalvetis; Balim Sulltan of Martanesh and the two abbots of Krujë were Bektashis; and Sheikh Fejza, founder of the monastery at Bulqizë, a dissident Bektashi. Sometimes it did not matter to what sect the buried saint belonged. Sheikh Hasan of Nangë was so renowned that the local population, even if not Khalvetis, took their oaths on his grave and never in the mosque, and Catholic as well as Moslem oath-takers came in serious cases to his grave from Shkodër, four days away. Sulejman Pasha's grave drew oath-takers from as far away as Martanesh; these had long since forgotten his history, and, though ardent Bektashis, did not care that he was a Sunni. Sunni Albanians are not so liberal however; taught to abhor the Bektashis as unorthodox Moslems, they left the graves of Balim Sulltan of Martanesh and the two abbots of Krujë to Bektashi oath-takers. Sheikh Fejza, abhorred by Sunnis as almost a Bektashi and by Bektashis as a backslider from their faith, commanded allegiance only among his own followers in Bulqizë. Oaths used to be taken in three mausolea in the Bektashi monastery at Krujë, but by 1930 the abbot refused to open one for such a purpose. Once, as an oath was being taken in this mausoleum, both disputants fell dead; there had been roguery on both sides as the buried saint was quick to detect. Ever afterwards the abbots restricted oath-takers to the two mausolea in which the saints seemed slower to wrath.

Among invocations of the Deity used in oaths, the following are recorded: 'By the Lord' (Perlat and Shkrel); 'By this Lord Who gave me life' (Perlat); 'By this Lord Who is in Heaven' (Shalë); 'By Our Lady' (Shkrel); and 'By the Blood of Christ' (Shalë). In all these the influence of the Church is evident, but there are hints in the Albanian originals that some are older than the Church.

The Deity was invoked by Moslems as follows: 'By that Lord' (Godolesh); 'By God' (Dibër); 'By God, with God, from God'[1]

[1] *Vallahi, billahi, tallahi.*

(Godolesh and Lumë). The first two phrases are evidently old Albanian and have nothing exclusively Moslem about them; the second (lit. 'May I see God') has even a Catholic ring. The third is widely known all over the Moslem world and in certain areas which were once under Moslem rule. But it is used in a magical rather than a religious sense. It is found in magical formulae among the Arabs of Egypt and the Christian Greeks of the island of Zea, next door neighbour to Euboea.[1]

The only invocation of the Deity which the author recorded among the Orthodox was in Shpat and ran as follows: 'By that Christ in Whom we believe.' It is evidently a Church formula.

There was no sign that any of these oaths was preferred to the others; they seemed to have equal value. Readers who know the Catholics and the Orthodox, the two religions which divided Albania before the Turks came in the fifteenth century, will be struck by the paucity of references to Christ and the Virgin Mary and by the emphasis on God; this may be a further indication that the oaths go back to pagan days when neither Christ nor the Virgin was known.

Formulae for invoking Catholic saints were such as 'By that St Nicolas' in Kurbin and 'By the candle of St Nicolas' among the Highlanders of Breg i Matit and Gurrëzë. Both were very grave oaths. The candle in the second is the wax taper lit before pictures of the saint by the devout; oath-takers seem to have feared that perjury would extinguish the flame of their life as easily as a candle could be put out. Of all their saints too, the Catholic Highlanders preferred St Nicolas. No Moslem saints were invoked as such; it was rather by their graves than themselves that oaths were taken. A strange oath, which comes from Surroj, was an exception. This ran 'By this patron saint of coffee'. Coffee, the peasants of Surroj explained, has a 'very important' patron saint. All over Albania coffee-house keepers make a libation to him every morning by pouring away the first cup of coffee that they make. They hope that after being placated in this way the saint will send them many customers. Some believe that he lies buried somewhere in the east of the Turkish empire, possibly in Arabia.

Catholic priests and Moslem clergymen—hoxhas and sheikhs among the Sunnis, abbots (*baba*, sing.; *baballar*, plur.) among the Bektashis—were respected as men of God, and Bektashi abbots

[1] See *Folklore*, Vol. xxxvii, p. 195 (June 1926).

even became saints at their death, but an oath 'by the priest' or 'by that hoxha' was never taken; it would have been regarded as sacrilege.

A most interesting oath was taken by both the Orthodox and the Moslems of Berat town and district. Its commonest forms were 'By Him of Tomorr' and 'By the Holy One of Tomorr'. The deity that dwelt in pagan days on the summit of Tomorr, the lofty, beautiful mountain that dominates the town of Berat, is still a living force in the district. He was, indeed, so dreaded that even in conversation he could not be named, but only darkly alluded to. 'By that mountain top' is no less solemn an oath than the more definite pair already given. No man had been known to swear any of them falsely.

By what was perhaps a survival of early nature worship, oath-takers sometimes invoked natural objects as in the oaths, 'By this bright light which is dawning', 'By this evening which is coming', 'By this night we have to-night'. These were all given by Catholics in Perlat. The first two were used for oaths taken in the morning and the third for those taken in the evening. Moslems in Godolesh and Labinot sometimes swore 'By this sun' and 'By this earth'. The latter was a very solemn oath, earth being weighty for two reasons: man was made of it and it lies heavy on a dead man who committed sins such as perjury during his lifetime. Apparently oaths were not taken 'by this fire' or 'by this moon'; perhaps both fire and moon lack the inevitability and stability that fitted dawn and darkness, the sun and the earth, for worship by primitive Albanians.

Among oaths by sacred buildings were such as 'By this church' among Catholics and 'By this mosque' among Moslems. They were chiefly employed conversationally, and meant little more than our own expression 'on my honour'. Indeed, a man of Lurë used them indifferently, irrespective of whether he or his hearer were Catholic or Moslem. But when a Moslem of Martanesh swore 'by this holy place' as he stood in Balim Sulltan's mausoleum, his oath was very solemn. So, too, were the oaths in Bulqizë 'by that shrine', the domed tomb of Sheikh Fejza; in Tirana by the grave of Sulejman Pasha, the seventeenth-century founder of the town; in Krujë by the tombs of two Bektashi abbots; in Nangë, Lumë, by the tomb of the Khalveti saint, Sheikh Hasan; and in Surroj, by the grave of Sheikh Hasan's brother, Sheikh Ibrahim. In the last case the formula was rather unusual; standing in the mausoleum (*teqe*) the

oath-taker began by saying 'May Sheikh Ibrahim cut short my life'.
In the other cases he used some vague formula such as 'By this
holy place' or 'By this shrine'.

Oaths by smaller sacred objects were all very similar. The formula
used in swearing on an altar was in Shalë 'By this altar'; on
a church door in the Malësi e Madhe and Kurbin, 'By these
things of the Lord'; on a crucifix or gospel in Mirditë, 'By this
holy thing of God'; in Kurbin 'By this thing of God'. The more
fanatical of the Moslems preferred to swear on the Koran under
a Turkish, or rather Arabic, name. Thus 'By this holy book' was
liked in Lumë, and 'By this sacred book' everywhere. Others, as in
Vinjollë and Zerqan, swore 'By this thing of God', or if in Godolesh,
'By the holy thing of this our God'. The last oath is very close to
the oath of Catholic Mirditë on the Gospel, and there is little doubt
that this Moslem oath was once Catholic or Orthodox. Indeed, it
may have been pagan. The vagueness of their phraseology made
the transference from one religion to another easy. A similar
vagueness characterizes most of the oaths in this paragraph. Its
origin lay in the simple Albanian's idea of respect for a sacred
object; he thought that naming a person or thing detracted from
the majesty of that person or thing. Besides preserving the efficacy
of ancient oaths through later changes of religion, this vagueness
also reduced any repugnance which a Catholic or Moslem in
a mixed jury might feel at being asked to swear on the holy book
of the other's religion. It has even led Catholics of Lurë, when
Islam was fast displacing Catholicism, to anticipate the future
conversion by swearing the essentially Moslem oath 'By this
hajmali (sacred book)' on the Christian Gospel.

A curious and most solemn oath among Catholics was 'by the
stone'. This was not any ordinary stone that the oath-taker might
pick up regardless of his religion, but was a special one found only
among Catholics. Triangular in shape, it had a hole in each of its
three corners for attaching the balance in which persons minded to
offer votive candles to church weighed the wax of which each was
to be made. It derived such sanctity from this association with the
church that an oath on it was as serious as one on the Gospel or
crucifix. Such an oath was in fact reserved for occasions of special
gravity, as when a man suspected of a heinous crime was put to the
ordeal, or a whole tribe swore to refrain from acts disturbing the
public peace, or a community took oath to stick together through

thick and thin. No memory of oath or stone survives in areas such
as Çermenikë and Lumë, which abandoned Catholicism some
centuries ago.

A number of very solemn oaths were taken on objects that had
no obvious association with religion, and these seem to date from
the oldest days of Albanian existence. Thus an oath in very common
use all over the country was 'By bread'. Among the Catholics
where the priests combated everything that they thought was
pagan, this oath was more often heard in conversation than in
ordeals, but among the Orthodox and Moslems it held a higher
place. The most solemn oath of the Orthodox of Shpat was 'By
that Christ in Whom we believe and by that bread we eat'. The
Moslems generally used a loaf, treating it like a Koran.

Sometimes at least in Martanesh an uncooked maize-cob served
instead of a loaf. Both in Martanesh and in Lumë salt was often
added; the formula then was in Lumë 'By the bounties of the
Lord'.

One advantage of swearing on bread was that the oath could be
taken, and peace made as soon as trouble arose. If two men who
had met in a house quarrelled, one accusing the other of letting
his animals stray into his maize-field or of cutting firewood in his
forest or the like, the accused could immediately clear himself,
provided two or three other men were present as witnesses; no set
jury was necessary. All he had to do was to lay his right hand on
bread and say, 'May the bread kill me'. This oath was known in
places as far apart as Labinot and Lumë. It has already been said
that though a woman could not make oath on the Koran, she might,
in Zerqan if accused of petty pilfering, make one on bread. Men
in Godolesh, which was an Orthodox village till 1910, sometimes
swore 'by this bread' but did not consider it one of their most
serious oaths.

The reason for choosing bread for such a serious occasion as an
ordeal is not certain. The Orthodox oath from Shpat speaks of
eating it so that the idea of its being the staff of life seems present.
Its conjunction with salt in Lumë and Martanesh supports this
idea. On the other hand, the influence of Holy Communion also
seems at work. The Orthodox of Albania as of Greece speak of it as
the Body of Christ, and on that account consider it sinful to cut
rather than break it before beginning to eat. Moslems regard even
crumbs of it as too sacred to tread on. Most probably the idea that

it is the staff of life is the oldest, and religious conceptions come later. As essential to life, it was suited to oath-taking; as shown by the oath 'May the bread kill me', it had power to punish perjury with death.

Two more formulae remain to be mentioned. The first was 'By my head', and the second 'By the head of my son'. The former was thought justifiable; one might do as one pleased with one's own head. But a man who swore on his son's head was strongly disapproved of; only a low fellow, it was thought, would risk his child's life by such an oath. Nothing less was involved, as appears in the following full formula for a land dispute. 'By the head of the son that I have, this land is mine. If it is not mine, may I weep for the son that I have.'[1]

When the time came to take the oath, both Catholics and Moslems behaved as if about to perform an act of worship. Catholics removed their caps and made the oath bareheaded; they also crossed themselves as they began. Sunni Moslems performed the ceremonial ablutions incumbent on them before they pray. By their preliminaries the Catholics sought to indicate respect for the Deity; by theirs the Sunnis sought also to make their oath binding —without them, so they believed, it would be null and void. The Moslems of Martanesh, being Bektashis, did not perform the ceremonial ablutions, but suspect and compurgator when taking the oath in a house had to stand facing Mecca, with the witnesses behind them. As each man's turn came, he advanced towards the Koran or loaf of bread, knelt, and laying hand on the book or bread repeated the prescribed words. This reverence for the sacred emblem was shown by both religions, sometimes with quaint little ceremonies. Thus, when the Catholics of Lurë swore in the open on the Gospel, as was their common practice, they picked up some grass or other greenery and held it over the book while they recited the oath; the purpose of the grass is not clear.[2] After the conversion of Vinjollë to Islam from Catholicism oaths were sworn indifferently, as has already been said, on the Gospel or Koran. When at a house, the sacred book was laid on fresh grass near the house or on a clean place in the farmyard. Each oath-taker kissed it three times, before venturing to put his hand on it and repeat the oath.

---

[1] The oath on a son's head is common to the Moslem world and if perjured involves the son as well as his father in eternal damnation.

[2] Possibly it involved the false swearer in withering like the plucked grass.

Ordinarily the Gospel might be open or closed and the Koran bare or wrapped in a cloth. A most interesting survival from Christianity comes from Fulqet, where the men, who now are all good Sunni Moslems, tapped their breasts with their fingers when making an oath; the gesture had lost the definite form of making the sign of the cross, but its origin seemed unmistakable.

The oath was taken in two stages. First the suspect swore in the presence of all the compurgators that he was innocent of the crime, and then the compurgators swore in the presence of witnesses that the suspect was innocent. He and they swore in the same manner. Bareheaded and making the sign of the cross if Catholic, with hands and face ritually cleansed if Moslem, each in turn invoked the Deity or laid his hand on the sacred object prescribed and repeated the oath. The compurgators did not as a rule take the oath until the suspect had done so and thereby assumed all possible responsibility before God and man for its truth. But, exceptionally, in Lumë a suspected murderer—and probably a suspected thief too—did not take the oath at all unless the compurgators, fearing that he had committed the crime, and lacking convincing proof one way or the other, wished to secure such evidence as his oath provided. In Zerqan a suspect took the oath only when the compurgators doubted his innocence.

Of the compurgators the accuser's nominees came first, headed by the suspect's nearest relatives and neighbours, the most responsible because the most knowledgeable of them all. As soon as the first two or three had taken the oath the others shed their fears of perjuring themselves and took it in their turn. Lastly came the suspect's quota, free of qualms. When the jury was large, the accuser often interrupted the proceedings before all the suspect's quota had sworn. Since his own nominees, 'good men and true', and the first of the suspect's quota had taken the oath, there could be no doubt that the remainder would do so. In Dukagjin, the Gjakovë highlands (Malësi e Jakovës), and a few other areas in that neighbourhood, only half of the compurgators ever recited the oath; the others merely put their hand on the Gospel and passed by. The first man recited the oath in full, the second touched the Gospel and passed by, and so on. According to the Franciscan priest of Theth the even numbers were there to vindicate the odd numbers, the only complete oath-takers, but Father Gjeçov describes the custom somewhat differently. He says that half the

compurgators took the oath and half stood listening with their
hands folded at the waist. As only the former touched the Gospel
they were called 'oath-hands'. Possibly Father Gjeçov's information came from a different area of Dukagjin, or even since his time
the details may have been modified.

The compurgators took the oath on the day officially appointed.
The suspect took it a few minutes, a day or several days earlier, as
best suited the general convenience, and generally in the presence
of the compurgators only. The taking of the oath by the compurgators was a more public affair. The accuser's presence was in most
places indispensable. If he would not, or could not, attend the
ceremony, he had to give up trying to get his rights by an oath and
had to find a private detective to take up the case. In Zerqan,
apparently, the accuser did not need to be present, in theft cases at
least. The number and quality of other witnesses varied in some
places, such as Kurbin, with the gravity of the case, and in others
with local custom. In Fulqet, Godolesh and Çermenikë it was
obligatory for the village to turn out; otherwise the oath was not
considered valid. In Mirditë the elders trying the case had to be
present and so too in Theth, Dibër and Çermenikë; if, however,
one of them found it inconvenient to attend, he could, in Dibër at
least, send a deputy. In Lurë the Catholic priest had to be present
when the suspect was Catholic, as had the Moslem sheikh of
Ceren when he was a Moslem. In the Malësi e Madhe, Bytyç and
Martanesh, an oath was valid if witnessed by the accuser and a few
of his friends.

In grave cases a whole family might be asked to take the oath. In
that event the master spoke in his usual capacity of household
representative, for the rest of the family as well as himself, and it
was forbidden to ask them to repeat his words. In Mirditë the
women and children were not involved, but in Malësi e Madhe all
the males of the family had to be present regardless of their age, and
the master held an infant boy in his arms while he swore that he
and they were innocent. In Martanesh, too, the accused had to
bring all his sons, all his brothers and all his brothers' sons to the
ceremony. The suspect had to swear to the whole family's ignorance
as well as innocence of the crime.

In most districts this oath was taken at any of the usual places for
oath-taking, but in Martanesh it was taken in the most solemn
circumstances possible, at the grave of Balim Sulltan. It was a very

serious oath, entailing the extinction of the whole family if the oath-taker perjured himself. This was symbolized clearly in the Malësi e Madhe ceremony. The master's perjury, if any, and its penalties would, it was believed, run through his body and the infant's like an electric current and destroy both. The wording of the oath seems to have been suitably strong as well as comprehensive. The only available example comes from the Malësi e Madhe, and runs, 'By this holy oath of the Lord, if I did it, may He reward me. As for the male of yours who has been killed, neither I nor my kinsmen, male or female, have killed him with our hands or our guns or with a guest's or agent's hands or gun.'

The family oath was reserved for men who were expected to deny a serious crime of which there was strong evidence that they were guilty. In the Malësi e Madhe, and apparently in Martanesh also, this was murder. So in these areas a family oath was tantamount to one with twenty-four compurgators. In Mirditë and Kurbin it was chiefly used in theft cases. If a sheep or goat in Kurbin was stolen, the thief had to return two sheep or goats to the owner, and pay a fine besides; if, however, he denied the theft, he must swear with his whole family that he was innocent. By contrast, a man who denied stealing an ox, a horse or a mule, was only ordered to take the oath with six compurgators. The theft of these animals was less serious than stealing a sheep or goat; for they only represented wealth, whereas the sheep and goats provided food for their owner.

In Mirditë the accuser had the right to ask a family oath of any man whom he strongly suspected, and could also say that he must take it with a jury. In that event he had to specify the various families in the village who were to compose the jury. For the Malësi e Madhe there is no evidence, but in Martanesh a jury was seldom required in family oaths. Group oaths were used in cases where the suspect, told to take the oath with twenty-four compurgators, failed to find so many ready to swear to his innocence and volunteered to take the oath with all the males of his family in Balim Sulltan's mausoleum. If he did so, nothing more was required of him.

In Mirditë, as Father Gjeçov informs us, a truculent accuser might also ask the oath by the head of the suspect's son; in that case the accused could not refuse to take it, unfair and dangerous to the child though it was. If there were more than one boy in the family, the oath had to be taken on all their heads. On the appointed day, the accuser went to the suspect's house, where the suspect gathered all the males in his family and drew their heads together. After laying his hands on their heads to establish the contact which would involve them in his perjury, if any, he took the oath, saying, 'By the heads of my sons, I have not done you the wrong of which you have accused me, and I do not know who has done it'. The gravity of this oath made it particularly useful in ending embittered disputes before they came to bloodshed, for only a man very sure of his position or one utterly unscrupulous would swear it.

Social oaths were designed to check lawlessness and breaches of the peace within the tribe and were the commonest types. In Document II, Mnelë and Gomsiqe swear¹ to stick together whatever may betide for mutual defence against external danger. Sometimes the tribe, or at least the brotherhood in the Malësi e Madhe, swore that they would not enter a certain house. Though this oath was never taken except to make the law-breaker obey a tribal judgement, it was not considered a good oath, and breaking it soon after it was sworn was advocated. Sometimes, too, a village would assemble and take oath not to send their animals to the summer grazing grounds before a fixed date or to cut wood in each other's forests. In Lurë irrigation rights still depended on oaths taken by the various claimants several generations ago and still binding on their descendants. This example shows how the perpetuity of oaths prevented renewals of litigation; a right once settled, remained settled.

When about to pronounce a decision or just after pronouncing it, elders frequently took oath that they had judged or would judge righteously. In all the tribal area they inevitably carried a stone on their shoulder to signify that they must carry it throughout eternity if their oath was false. In Shalë their formula was, 'With body and soul, with good luck and good fortune, so far as I can tell I have decided this matter without guile, without bribery and without prejudice'.

¹ See Appendix, Document II, p. 262.

CHAPTER XVIII

THE OATH

III. VERDICT AND PENALTIES

The only way of bringing in a verdict in the suspect's favour was, as has already been said, by his taking the prescribed oath himself and inducing the prescribed number of compurgators to repeat it. This done, he was acquitted (*u-la*, lit. 'he was washed').

By contrast, there were several ways of reaching an adverse verdict. The suspect might pronounce it himself. Sometimes superstitious fear made him refuse at the first asking to take the oath. This only occurred when he knew he was guilty of the crime, or had no lawful right to the disputed property. Sometimes a bolder suspect got as far as the door of the church or mosque, and then was stricken with sudden fear of the perjury he was about to commit, confessed to the crime and faced up to the consequences. A slyer suspect, hoping that the matter was forgotten, sometimes let the day for taking the oath pass. But the accuser was generally on the watch and frustrated his hope. First he informed his own elder that the appointed day had come and gone without the oath being taken. This elder having passed on the information to the suspect's elder the two dignitaries went together to the man's house, pointed out that the term was up and declared that since he had not taken the oath he had lost his case.

There were at least three ways by which the compurgators might bring in a verdict of guilty. The first was when three out of twenty-four compurgators, two out of twelve or eight, and one of a smaller number, informed the suspect soon after their nomination that they did not have enough confidence in his innocence to take the oath that would clear him.

Again, if the compurgators did not believe the suspect's oath, they could take one of two courses. They might tell him there and then to go and pay the penalty for his crime because they did not believe his oath and must refuse to acquit him with their own. Some of them were, of course, certain to know the truth from other sources and so could check his oath. Or they might wait till the day of taking the oath and then, without giving the suspect any warning, fail to turn up. If even one so failed, the suspect was declared guilty. Indeed, the easiest and least obnoxious way of convicting the suspect was not to turn up for the oath. Such was the almost universal rule. In the Malësi e Madhe, however, a message was sent to a missing compurgator to make sure that he had not merely forgotten the date. If he replied that he had not come on purpose because he thought the suspect was guilty, the case ended, a verdict of guilty being returned. If he replied that he was absent for personal reasons, an attempt was made to find two others to take his place at once; if this succeeded, the oath was taken. If only one compurgator did not attend in Bytyç, the oath could be taken, particularly if the reason for the compurgator's default was the newly discovered pregnancy of his wife. These rules applied only to the accuser's quota. If one of the suspect's compurgators failed to turn up, any bystander who could be persuaded to join the jury might be substituted. As the suspect was not bound to disclose the names of his quota, the public was often unaware that the second man was a substitute and not the suspect's first choice.

In Mirditë the verdict was virtually known before the taking of the oath. When the suspect felt ready to take the oath he invited the compurgators to a meal in his house. If they declined his invitation it meant that they thought him guilty and would not take the oath. If they accepted his invitation he could sleep in peace, secure in the knowledge that whenever the time came for them to take the oath, they would do so. Once they had eaten his food, the oath was as good as taken. This custom may have developed because the suspect had to assemble the compurgators to hear him take the oath and was forbidden by his instincts of hospitality to leave them unfed. In Labinot, Çermenikë and Zerqan, the suspect also offered the compurgators a high-class meal, with meat and rice pilaff, but not till after they had taken the oath, and only if he had been cleared. The meal was thought to ratify the oath and to reward the compurgators in some measure for their trouble.

A loser who did not abide by the verdict of the oath lost 'face'. Some years ago, a family in Fulqet died out. Two neighbours, more or less related to the family, claimed its land, one taking possession of it and the other gathering a stackful of hay from it. Even the women quarrelled so fiercely over it that they had to be separated by gendarmes and the elders intervened and said that the relative in possession must take an oath with twenty-four compurgators that the land was his. He took the oath, but the other refused to accept its verdict and the quarrel continued. The whole village denounced this as 'very shameful'.

Some losers were made to accept the verdict by the realization that resistance would only plunge them into the difficulties of a blood feud, and others submitted in fear of losing 'face'. The elders had normally little machinery for enforcing the verdict. In one difficult case observed by the author in Çermenikë however, they succeeded by the unusual device of putting both claimants to the oath. An old, forceful man had quarrelled about irrigation water with a young rascal who was his distant relative. The elders decided that if the young man could take the oath, he should have the water; if he could not, the old man must not think the water his but must take oath on another day that it was his by right. As the young man was a notorious liar, it was not expected that he would be able to muster the requisite number of compurgators. But to the general surprise he succeeded, and took the oath. The elders decreed that he should have water for six hours every five days. The old man seemed at first to acquiesce in this decree, but later held up the water and turned out his own compurgators to take oath along with himself that it was his. But the elders would not countenance such disobedience, particularly as he had originally submitted to the verdict of his relative's oath; and by refusing to come and witness his oath they prevented it from being taken. Eventually he gave in, and allowed the young man to have water according to the oath that he had sworn as prescribed by the elders.

Another interesting case occurred in Dibër about 1935. Cen Elezi was asked to arbitrate between two cousins in Çajë, in south Lumë, who were quarrelling about a piece of land. He asked a fee of twelve napoleons from each, and accepted their tobacco boxes in pledge thereof. The boxes were silver but not worth anything like his fee, so they were only a token pledge. Cen then went to see the land and discovered that neither cousin knew exactly where its boundaries lay. He pointed this out and said that this and their relationship made arbitration difficult. One of them, whom he named, must therefore take oath with six named and six unnamed compurgators that the land was his. First of all, however, he must set up the boundary stones in their proper places. On the day arranged Cen could not go himself to witness the oath. He sent the cousins word to that effect and said he was sending a deputy. When the latter arrived, he found the named cousin ready to take the oath but no boundary stones in place. He refused to witness the oath because Cen's condition had not been observed. The matter was referred back to Cen, who said that since the cousin put to the oath had been unable to take it as enjoined, the other must have the land. If they did not wish to accept this judgement, let them bring him four napoleons each as his fee for the incomplete oath, and let them find another elder and he would pay his expenses; he was no guarantor to make them accept his judgement. The cousins prepared to accept his decision, but when the winner began to plough the land, the loser shot one of his men dead and wounded another; the feud continued for many years.

The oath derived its efficiency as a legal instrument from superstitious fear of punishment for perjury. God, as the Almighty, was naturally the chief agent of this punishment. 'Don't let God catch a perjurer', said the aphorism. In invocations the connexion between oath and Deity was simple. The oath-taker called God or one of His saints to witness to the truth of what he was about to swear, and did so in the full knowledge that if he angered Him by perjury, he must expect a manifestation of Divine wrath. There was a very definite belief that God was watching. In oaths sworn on a sacred object or building, such as 'By this good thing of the Lord', there was an indirect invocation of the Deity, but also while the oath-taker swore, he had to keep his hand on the sacred object— Gospel, crucifix, altar, church door, Koran, saint's grave—just as a witness in an English law court must take the oath with his hand on the Bible. This act established physical contact between the oath-taker and the Deity or saint with which the sacred object or building was associated. To a simple tribesman this was a very solemn thought. On this account these contact oaths were preferred above all others. Probably the contact also made the tribesman think punishment more certain. All over the Near East the principle of direct contact with holy things plays an important role. This is most familiar in cases of sickness, as when people knot rags to sacred graves or trees; the holy influences with which they have thus linked their persons penetrate their whole being and cure their maladies. Many instances will be found in the author's book *Christianity and Islam under the Sultans*. But suppliants for such favours must placate the holy influences with prayers or other offerings. If they irritated them, as an oath-taker would do by perjuring himself, they could only expect punishment.

A most interesting example of the working of physical contact which is certainly of pagan origin was found in the Moslem district of Sulovë, south-west of Elbasan. There the most hardened oath-taker dare not forswear himself in a serious case, for he must then take the oath with a coin in his mouth, and perjury would bring him certain death. The coin was clearly Charon's obol, as was the coin slipped on to the chest of Albanian dead in many widely separated areas.

In the exclusively Catholic oath 'by the stone' the solemnity of the oath came from the contact with a holy thing, and punishment for perjury was inflicted in any form that the sacred object chose. When, however, elders swore their equally solemn oath with a stone, log of wood or other weight on their shoulder, or when a man, stone on shoulder, claimed repayment of a dead man's debt, no principle of contact was involved. There was rather a quite crude belief that a perjuring elder would be punished by having to carry the weight for ever and ever in the next world.

God punished the perjurer both in this world and in the next. When the man died, his soul was lost, for being 'heavy-laden before the Lord' it had nowhere to go. If he was an elder who had taken an oath with a stone on his shoulder, he was doomed to carry the stone through all eternity. The first of these terrors was evidently inspired by the Church. The second is an older fear. The elder, when taking the oath, often expressed his willingness to carry the stone in the next world if he perjured himself, but an accused man left his future condition to be inferred, except for the cryptic phrase 'If I did it, may He reward me', which he sometimes inserted in his oath. When he was thinking only of himself he meant, according to the Catholics of Kurbin, 'If I lie may God kill me. If I tell the truth, may He forgive me my sins.' When he contrasted himself with his accuser he meant, 'If I did it may I suffer for it. If I didn't, and you've made me run the risk of taking this oath without due cause, may *you* suffer for it.' This sentence seems to have died out among the Moslems.

Death was the commonest, and most dreaded, form of punishment in this world. In the most solemn oaths it was specified—a son's in the oath by the child's head, the oath-taker's own in the oaths by his own head, with Charon's coin in his mouth, and in such phrases as 'May Sheikh Ibrahim cut short my life' and 'May the bread kill me'. Sometimes the mechanism was crude and obvious, as in Jove's thunderbolts, the lightning that struck the perjurer dead, set his house on fire, or killed his livestock. Even if a perjurer escaped death, it was expected all over the country that he would fall ill or go from bad to worse till he came to ruin. Poverty and sickness must be his lot. His family might even die out, most dreadful of calamities. His son might be born with a physical defect, lame or blind or with a withered arm or too many fingers to his hands. A man of Tërnovë, near Martanesh, took a false oath, and as a result one of his eyes a year later was as large as his fist.

There were also social penalties to be faced. A man detected in a false oath became an outcast, despised and condemned by all his fellows, and was never again invited into any house in the tribe. In grosser cases in the Malësi e Madhe he might even be expelled by the tribe. In Mirditë his family was branded with shame for seven generations. All over the Catholic areas he was also fined. In Mirditë there were elaborate rules for these fines. If there had been a jury of twenty-four, the perjurer had to pay 100 rams and an ox to the Gjomarkaj family. If the jury had been smaller, the fine, which was presumably of the same amount, went to the tribe. In addition, the perjurer had to pay a fine to the Church and 500 grosh to each compurgator for leading him into perjury and outrage to the Church, and so exposing him to the usual punishments for perjury and sacrilege. For the Divine wrath fell on an unwitting no less than on a witting perjurer. It was no excuse for a compurgator in God's eyes that he had forsworn himself in reliance on the suspect's oath; he had had the responsibility of ascertaining the facts for himself. The compurgators and the perjurer had to go to church in order to obtain absolution for their sins. Just before leaving, the perjurer had to leave money on the altar to pay all the fines he had contracted to pay when he took the oath before the compurgators. In the Malësi e Madhe he had to give six purses to the Church as well as one to each compurgator. In Martanesh which is, of course, completely Moslem, the same compensation was payable to each compurgator in a perjury case, but in neighbouring Zerqan the practice was unknown. The fine was obviously a considerable deterrent to would-be perjurers, especially when the jury was large.

As Father Gjeçov remarks, perjury harmed the soul, imposed a fine and disgraced the man in the eyes of his fellows. All three consequences worked powerfully in their different ways to keep oath-takers on the path of truth. A thief, for instance, might get as far as the door of a church or mosque, but there his heart would fail him and he would exclaim, 'Forgive me, I did steal it'. Then he would proceed to make the usual reparation. Even innocent men dreaded the oath and took it with great reluctance. In poverty-stricken Theth many were so afraid of it that even when wrongfully accused, they preferred to pay whatever fine was due for the crime. In Lurë people professed to fear nothing so much. 'You may rob me of my life, but I will not break my oath', they used to say. As for oaths taken to settle disputes, generations afterwards the descendants of the original disputants were afraid to break the oath of their ancestors. This fear kept boundaries that had been trodden out by an elder under an oath immovable for all time, and preserved water rights. In modern Lurë there is some maldistribution of irrigation water, but no attempt is made to remedy this by force of law. Many years ago, the people say, their ancestors took an oath about the irrigation rights of each family and they dare not violate this oath. One of the derisory stories told in sophisticated Tirana about the Highlanders relates that they were such poor stuff that one said, when brought to court, 'I have sworn a solemn oath not to tell, but press me a little and I will speak'.

There were occasions, however, on which perjury was thought permissible or even commendable. A man of Lumë, when asked to be compurgator in a murder case, would sometimes consider whether he might help to make peace between the parties if he forswore himself. If he decided that 'giving a living man for a dead one was no way of doing', he would swear a false oath. In the Malësi e Madhe, a village ward or a tribe had sometimes to swear not to enter a malefactor's house; when this punishment came to seem excessive it was thought advisable to break the oath.

In general, the modern mountaineers drew a distinction between their own old jury system and the law court that was superseding it. Reluctant though they remained to forswear themselves by their old system, they would do so joyfully in the modern court, especially if this saved a friend or relative or concealed their possession of a rifle; this weapon being their chief treasure, they would deny '500 times' on oath that they had it. Instead of public censure they met with public commendation in such cases. The modernity of the court-house was against the oath; there had been no time for the growth of stories about punishment for perjury in it. For the same reason the new church in Nikaj was not thought so good a place for taking an oath as was the old one.

It happened inevitably that some men were sceptical or sacrilegious enough to take a false oath and plausible enough to persuade the requisite number of compurgators to swear to their innocence. A thief could send a stolen cow to graze with his own, yoke the stolen ox into the plough with one of his own and hang a bell on the neck of the stolen sheep or goat. The real owner might recognize the animal, but he could not claim it. The public too might recognize it, but they had to shut their eyes. The law said, 'what is won by an oath belongs to him who wins it'. The law disliked this principle but had to accept it because there was no way of bringing home a crime to a man who had been cleared by an oath. This legal defect made it essential that honourable and knowledgeable compurgators should be chosen. The same defect made every tribal authority, in the interests of justice, foster the general fear of perjury to the utmost.

In spite of the fear of punishment for perjury, some jesting stories, which are possibly apocryphal, were told of perjurers. Once there was a headman in the village of Peladhi, near Zerqan, who wrapped up a block of wood in a cloth as if it were a Koran and summoned the village to swear on it that they would no longer go and cut wood illicitly in each other's forest. They took the oath and, believing they had done so on the Koran, kept it. He too took the oath, but knowing it to be void because taken only on a profane bit of wood went afterwards to his neighbour's forest and cut all the wood he wanted.

CHAPTER XIX

WITNESS (KËPUCAR)

While compurgators empanelled for an ordeal by oath were collecting evidence about the case, neither they nor their informants were on oath, and the verdict depended on whether they judged it right or wrong to swear to the suspect's innocence at the conclusion of their inquiries. Many cases, however, were decided on the evidence of a single informant known as a *këpucar*, who was generally sworn in before being allowed to speak. As he was also severely cross-examined by elders and the verdict depended on the impression made by his evidence, he approximated more closely to the English witness than did the compurgators to the English jury.

An informant was a man who gave information leading to the detection of a criminal, above all when a secret murder or a cunningly concealed theft had taken place. His information had to be based on personal observation.

It was believed that all criminal problems could be solved either by oath or a witness. In some of the most secret crimes, as when a haystack was burned or a dog killed in his own farmyard, there was practically no hope of discovering the criminal save by witness. There were other occasions on which trial by witness was chosen in preference to ordeal by oath. If a witness was known to exist, many elders, particularly in Mirditë, declared forthwith that an oath was superfluous. In Martanesh and Zerqan they often waited to see if a witness would come forward before they ordered the suspect to take an oath. In other cases the accuser was allowed to choose between the two methods. He might do so at the outset of the case, when everything was still vague. In Labinot, for example, as soon as the Village Assembly was notified of the crime, both accuser and suspect being present, the headman habitually asked the accuser which method he was using. Whatever his reply, the suspect himself, in a fury at being under suspicion, gave the accuser the choice of method. Or the choice might be offered when the preparations for the suspect's taking the oath were almost concluded. In Mirditë, for instance, as soon as the compurgators announced that they were ready to clear the suspect, the elders bade the accuser come and witness their oath or produce a *këpucar*. An accuser who had good reason to be dissatisfied with the suspect's acquittal was entitled to pursue his inquiries and, securing fresh evidence of the suspect's guilt from an eye-witness, to lay this before the elders with a demand that the case should be reconsidered. Indeed, many elders after delivering a verdict of 'not guilty' reminded the accuser that if he was dissatisfied he was at liberty to find a *këpucar*. He could not, of course, have the suspect put to the oath a second time; 'oath upon oath' was not allowed by the law.

An eye-witness had always to come forward of his own accord; the accuser could not go and look for him directly. In ordinary cases, the accuser let it be known through private channels that he would be glad to find one, but in the cases of arson and murder of a dog already mentioned, the Village Assembly might issue a public appeal for information. No time limit was ever set. Information given a year or more after the crime had been committed was treated as seriously as if it were only a day old.

In every type of case the witness first approached the accuser saying, that he had found the stolen property, the murderer, or the falsity of the oath as the case might be. The accuser then had to go to the suspect and demand restitution. In Mirditë, at least, he had to be accompanied by two friends who were sometimes asked afterwards to confirm that he had warned the suspect. If the latter refused to make atonement, the accuser had to warn him that he had a witness. If the suspect persisted in his refusal, saying, 'Produce your witness', the accuser then, but only then, settled the witness's fee and secured his information. The elders then formed a committee for the purpose of cross-examining the witness. In Zerqan this consisted of five or six men appointed by the suspect and two or three friends of the accuser. In Mirditë it was selected from the *pritëtarë* (sing. *pritëtar*), men fitted to be judges or compurgators by their honour, wisdom and experience in cross-examining witnesses. In the Malësi e Madhe the committee was formed by the bajraktar and one to four headmen; the qualities which such personages were believed to inherit along with their position were thought sufficient equipment for dealing with a witness. Elsewhere one elder was considered enough in simple cases; he was chosen by the suspect at the bidding of the accuser, by the two together, or by the other elders.

With a few exceptions, the greatest precautions were taken to conceal the witness's identity, as the criminal would have killed him if he had discovered who he was. In Mirditë he was allowed to object to the nomination of men whom he thought too indiscreet to preserve his incognito, and those eventually selected had to take an oath that so long as they lived they would not without his permission divulge his identity. He was always interviewed in all secrecy; often the accuser alone knew who he was. He might be taken to an empty house where the elders awaited him, or led at night to the house of an elder who questioned him from a balcony while he stood unseen by all the inmates, the elder included, in the dark farmyard. In the Malësi e Madhe he was often given a rendezvous by night in another village altogether. In Zerqan he usually met the committee in some lonely spot at sunset, with them on one side of a thick hedge and him on the other so that they could not see him. However often he was interviewed, it was always in the same secrecy.

No doubt owing to the danger involved in trying to bring a criminal to justice, a witness was always given a fee. With the delicacy characteristic of Albanians the fee was cloaked under the name of *këpucë* (lit. 'shoe'), presumably in allusion to the shoe-leather which he wore out in finding or conveying his information. Consequently, *këpucar* means literally the 'man who gets shoe-money'.

In the case of theft the witness's fee was not allowed to exceed the value of the stolen property. It was generally determined by agreement between witness and accuser at their first meeting, often after lively bargaining, particularly if the witness was greedy enough to ask more than he should. When the accuser let it be known that he was looking for a witness, he often specified the fee he was willing to pay. When the theft took place in a house, the fee was doubled, because human life had been endangered and the house's honour tarnished; house-breaking always implied that the men in it were weak or the womenfolk light. In Kurbin and Lumë, for example, four napoleons were paid to an informant who found an ox that had been stolen from the farmyard or stable under the house, but only its value, which was always less than four napoleons, in those districts when it had been stolen while grazing outside.

A man who disclosed a woman's adultery to her husband received no fee; and a friend was not allowed to take money for such a service. In this type of crime there was, of course, no trial in view; the husband's rifle was the only possible arbiter.

The examination which an eye-witness had to pass was very stiff. As a first step, he had to take oath before the elders that he would tell the truth without prejudice or spite; the man he accused was not to be troubled till his accusation was proved to be just. The only extant example of his oath, which comes from Çermenikë, runs, 'Look upon this earth, these mountains, these plains, this sky. You must carry them (through all eternity) if you lie', said the elders. 'Let me carry them. It is as I say,' the witness replied. Sometimes an elder recognized the witness and, knowing him to be of good character, did not ask him to risk his future by taking an oath. Even if he did not recognize him but only liked his manner and general appearance, he might excuse him.

When everything was set for cross-examination, the elders questioned the witness closely, noting any discrepancies in his statements, and looking out for any sign that the accusation was false. If it was a case of perjury, they had to be specially patient and careful as the penalties involved were so much heavier. The witness was not a professional like our detectives. Often he was a man so trusted by the thief that he had constant access to his house and so was in a position to see the stolen goods as soon as produced.

The witness had to give a detailed description of the crime and stolen property to the elders. In most cases of theft he must have either seen the thief in the act of stealing or leaving the scene of the theft or observed the stolen goods in the house or hand of the thief. When an ox had been stolen, he had to say where he saw the animal, where the thief had killed it, sold its hide and so on. When several oxen had been stolen he had to report according to their colouring that one was black, another white and a third dappled, that the thief took first this road, then that, killed one ox at such and such a spot and sold another to so-and-so. Whatever he said was subject to confirmation. When he alleged a sale, the elders sent independent agents to inquire whether it had really taken place. When he said the ox had been eaten, he had to produce concrete evidence, a token such as a bit of the skin, a horn, or some other part. This was the most conclusive of all possible evidence.

If the witness stood up well to the cross-examination, the elders declared that the suspect was guilty and must make the statutory atonement. If the witness had come forward after the suspect had taken an oath and been acquitted, the elders declared the suspect's oath invalid, pronounced him guilty, and sentenced him, not only to the usual penalties for his crime, but also to punishment for perjury.

Apart from what his perjury, if any, cost him, the convicted thief had to pay the value of the stolen property, the witness's fee and the elders' fee. He had to hand the witness's fee to the owner of the stolen goods, who had to pass it on to the witness, whose anonymity was thus preserved. In order to extract the witness's fee the elders commonly valued the stolen property at a good deal more than its real price; when the thief paid up, the owner retained the real price and handed the surplus to the witness. In Mirditë, says Father Gjeçov, the accuser who failed to warn the suspect at the outset that he had a witness, could not, even if the suspect was convicted, recover more than half the witness's fee. There does not seem to have been a similar law elsewhere.

If a thief continued to deny the theft and refused to pay his various fines after being declared guilty on a witness's evidence, the elders said he must take an oath that he was innocent, and then the compurgators stepped in, forbidding him to perjure himself and so confirming his conviction. This was in Mirditë and Lumë. In Martanesh, the law apparently went further. If a man convicted by a witness of having stolen from a house—the worst type of theft—denied the theft, was ordered to prove his innocence by an oath, and succeeded in doing so, and if the accuser still persisted in his accusation, the latter was asked to produce his witness before a new committee of elders. If a searching cross-examination convinced these that he was telling the truth, they ordered the thief to swear with forty-eight compurgators that he was innocent. This was double the number usual even in murder cases, and far more than he could ever hope to find.

The cross-examining elders sometimes concluded that the witness was lying. In Dukagjin, when quite certain of this, they made him instead of the thief pay for the stolen property. In the Malësi e Madhe, attended by their followers, they went and burned down his house, killed him if they caught him, and confiscated his property, making it common land on which all were free to graze, although none could plant grapes or sow maize. If some time elapsed before they discovered he had lied and if in the meantime they had punished the man he denounced, they repaid any moneys taken from this man out of the false witness's property, selling a portion of it if necessary.

In some southern areas manners were softer. In Çermenikë and Zerqan a lying witness was dismissed with a contemptuous word, suffering only disgrace in the accuser's eyes. Since his identity had never transpired, the public thought neither more nor less of him than before.

Sometimes the witness convicted himself of being the thief. This happened especially when he knew too many details, describing too exactly, for instance, the colour of a stolen animal's hair, the number of its spots, or the shape and twirls of its horns. The elders then called him the thief outright and sentenced him to pay their fee as well as the value of the stolen property and the amount he had extracted from the accuser as his own fee. 'So you wanted to steal twice over from him, did you?' they would exclaim. In Martanesh they also disgraced him publicly. The elder in whose yard he was being secretly examined called out to the accuser to come and seize him like the thief he was; during his cross-examination the accuser had remained, as was everywhere customary, out of earshot. As the yard was bolted for the night, the thief could not escape. Next day he was led out in front of the assembled village, denounced by the elders, and publicly sentenced to pay the sums described above. It often happened that they saw him then for the first time.

In Mirditë, it sometimes happened that a witness, observing that he had failed to convince the elders, and certain of his evidence, came forward publicly, seized the thief (or murderer) by the arm and denounced him as the criminal. Such courage never failed to win credence for his story.

If the witness was dismissed as a liar or convicted as the thief, the accuser lost the money he had paid him as well as the value of his lost property. That explains why a suspect could not be put to the oath a second time, yet could be retried as it were on a witness's evidence. It cost the accuser nothing to make a suspect take an oath, so that if the law had allowed 'oath after oath', a litigiously minded man might have made himself an endless nuisance to suspect, elders, compurgators and general public. But there was no such risk with a witness. The accuser had to prepay him whatever fee they agreed on, and if he had been foolish enough to trust an unsatisfactory person, he lost his money.

202

CHAPTER XX

THEFT AS A CRIME

Most of the material on theft comes from the history of Turkish times. The Turks, none too efficient in the towns, did not even try to control the mountaineers, and theft was, therefore, very common. During the twenty years between the Great Wars, the only period of independence that Albania had enjoyed for 500 years, theft was not one of the major crimes. This was often commented on by Major-General Sir Jocelyn Percy, who, as Organizer in Chief of the Albanian Gendarmerie, had cognizance for twelve years of every crime committed in the country. When the first British officers arrived in Albania in 1943, the machinery of modern government had already broken down. In view of that fact, and of the general effect of war conditions, it was not surprising that they should have found the mountaineers stealing frequently and on a large scale.

In the eyes of the law, thieves were divided into several categories according to the gravity of their crime. In Mirditë they were pilferers, robbers or highwaymen. The pilferer 'pinched' a small article from a house; the robber stole a beast with his own hands; and the highwayman robbed with violence. In Fulqet the categories were pilferer, timid thief and complete thief. The pilferer was a bad type because he came near enough to a house to steal clothes on its fence; the timid thief stole sheep in the forest; and the complete thief broke into houses and was ready to kill as well as to rob. In Dibër a thief with sandals was never so bad as a thief in shoes, stealing only a sheep or two, whereas the thief shod and dressed in European fashion was a serious menace. Here there was a sly reference to government officials and gendarmes, the only persons dressed in the 'French' manner whom the average Dibian knows.

Thieves were also classified according to their motives. A pilferer was usually prompted by innate wickedness and was consequently incorrigible. Others, especially the Highlanders of the north-west, stole for fun and were, therefore, worse than murderers who had some compelling motive for their crime. Many stole because everyone else did, and they would only have been laughed at if they had refrained. As the proverb says, 'One bunch of grapes, seeing another ripening, then ripens itself'. Then there were incidental offenders: a man who could not recover a debt might distrain on his debtor by turning highwayman and seizing his pack-pony or sheep on the public road; or men might steal out of spite. The debt recovered or the spite vented, such thieves usually became law-abiding citizens again. Though poverty is, and always has been, extreme in this mountainous land, hunger rarely made a man steal. Few broke into a house to help themselves because of the risks involved. Many, however, would catch a lamb or kid on the mountain where the risks were less and, after killing it, make a cooking-vessel of its paunch and boil the meat over a gipsy fire. Sheep stealing often took place on a grand scale between family and family, village and village or tribe and tribe. There are many popular tales of forays for fun or glory. 'Ragging' the other house, village or tribe and, more especially, the hated Serbs and Montenegrins, was a recognized sport, and the bigger the booty the greater the glory. There was a picnic atmosphere about such expeditions. A hundred men might go, half to drive the sheep and half to take pot-shots at pursuers. As soon as the first party found the flock they killed the bell-wether and cut off its head. One of them held this out, bell and all, to the other sheep and ran off at top speed. As the sheep galloped helter-skelter after the head, the rest of the party ran hither and thither shouting and cursing, laughing and beating the sheep with sticks to make them run faster. Being pressed for time, they left the leader's carcass on the ground. They usually disarmed the shepherd and carried him off to prevent his giving the alarm. On releasing him they gave him what they pleased.

On the whole there was little shame about individual and group thieving, although there were many expressions of disapproval. The men of Lumë had a saying, 'Better be a good-for-nothing than a thief', which was in direct contradiction to their reputation. The Malesors asserted that all other tribes were thieves, but that they themselves never stole. The Catholics of Kthellë used to say that it was better not to sleep too softly like the Moslems of Mat, whose oxen had often been driven away, killed and eaten before they got out of their beds. The man who stole because he had been stolen from evoked universal admiration. There were, however, two forms of theft which were no less universally regarded as shameful. A man who stole from another with whom he had broken bread as host or guest disgraced himself for ever. A woman must not steal for fun or spite. If she did, not only her husband's family, but the whole village felt ashamed and took steps to deal with her.

The accomplice who helped the thief, the host who fed him and the receiver who hid the booty were all considered as no less guilty than the thief himself. 'A thief and his host are the same', and 'Like thief, like receiver' were common sayings. All had to suffer punishment in proportion to their share in the crime and booty. The owner of stolen goods had the right to remove them from the premises of a receiver and to claim compensation, and the receiver had no legal claim for redress as against the thief. On the other hand, if a man bought stolen goods in good faith he had to give them back to the rightful owner, but he was entitled to recover what he had paid for them from the thief.

All possible means of protection against theft were adopted by the mountain peoples. Every man carried a gun by day, and slept with it beside him at night. Dogs were kept in every house and sheepfold. Domestic animals were branded with a mark that could not be destroyed, as when sheep had both their ears notched. Farmyards were surrounded by walls too high to scale and had stout wooden gates heavily bolted at night. Thieves, however, could make holes in the mud and stone walls, and frequently forced an entry that way. The walls of many village shops were lined with wood, so that a thief's chisel, striking it, would make sufficient noise to put the householder on the alert.

In Turkish times many villages sent out armed patrols every night, composed not of professionals like the night watchman of the towns, but of unpaid villagers who served in turn as directed by the village headman. When there was danger of sheep-stealing on a large scale, the threatened villages sometimes bought the protection of some strong man. For example, the villagers of Reç, now in Yugoslavia, hired protection from sheep-stealers of Dibër by paying the Kaloshi family of Dibër a thousand napoleons a year. Nor were the parties deterred from contracting together by the fact that the Kaloshis were Moslems and Albanians, and the villagers of Reç were Orthodox and Macedonian Bulgars.

In the extreme north and south of the mountains, guns could legitimately be used when a thief was caught in the act of breaking into a house or sheepfold, though in some districts the house-holder or shepherd had to warn the thief three times before shooting in order to avoid a blood feud. The local law said, 'A thief's blood is lost'. In Mirditë, however, there was a saying that 'A blood feud is not stopped by felony', and there it was forbidden to kill a housebreaker at sight. This prohibition had been introduced to prevent men killing their enemies and placing their dead bodies in the farmyard to give the impression that they had been caught in the act of theft.

A man who robbed a child or a woman, stole a loaded packhorse, or another man's gun, could be shot even when not caught in the act, though a blood feud might follow such action.

In Turkish times, the authorities had to be informed of the death of anyone in the act of theft, but they did not punish the man who had killed him. They required only that he should keep watch and ward over the body till some official arrived and send word to the relatives to make arrangements for burial. After the funeral, the relatives and the killer resumed ordinary relations. Strong men, of course, sometimes overrode the ordinary rules and decencies. Thus Deli Beg, the overlord of Preze, an old market centre, was so determined to stop all raids on his flocks that he not only killed all thieves, but shamed them when dead. He tied their bodies on horses, with the heads propped up with a muleteer's forked stick, and drove them through the village streets. He never troubled to inform the authorities of the deaths.

There were elaborate rules for the detection of the thief who succeeded in escaping with his booty. In Lumë the village authorities had the right to search one house after another for the stolen property. Everywhere the victim might try and find it for himself. He would follow the tracks of a stolen animal, generally in the direction of the home of someone known to have a grudge against him. When the tracks ended at a house or its immediate surroundings, the master was regarded as convicted of the theft. 'Track on the ground, animal found', and the owner had the right to take it away immediately if it was still alive. The thief might refuse to produce it and the owner could then ask leave to search the premises. If such permission was not given, the owner had to turn to the elders to enlist their help, as he also had to do if it were found that the animal was dead.

When the beast's tracks stopped between two houses, the

formula then applied was 'The beast or an oath'. Each house had to make oath separately that it did not harbour the stolen property. The same routine was followed when the tracks stopped between two villages, the villages as a whole having to take oath.

The tracks of an animal might be destroyed by the thief, or the property stolen might not be an animal at all. In such cases, the owner had to rely on information supplied by third parties, and this was seldom lacking in small communities where there were few secrets. If the whereabouts of the stolen property was discovered, the suspected thief might admit the crime, and if so, the owner and he might settle about repayment themselves, or leave it to the elders to do so. If the suspect denied the theft, the owner informed the village headman of his loss and of the identity of the suspected thief, and the latter called an Assembly to which he summoned owner and suspect. A suspect who did not appear was declared guilty and ordered to pay for the stolen goods. If the suspect came, the owner was given the choice between ordeal by oath and trial on the evidence of an eye-witness, and the proceedings then took the ordinary form.

The convicted thief had first of all to make restitution in accordance with the 'twofold' or 'two-for-one' rule, which exacted twice the value of the stolen goods in kind or money. In Mirditë, when animals were given in restitution, their selection was left to the thief, and, to quote from Father Gjeçov, 'it sufficed if they could walk on their feet'. In Martanesh a committee of two or three was appointed by the thief to make the choice, and this committee had to be accepted by the owner. In addition to restitution, a penalty might be imposed, either in the form of a fine or by ordering an extra number of compurgators if the oath was to be taken. The amount of the fine was largely fixed by tradition though the elders might vary it according to extenuating or aggravating circumstances.

There were various generally recognized kinds of aggravating circumstances. For instance, if a thief lost, spoiled, or ate what he had taken, the penalties were often heavy. In Martanesh and adjoining districts a loser could put any value he liked on a stolen article that had been destroyed. In Zerqan, it was regarded as a disgrace to the owner of a stolen sheep if it was eaten by the thief on the mountain. Punishment then was not only for the theft, but for the injury to the honour of the victim.

Another aggravated form of theft was that which took place on the public highway. There was a rule that 'the public highway must not be cut'. If a robber stole a wayfarer's horse, mule, donkey or sheep, shooting inevitably took place; if the thief survived, he had to return the animal, and to pay whatever the Village Assembly decreed. A man very often turned highwayman because he thought his victim was in his debt. If this belief turned out to be mistaken, he had to pay a fine for cutting the highway, besides returning the stolen animal and compensating the owner for the loss of its services. When a sheep had been taken, and was not returned at once, the thief might even be expelled from the village with all his family.

Robbery of a Catholic church was sacrilege and a very serious view was taken of it. The thief was shot by the tribe and could not be avenged. His family was expelled and his nearest relatives bought his land, the price going to the church. Stealing from the priest's house or from church lands was still sacrilege, but not so severely punished. In addition to returning two-for-one, the thief had to pay a fine for violating the sanctuary of the house or lands and another to the community for the threat to it. In Mirditë the same penalties were imposed if the theft occurred elsewhere but the booty was hidden in the church.

Thefts from Orthodox churches and Moslem shrines were also regarded as sacrilege, but not thefts from the houses of Orthodox priests or Moslem clerics, as they were usually at some distance from the places of worship and no sanctity attached to them.

Breaking into any house in order to steal was regarded as a very serious crime, for it brought dishonour as well as material loss to the householder. Opening the farmyard gate or the house door, without giving due warning and being invited to enter, was regarded as housebreaking and punished as such. In Krasniqë, the fine for burgling a house was four times that for burgling a sheepfold. Stealing out on the lonely mountain was regarded as still less heinous, and only one article had to be given in restitution; nor was any fine imposed.

A man might be dishonoured by other forms of theft than that of housebreaking. In the Malësi e Madhe, a fine of 500 grosh was imposed on the man who helped himself to another's tobacco box or cigarette, and a mere touch on another's pocket might bring a fine. A story is told of a man who was shot at a General

Assembly by his neighbour from whose tobacco box he had inadvertently rolled a cigarette. In every tribe and village, a man's honour was so stained by the theft of his gun or his wife that he had to shoot the thief and take the consequences of the ensuing blood feud.

The penalties imposed depended also on the nature of the articles stolen. North Albania was predominantly pastoral and, as the safety of the flock of sheep depended on the bell-animal, penalties for stealing this animal were heavy.[1] In Lumë the owner could demand six or seven sheep for the thief: 'as well steal the whole flock as its leader.' In Perlat stealing a bell-wether was such a disgraceful act that in the blood feud against the thief's family, even a woman could be killed. The bell of the leading animal was even more precious than the animal itself, and in Perlat, if it were stolen, it had to be returned and a sheep with it. In Labinot, the bell was thought too unlucky to be hung round an animal's neck again, and instead of returning it, the thief had to pay twice its value or be shot. In Mirditë a fine of 500 grosh was imposed for the dishonour done to the owner.

The two-for-one rule was applied to thefts of all farm animals, with the exception of pigs and cocks. The man who stole a pig had to pay 500 grosh in hard cash. This sum was often ten times the value of the animal, but the pig was the mainstay of the poor man and required special protection. The same sum of 500 grosh had to be paid for a cock, as 'the cock is the poor man's watch'. It was said that in Krasniqë an actual watch had to be paid instead of the money penalty.

Firewood was usually collected by women, and when they stole it their husbands were held responsible. It was common practice to seize the axe with which the thief cut the wood and the rope with which she slung it on her back. These articles were sometimes used as visible evidence of her guilt, sometimes retained as compensation, or as a guarantee for the payment of the penalty, or of the fee due to the elder who dealt with the case. Women might steal other things than firewood, and responsibility was always placed on the husband. It is recorded that, during the reign of King Zog, men might even be imprisoned for their wives' thefts. It was they who had to take the oath if an oath was required. The woman did not, however, get off scot free. In most areas she was

[1] Vide supra, p. 173.

beaten by her husband, and no matter how severe the punishment, her brother, who was her natural protector, would be too ashamed of her conduct to interfere. If a thieving woman did not mend her ways, her husband usually divorced her. The southern Catholics, anxious to reform erring wives and to avoid divorce, sometimes sent wrongdoers to spend a night in the lonely church of Shen Ndue in the forest above the village of Laç in Kurbin. This treatment is said to have been effective in many cases!

By the laws of hospitality, a man never robbed his guest nor a guest his host. If a third party robbed either, the other did his best to find the thief and the stolen goods. But such laws were not always respected, and penalties were prescribed for their breach. In Mirditë a guest who stole was ostracized as well as having to pay the usual penalty. In Kurbin he was expelled for ever from the tribe. If a guest in Mirditë was robbed by a fellow-guest, their host demanded double redress from the criminal—for the injury to his guest and for housebreaking. If a guest was robbed after leaving his host's house, it was still the host's duty to punish the thief, as the latter would know where the victim had been.

CHAPTER XXI

MURDER WITHIN THE FAMILY

When a man murdered his son, father, brother, paternal uncle, paternal uncle's son, or brother's son, the usual verdict was that in killing so near a relative the murderer had 'killed himself'. The victim's blood was therefore lost, 'no one sought-to-avenge him', and it had only been his 'ill-luck' so to die.

From another point of view it might be argued that since the murderer was the victim's nearest relative, other relatives could not act over his head and avenge the dead man. For example, when a man murdered his paternal uncle, if the latter left neither son nor brother, his blood was lost, for the murderer was his nearest relative and by killing him had only killed himself. On the other hand, if the uncle left either a son or a brother, that son or brother was nearer to him than the murderer and avenged his death. In view of his relationship to the criminal his vengeance generally took the form of exacting blood money. In the same way when a man murdered his brother's son, the victim's blood was lost if he left neither father nor brother. But if he left either, the murderer had to pay blood money. The rule of the nearest relative failed only if one brother killed another while their father was alive. Though the father was the nearest relative of the victim, the fratricide being only a neighbour by comparison, the victim's blood was lost. The father could not avenge him except by killing his surviving son, and even from the best of motives no decent father would kill a son.

The motive of the murderer seldom affected the situation. The murder of a son, an extremely rare occurrence, was oftenest due to his adultery with his young stepmother. His blood was lost, not because of his sin, but solely because the father who murdered him was his nearest relative. Again, one brother sometimes fell in love with the other's wife, and knowing, especially in north Albania, that if she became a widow he could by customary law marry her, could not always resist the temptation to make her a widow. The victim's blood was lost in spite of the murderer's motive, and the fratricide married the widow and suffered no disability except some loss of face. At Krujë in 1930 when the authorities sought to punish a man who had murdered his brother during a quarrel, the widow swore that the pistol had gone off accidentally when her brother-in-law was trying to wrest it from her husband, who had threatened suicide. Having thus prevented the authorities from taking action, the widow made no effort to keep the true story of the murder quiet, but repeated it every day during the month when the women met for the ceremonial 'keening'. She was also openly commended by the public for preventing the government from shaming her husband's family by arresting the murderer.

Exceptionally, if the murderer's motive was bad by tribal standards, his relative was well avenged. For instance, if a man killed his cousin or nephew to get his land, the crime was considered so anti-social that the murderer was killed by the community, his blood was lost, and his family expelled. Again, exceptionally, a motive might be so good by tribal standards as to win the murderer public admiration. Thus children in Shalë were taught with great pride that once a tribesman killed his brother for killing a guest, for an Albanian's duty to his guest transcends the claims of blood relationship.

Two modifications of the general rule are to be noted. In Mirditë in spite of the victim's blood being lost, the murderer had to pay the tribe the fine due in cases of ordinary murder, 100 rams and an ox. In the Malësi e Madhe if the two brothers had separated the fratricide had to pay blood money to his brother's dependants. If the widow had no children, she took all the money; if she had a daughter only, she again took it all, for when the time came for the girl to marry, she would as 'head of the family' have to pay the wedding expenses; if she had a son, he took all the money, for his father's death had made him head of the family. The blood money was therefore alimony payable to the widow and orphans who had been robbed of their breadwinner. If the two brothers had not separated, the fratricide as a matter of course supported the widow and orphans along with the other members of his household and the question of alimony did not arise.

Parricide was thought the most abhorrent of all murders within the family. In a sense a father had the right to kill his son without being asked by anybody what he had done, but a son unnatural enough to kill his father could surely not have been got by that father, but must be a bastard. Even where his crime was regarded as suicide so that he escaped with his life, and that was the commonest result, he was treated as 'a low-class fellow', visited by none but bad characters, and, if a Mohammedan, never given the greeting 'Peace be with thee'. In Mirditë, always more rigorous than other districts, he was considered so anti-social that he was either killed or expelled in perpetuity by his kinsmen, or, according to another version, by the whole village along with his kinsmen.

The murder of certain relatives did not concern the family. Thus, if a man murdered a relative by marriage, such as his son-in-law, father-in-law, wife's brother, or sister's husband, the crime ranked as an ordinary murder and was expiated with a life or with blood money. The marriage tie was disregarded; the important point was that, unlike two brothers living under separate roofs, murderer and victim belonged to different families. Such murders were very rare, for marriage relationships were always contracted to secure a valued friend, and no Albanian in his senses ever threw a friend lightly away. Again, if a man murdered his maternal uncle or his sister's son, murderer and victim belonged to different families, and blood money at least was payable for the crime. The contingency rarely arose, since a maternal uncle was regarded as a father and a sister's son as one's own child.

If a woman was taken in adultery, and her husband killed her and her paramour together—'kerchief and cap together'—he incurred no feud; their deaths went unavenged; it was a case of 'blood for blood', one equal to the other. To prove them guilty he sent for his wife's brother and her lover's brother to see them both lying dead; his message would run, 'I killed her because I caught her sinning'. The wife's brother would hand him a cartridge, saying, 'Here is a cartridge for my sister. Bravo for doing this'. The paramour's nearest relatives came to the house, drank coffee, and took away the corpse; the murderer accompanied them to their house, drank coffee, and so peace was established between them. If the paramour's brother was 'a gentleman', 'a man', he would give a cartridge to the husband, saying, 'I pardon your crime because my brother has sinned'. Even the father of the paramour might say to the murderer, 'A blessing on your rifle', and give him coffee as a sign that there was peace between them. In modern times the government accepted the evidence of the two bodies lying together and punished the husband with no more than two or three weeks' imprisonment.

This custom of the wife's brother giving a cartridge to a husband who had murdered his erring wife explains the phrase often heard in Albania, 'a bride with a cartridge on her back'. In Martanesh it was an old, but long disused, custom to tie a cartridge on the back of a bride's veil as she left her father's house; this cartridge she was to give to her husband on her wedding night, and he would keep it against the day when he found her unfaithful and then kill her with it. This custom, if it existed elsewhere, has been forgotten, but the phrase is universally known.

In Lumë, if a husband suspected his wife of illicit love-making, he could not tell her people because he was being disgraced. He could only lie in wait till he caught the pair together and then kill them. Sometimes when he could not catch them together, he divorced her; in one instance a man did so on the insistence of his kinsmen, who thought themselves as well as the husband disgraced by the wife's notoriously loose living. He admitted that he could not manage her, divorced her for the sake of the family honour, and then, being too poor to pay the bride-price of another wife, lived alone. Divorcing the wife also ensured that the husband ran no risk of having a feud with either her brother or her lover's family. The Highlanders held similar views—the husband could not question his wife or tell her lover not to come to the house; he could again do nothing but lie in wait until he caught them. A few Highlanders held that the husband might inform her people of her misconduct; if they believed him, they would say, 'Kill her', or perhaps kill her themselves; in either case her death went unavenged. They preferred to kill such a wife for they were Catholics in the main, and as such could not remarry if they divorced their wife. As it was permissible in Martanesh to kill the guilty pair separately, an adulterous wife was never divorced but always killed. If a woman was divorced in Mat, her brother always asked what wrong she had done; if she had been an adulteress, he killed her, provided that the husband first killed the lover. In north-east Albania, if the lover was the husband's brother, divorce was thought the easiest way out. Only an exceptionally brutal man would kill his brother; the average man would prefer to say to his wife, 'You have committed this sin, and are divorced'.

If the husband killed only his wife, her brother avenged her death in most cases; without seeing his sister dead by her lover's side he was unwilling to believe in her guilt and apt to think the husband had killed her out of ill-will. After her brother had killed a male from his house, the husband would kill both her brother and her lover; then peace would be made between all three families. In Martanesh and Lumë if the husband did not kill the lover as well, the wife's brother, when threatening vengeance, would say, 'You killed the bitch; why didn't you kill the dog also?'

Sometimes a husband had not the courage or the heart to kill his wife; then perhaps his people killed her. Or perhaps he sent word to her father that he had found her sinning and asked him to kill her. But the father generally replied to such husbands, 'Kill her yourself, because I gave her to you to look after'. If the wife suspected this interchange of messages, she might run away to her father. In that case her husband sent him word saying, 'Either kill that bitch or see me destroy you root and branch'. The father then either killed her or sent her to her husband to kill. If the father protected the wife, a blood feud began between him and the husband, for the latter could not bear the world to think that he had swallowed such a disgrace.

In Martanesh, it should be noted, it was permissible, as it was not elsewhere, to kill the lover and the wife separately, if they could not be found together. This seems to have been the case in Dibër also. About 1916 a man in Vleshjë (Dibër) found his wife unfaithful and killed the lover. The wife ran away, but the husband caught her, poured paraffin on her, and burned her alive, yet seems to have escaped her brother's vengeance.

If the outraged husband killed only the lover, then he had to fear vengeance from the lover's family. In Lumë on the principle that 'vengeance is not abandoned because of guilt', vengeance was sometimes taken by a 'bad' brother for a man killed in adultery. He might kill the husband, forgive him, or demand blood money.

A gruesome story of collective punishment of a guilty pair comes from Martanesh. About 1912 a young man was caught with a young wife. The 'circle' of the young man took him and the 'circle' of the wife took her out to an appointed spot where they stood them up together. The youth's uncle shot him dead, and the girl's brother shot her, while the drums beat and the other men danced. The honour of the two families being thus cleared, they buried the two close together, but in separate graves, at cross-roads; no hoxha was present to commit them to the grave, nor were they washed and changed. In the neighbouring Zdrâjshë also a guilty couple were buried in any sort of hole, but in separate graves, without a hoxha or being washed on boards and changed. In Lumë other customs prevailed. Both were buried in the cemetery in the ordinary way, unless they had been caught outside in some wood or thicket, in which case they were buried where they were killed.

Public opinion is growing against such double murders. It was too often the custom to give young girls to old men, with the inevitable result that the young wives were apt to fall in love with men more of their own age and had therefore to be killed by their fathers.

At Zdrâjshë, when a bride was found on marriage to be pregnant by another man, the unusually mild divorced her at once, but the general rule was to have her killed. The groom locked up the bride, sent for her father, and bade him find her lover. The father always asked for three or four days' respite during which he made inquiries. If the bride had indeed done wrong, an honest father sought out and killed the lover and then came to shoot his own daughter. Or perhaps he gave the bridegroom a cartridge and bade him shoot her with it. All the principles involved are well illustrated by a story from Lurë, still the most undisciplined of all Albanian tribes. About 1928 Metë Hoti, having taken a bride from Vehib Runa in Gur, found her within three months of bearing a child by another man. He sent her back to her father, bidding him find the lover and kill them both. The father would not kill his daughter and persisted in his refusal in spite of Metë's threats to kill the whole family if he did not do so. The father's kinsmen supported Metë, and when he came one night and killed the father, mother, daughter and infant and four other people in the house, they refused to avenge these deaths because the father had transgressed against the unwritten law. For the same reason the government merely imprisoned Metë for a few months.

A woman might be killed for various reasons by a man in her husband's or her father's family. For example, her husband or his representative had leave to kill her for heinous crimes like adultery, incorrigible pilfering, or murdering one of his relatives, but if they killed her for any other reason, her father killed one of them. Two principles were involved: one, that a man bought only the services of his wife and not her life; the other, that a woman retained till her dying day her right to protection by her father's family. Her son by the murderer could not avenge her, because killing his father, his only means of doing so, was forbidden. Her son by another husband, belonging as he did to another family, was free to avenge her. If a woman's son killed her for any but the above heinous crimes, her husband could not avenge her, since to do so he must kill his son. In Mirditë her brother could kill her son or other male in his family, but elsewhere it was held that her brother was as helpless as her husband because her son was a nearer relative and her nearest relative having killed her, her blood must be lost. If she was married for the second time and was killed by the son of her former marriage, her husband could kill his stepson, but as before, her brother's hands were tied, except in Mirditë, by the law of nearest relative.

When a man killed his brother's wife for any other reason than those stated above, her husband took no action if he and the murderer had not separated; the murder was a family affair. Her brother, however, killed one of them. If the two brothers had separated, the murderer had to pay blood money to her husband. If the husband did not exact it within a year, her brother killed either the murderer or her husband. Her husband never killed his brother: 'I'd never kill my brother for the sake of my wife', was a common saying.

When a woman was killed by her father or brother, her blood was always lost by the rule of nearest relative. If she was married, her husband did not, in most districts, continue friendly relations with the murderer, but in some, such as Krasniqë, he asked him for another girl and on receiving her forgot his annoyance at the other's murder. The same was true if the murdered woman was only betrothed, for a betrothed girl 'is counted the man's wife'. When a woman was killed by some other man in her own family, by her uncle or her nephew for instance, by the rule of nearest relative her blood was lost if she was neither married nor betrothed. If she was either and was not killed for a heinous crime, her husband felt he had been disgraced and avenged her by killing a male in her family.

When murders were committed by women, the situation was complicated by the fact that women belonged to two families, their husband's and their father's.

If a woman murdered her husband, both his family and her father's were involved. The important factor was her motive, which was usually love for another man who had probably bought the necessary rat poison in the bazaar. If her lover was her husband's brother, she married him and her husband's blood was lost exactly as if he had died by his brother's hand. If her lover was an outsider, her husband's brother killed her. He had the right to do so, woman though she was, for a question of honour was involved, and for questions of honour women might lawfully be put to death. Her son by the dead man could not kill the murderess because matricide is not allowable. Her husband's son by another wife was under no such inhibition, for he was only her stepson and therefore no relative. If her father's family believed in her adulterous motive, they sent a cartridge to her husband's brother, thereby signifying that they gave him leave to kill her and would not avenge her death. If they did not believe in the alleged motive, they avenged her by killing a man in her husband's family and an unusually bitter feud resulted.

Sometimes her husband's brother was too high-spirited or too angry to rest content with killing the murderess and killed one of her male relatives as well; he would plead that a woman's blood could never equal a man's and that her male relatives were responsible for her misdeeds. Sometimes a murderess escaped alive to her father's house. In that case she was held to have escaped from the suzerainty of her husband's family and became a stranger; as a stranger she must expiate her crime, but her sex shielded her personally and threw the onus of expiation on her male relatives— 'Women don't have blood feuds'. Her husband's brother was therefore bound to kill one of her relatives. To avoid losing a male for his daughter's crime her father sometimes killed her himself, a desperate act that always satisfied her husband's brother.

A woman rarely murdered any other man than her husband. If she did murder her brother, it was assumed that it had happened by accident as he was her surest protector. There are no records of the murder of father or paternal uncle by a woman.

The last category of murders within the family includes the very rare cases in which a woman murdered a woman in her husband's or her father's family. If she murdered her mother or her daughter, both most unlikely contingencies if she were sane, the victim's blood was lost by law of nearest relative. In all other cases the result depended on whether her victim was single or married. Thus the murder of her unmarried sister, paternal aunt, brother's daughter, counted as a suicide and the victim's blood was lost. If she murdered her husband's sister, the victim's blood was again lost because the only possible avenger was the woman's husband, who was not likely to kill the wife, who had cost him good money, for the sake of his sister, though he was more likely to do so for the sake of his father or brother. If she murdered a married woman of her own kin, her victim's husband exacted blood money from the males of her family or perhaps another girl. If she murdered a married woman in her husband's kin, his brother's wife, for example, or her own brother's wife, her victim's brother exacted blood money or even a life from the males in her family.

When a woman killed the wife of her husband's brother, her victim's husband had to suffer the loss of his chattel in silence. He could not kill the murderess because a man might not kill his brother's wife for any reason other than adultery or thieving. Nor could he kill her husband because a man might not kill his own brother. In his default his wife was avenged by her brother, who might kill either him or his brother if they were not separated, but only him if they were. Whatever the issue, her sex saved the murderess from expiating her crime.

When a woman killed her mother-in-law or her daughter-in-law, her sex again saved her from expiating the crime. Her victim's brother was the only possible avenger, for no member of her husband's family could kill the murderess for anything except adultery and thieving. The avenger could kill any male in the family of the murderess; the marriage relationship did not count.

CHAPTER XXII

BLOOD FEUD

I. FAMILY VENGEANCE AND COLLECTIVE VENGEANCE

To understand the fabric of the Albanian blood feud it is essential to remember several things. Till after the 1914–18 war communications in Albania were so bad, government centres so few and the gendarmerie so ill-organized that communities were largely self-governing. These communities consisted in the narrower sense of the family, and in the wider sense of the tribe. If a person was injured, the family in most cases, and the tribe in a few cases, by the law of self-government punished the wrongdoer. Since the individual was almost completely submerged in his family, an injury to him was an injury to the whole family and might be punished by any of its members. When the tribal community was involved, the injury might again be avenged by any of its members. When the injury took the form of murder, vengeance generally took the Mosaic form of a life for a life, but sometimes was achieved by the exaction of blood money or the imposition of exile.

When the family of a murdered man, in default of government action, took the punishment of the murderer into its own hands and killed him or one of his male relatives, the head of his family might admit that both sides were equal and make peace. On the other hand, while still admitting that both sides were equal he might prefer to continue the feud by killing a second male from the avenging family; that done, a second life was forfeit on his side. In this way the feud might rage backwards and forwards for years or even generations, each family being in turn murderer and victim, hunter and hunted. 'To take vengeance' was 'to take the blood' (that is, of the man already killed, not of him who was to make atonement); the criminal was called 'the bloodstained', and avenger and criminal thought of each other as the 'enemy'. In north Albania the criminal was also called the 'agent' and the avenger the 'master of the blood of the victim', i.e. the master of the house in which the victim lived. 'To incur a feud' was 'to fall into blood' or 'enmity'.

This simple outline was filled in with all manner of elaborate details; vengeance could not be taken indiscriminately, but was governed by a multiplicity of rules. Thus, a murdered man found his most natural avenger in his brother, especially if they had not separated. If his father was not too old, and his son too young, to bear arms, they shared the brother's obligation. In slightly less degree so did his father's brother and cousin in the male line, and their sons and grandsons, that is to say, all the other males who were in the collective sense his 'father', 'brother' and 'son', through being at the time, or having recently been, members of his household. If his son was in the cradle, the child's mother and the neighbours told him of the crime as he grew up and urged him, failing another avenger, not to rest till he had done his duty. No matter which of these relatives took revenge, his 'rifle could be hung up' and 'go to sleep', to quote the picturesque phrases of Dibër and the North. The lawful representative of his murdered kinsman because he belonged to the same household, he had only made the two sides equal, with one of two results; either peace could be made or the feud continued between the same two families.

A man might kill his enemy where and when he could—in a chance encounter, in a meeting deliberately sought or in a carefully laid ambush. If he was 'strong' with plenty of good shots in his house, he and his family went alone on set expeditions. If he was weak he was probably accompanied by friends, who included friends in the ordinary sense, relatives by marriage, dependants and servants. They came, not for pay, but on his invitation or of their own accord. Invitations, always verbal, requested the recipients to come with so many rifles to such-and-such a place by such-and-such a day and hour. Those invited were bound to come; those who volunteered were praised by the public for their bravery and devotion, a much coveted distinction. The distance from which they came was immaterial; a feud had no geographical limits.

If the enemy fell to the rifle of a friend, the shot was always credited to the 'master', who was expected to assume responsibility for it. The enemy accepted the kill as a bout in the feud and either made peace or continued the feud with his original antagonist. The friend who fired the fatal shot could 'hang up his rifle' and let it 'go to sleep'; he did not need its protection for he was quit of the affair. If he had been alone when he killed the man, he would have 'brought the feud home', i.e. involved himself in a separate feud with the victim's family while leaving his friend's feud unaffected.

In a few cases vengeance was lawfully taken by men who were not, strictly speaking, members of the victim's family. Theoretically, the man who had 'drunk blood' with the victim[1] and so had become his foster-brother could not go alone to avenge him, for he had not been an actual member of his household. In Lumë and Labinot such a man was held to the letter of the law, and could take vengeance only when accompanied by the victim's 'brother'; taking it when alone involved him in a separate feud with the murderer, with no benefit to the victim's family. In many other districts it was recognized that great love must have existed between the two men before they swore blood-brotherhood, and in virtue of that love one could, even when alone, lawfully avenge the other. In Dibër, indeed, he had no choice but to do so, and often outstripped a brother by birth. In Shkrel such vengeance has been taken 'five hundred times'. On the other hand, a compromise was the rule in western Mat. Solitary vengeance by a foster-brother was theoretically as unlawful as in Lumë, but in practice it was generally legalized by the 'master' of the feud, who sent the foster-brother a cartridge and so recognized him after the event as his emissary. Wherever foster-brothers had the right to take solitary vengeance, they seem to have derived it from their community of blood with the victim. For only those united by the drinking of blood possessed the right; those united by any other ceremony, by hair-cutting, for instance, were denied it. And in districts where they had the right, one could not go alone to avenge any relative of the other's. During their lifetime each regarded the other's relatives as father, brother, etc., and was regarded by them as son and brother, but when one was killed, the other ranked as an alien by blood and household and could only avenge his foster-brother by joining an expedition led by their 'master'. And almost everywhere blood-brotherhood was recognized as a complete bar to marriage between the two families.

Relations on the female side could always avenge a murdered man by joining an expedition led by his 'master'. Opinions differed about their right to avenge him when alone. Shkrel, the Malësi e Madhe generally, and Labinot held to the logical view. A sister's son, they said, although called 'nephew' like a brother's son, belonged to his father's family and was an outsider in his mother's. He had, therefore, no right, joint expeditions apart, to

[1] I.e. had sworn blood-brotherhood with him.

avenge or to be avenged by his maternal 'uncle', that is to say, the males in his mother's family. The two men belonged to different households, and if one attempted independently to avenge the other, he meddled in business that was no concern of his and so could only involve himself in a separate feud. The men of Shkrel in the Malësi e Madhe who felt so little duty towards their maternal 'uncle' that they would entertain his murderer were therefore within their rights. On the other hand, in central and east Albania— in Çermenikë, Dibër, Kurbin, Lumë and Martanesh—it was held that a man could not avenge his maternal 'uncle' but could be avenged by him, a law said in Kurbin to have been of Skanderbeg's making. As a corollary, if a native of these districts did avenge his maternal 'uncle', he plumed himself on the deed more than a nephew in the male line could have done; the latter, as a member of the dead family, could not escape the obligation and would not have been involved in a new feud as he, the outsider, had been.

The confused practice is locally explained as follows: A man could not avenge his maternal 'uncle' because he was the son of his mother and she as a woman had no rifle, presumably to hand on to him with all its offensive and defensive possibilities; the rifle he carried came to him as a member of his father's family. On the other hand, he could be avenged by his maternal 'uncle' for the same reason that the latter was entitled, when his 'sister's' daughter was married, to receive a 'maternal uncle's fee' at the time of the wedding and, if she was afterwards killed, to avenge her. For the maternal 'uncle' regarded his 'sister's' children as his own and as part of his own household; in Kurbin, indeed, a man owned a quarter share in his 'sister's' son. Further, since a woman could not carry a rifle, a 'sister' could not defend herself, and therefore, retained the right for herself and her children to be protected by her 'brother'. In Dibër, where rich and powerful men were so few that girls must often be given in marriage to men who were neither, this feeling that 'sisters' and their issue might require protection was pronounced.

In south Albania, on the other hand, a man would both avenge and be avenged by his maternal 'uncle'. A classic instance of the former process at Melesinë near Leskovik is commemorated in the song beginning:

> Melesinë on a hill,
> For his uncle fights a sister's son.

This want of restrictions may be attributed, partly to the smaller emphasis which south Albanians lay on descent in the male line, partly to the greater store which, probably under Greek influence, they set on relationships in general. North Albanians, when sent to work in south Albania, always expressed lively astonishment when they found, for instance, a southerner claiming as a relative a man who was only the brother of his wife's brother.

It occasionally happens that a young widow with a son remarried in another family, who probably lived in another village or even district, and had a son by her second husband. Almost without exception the son by her first husband remained with his father's family, so that the two boys grew up apart. Even if the first son accompanied his mother on her remarriage, he had at an early age to return to his father's family. There never was any doubt that the two boys belonged to different households. They recognized each other as brothers, however, and if one was killed, the other had as much right as a full brother on the father's side to avenge him. But if either wished to avenge another male in the other's household, he could only do so by joining an expedition led by the master of that household; he could not do so independently, for except to his half-brother he was an outsider.

'Women do not have rifles' ran the Kanùn. As a corollary 'Women do not have blood feuds', it continued. One result of these Kanùns was that women could not properly avenge their murdered relatives. It was also recognized that they were generally too timorous to do so. A few 'strong characters', however, had been known to lay aside their feminine fears and to kill an enemy. Thus the virgin Emin of Orenjë in Çermenikë avenged her father. When he was killed she was still in the cradle and as she grew up she became aware that her four cousins, the only males left in the family, did not show too much zeal in avenging him. When she was fifteen, she secretly bought a rifle and, seeing the enemy one day come within range of the windows of her home, she fired at him and killed him with the third shot. Then her cousins were trebly annoyed. She, a woman, had proved herself their superior in courage; for her crime one of their lives was forfeit; and they had hoped to compound the feud without further bloodshed, a hope she had destroyed. In fact, she had embittered the feud by putting the enemy to the shame of losing a relative at a woman's hands. Again, a woman from Tërbaç, near Elbasan, hearing that her son had been killed at a third person's instigation, took his revolver and killed the instigator. Unfortunately for her, the date was about 1923 when a modern government was already functioning; she was arrested and tried for murder, but in view of the circumstances she was condemned to no more than a year and a half's imprisonment. The public were astonished to find that the government had punished a woman on much the same terms as a man.

Assuming that a woman could steel herself to murder anyone, it is natural to find her avenging her father, son or brother. Given primitive Albanian ideas about the proprieties between husband and wife, and the feeling that the wife remained a member of her father's household, it is somewhat surprising to find one avenging her husband. A woman of western Mat went one day to the bazaar and there saw the man who had murdered her husband. In spite of the press of people she drew a revolver and shot him dead; as she had come provided with the weapon, there is little doubt that she did not act on the spur of the moment. About 1883 Fatime Almetaj, a woman born in Kostejë near Martanesh and married in Përvall, was busy baking one day while her husband talked to a neighbour. On hearing a gunshot she rushed out to find her husband already dead and the neighbour running away. She ran inside, seized her husband's rifle and again rushed out. The neighbour had already reached his own doorstep when she fired. As soon as she saw him fall dead, she re-entered her house and resumed her baking; her husband had been avenged, there were others in the family to feed, and the dough was getting cold. In neither of these cases do records show whose life the enemy took in return for the one she had taken; by right it should have been one of the males in her husband's family.

In certain cases both the avenger and the expiator of a murder might be drawn from outside the household directly concerned. For instance, if a murderer and his brother were separated, the avenger might kill the latter while his blood was boiling, a period estimated in Dibër at one hour and in Mirditë and elsewhere at twenty-four hours. When his blood had cooled he must not molest the separated brother, and might be required to find a guarantor that he would not do so. Conversely, a man separated from his murdered brother might avenge him during the regulation period, but not afterwards.

Sometimes the rule of 'boiling blood' was extended to larger units. For twenty-four hours after a murder in Lumë, a district peopled by little groups of kinsmen, any man of the victim's kin might avenge him on any man of the criminal's kin. So long as members of this group survived no other would move. If they were killed off, other groups, beginning with the nearest neighbours, might seek vengeance. Within living memory this licence found dreadful expression in Theth, the beautiful northern part of Shalë. About 1890 a man who lost a lamb promised to give a cartridge to a shepherd if he found it. When the shepherd succeeded, the man went back on his promise saying he would 'give him five'(sc. fingers on the trigger) instead. For the moment the shepherd let the matter drop, but later met the man and asked once more for his promised reward. Again the man refused it, not too courteously, and was immediately killed by the incensed shepherd. Unfortunately, it was Easter Sunday and the murder took place in a meadow where all the men of Theth were gathered for the festival. Immediately the dead man's *vllazni* (brotherhood), comprising all the males descended from the same ancestor, sought vengeance on the murderer's brotherhood. These were not backward in replying, and within an hour fourteen men lay dead for the sake of one cartridge.

Whole tribes might be affected by the rule of 'boiling blood'. In the Malësi e Madhe if a Kastrati tribesman killed a Koplik man, any member of the latter tribe had licence for 24 hours to kill any man from Kastrati. The murderer was, therefore, bound to announce his crime at once so that his fellow-tribesmen might take cover. The time limit elapsed, vengeance lay as usual between the two households. In such cases of inter-tribal aggression each tribe became temporarily a single family in which each member represented the whole.

In Çermenikë, kinsfolk were sometimes fused into one family, not by boiling blood as described above, but by a particularly atrocious murder such as that of a guest by his host, when 'circle after circle' was the rule. The guest's 'circle', consisting of his own household, his kinsmen in separate homes, his neighbours and the sons of the married daughters of his family, wherever these last might live, tried to kill the murderer, and failing to find him or other members of his household, they might kill one of his 'circle'. On succeeding, they held that they had avenged their relative's death, and their victim's family agreed. In other districts they

15   H A M

would have found themselves involved in a new feud with the household of the man they had killed, but by the local rule of 'circle after circle' he died as proxy for the real criminal and no new feud entered into the question. There seems to have been no time limit to their extended vengeance.

National solidarity was recognized in the debatable border lands where Slav and Albanian lived side by side. If an Albanian was killed by a Slav, any Albanian would kill any Slav in revenge. The crime, it was felt, had pitted the Albanian family against the Slav family. This national sentiment was so strong that though there has never been any love lost between Gegs (north Albanians) and Tosks (south Albanians), no Geg would allow a Slav to kill a Tosk without seeking in return to kill any Slav he could find. The less warlike Tosks did not feel a similar impulse. If one of their number or a Geg were killed by their Bulgarian or Greek neighbours, they left vengeance to the victim's family.

The community also acted as a single family when certain public servants were killed. If the victim were a Roman Catholic priest, he might lawfully be avenged by his parish, the tribe in which the parish lay, and his own family. If action were taken by the parish or tribe, the matter ended. The avenger's act closed the feud, and, fearing no retribution, he could hang up his rifle. If the priest's family afterwards killed another of the murderer's men, they began a new feud. Generally the family did not wait for the parish or the tribe to act. When a Mohammedan or an Orthodox priest was killed, it fell to his relatives to avenge the crime; the feeling that sacrilege had been committed was too slight to drive their parishioners into action.

If a field-guard of Lumë were killed, he was publicly avenged. If the murderer was from another village, any of the field-guard's fellow villagers could lawfully kill any man from the murderer's village during the first twenty-four hours, and afterwards he could kill the murderer or any other man in his household. In either case he could hang up his rifle. If the field-guard were killed by a fellow-villager, the village expelled the murderer. On the other hand, if a miller were killed, vengeance rested with his family; the village could not act. A field-guard was a public necessity; without his services the village economy would suffer, and he must be given public protection. A miller had taken up his work for the sake of private gain and was not a public necessity; if he were not at the mill, the villagers themselves could work it; the miller was therefore not entitled to public protection. The village blacksmith, with few exceptions a gipsy, was in even worse case than the miller. He was a public necessity, since Albanian peasants will not make horse shoes or farm implements, but he was only a gipsy and no Albanian community would trouble about so low-class a creature. If he was murdered, only his family would avenge him, and they probably lacked the spirit to do so.

CHAPTER XXIII

BLOOD FEUD

II. COURSE OF THE FEUD

The fatal shot fired, a murderer's life was in such instant danger from the avenger that it behoved him to fly with all speed. But often his 'blood seized him' so that 'his legs gave way under him' and he was rooted to the spot from shock. Custom therefore prescribed in Shkodër, Lumë and Godolesh that he must drop on the ground a cartridge or an article of clothing such as his fez, sash, or handkerchief; in Elbasan, Shpat and Çermenikë that he must lick the muzzle of his rifle or pistol; alternatively, in Elbasan that he must inhale the smoke of the gunpowder or let his comrades slap his face; in Labinot that he must hold the cartridge case in his mouth and bite his little finger and suck the blood, and in Mat that he must eat a little gunpowder. That done successfully, 'his blood was set free', 'the seizure passed', and he was able to run away.

When an article of clothing was left behind, it served to identify the murderer; where none was left, word had to be sent to the victim's family. It was everywhere 'held dishonourable' to kill and not to tell. It was also thought unfair for reasons that varied with the locality. In Mirditë the victim's relatives might go mad if they did not know the identity of the murderer; in north Albania the murderer's kinsmen would not know to hide while the avenger's blood was boiling; in south Albania the crime might be laid at the wrong door. Besides, the normal murder was matter for boasting; committed only to avenge some wrong or insult, it showed that the murderer was spirited enough to resent ill-treatment.

Latterly, when the government was attempting to repress murder, the murderer, certain of arrest, left no token and did not inform the relatives. The community, however, was always on the watch and from its members' observation of those who came from the direction of the shots and from their knowledge of the whereabouts of the victim's enemies at the time, the murderer's identity was established—at all events to the satisfaction of the community.

In the early days of a feud the father or brother of the victim might in his furious rage kill the murderer and shoot a second time

at the lifeless corpse. When the feud was older, it was not permitted
to kill and shoot again. A murderer seldom looked at the corpse,
a fact which gave men quick-witted enough to feign death a chance
to escape. In some places, such as Mirditë, the murderer was
expected to turn the dead man in the right direction for one of his
religion—with his head towards the east if Christian, whether
Catholic or Orthodox, towards Mecca if Mohammedan, and to
rest his rifle against his head; if unable to touch him, he had to tell
the first man he met to attend to those matters. In Shpat the
murderer left the cartridge-case by his victim, allegedly not to
'set his own blood free', as in Lumë, but to avoid carrying away
a thing that was unlucky because stained with blood and sin. In
Mat and the Malësi e Madhe, the murderer's own life being in
grave danger from the avenger, it was thought 'brave' to tread in
the victim's blood as a last insult.

A murderer must not rob his victim; he had killed him only to
defend his honour and not to enrich himself. As was popularly said,
'low-class fellows' take a man's rifle, watch, money or clothes;
'good-class men' take only vengeance. In some places sanctions
reinforced public disapproval of the robber-murderer. In Lumë
he saddled himself with one and a half feuds, i.e. the need to pay for
the murder with blood money as well as a life; in Mirditë, where
he was expected to lay the dead man's rifle against his head, he
incurred two feuds. Certain exceptions to the rule were admitted.
A murderer could everywhere, except in Mirditë, take his victim's
rifle to prove that he 'had really trodden in his blood', but he must
afterwards send the weapon to the family. On similar terms he
might take the dead man's watch also. When the murderer was
a hired assassin, he commonly took a token from his victim, usually
his cap, to prove to his paymaster that he had earned his money.
When a man's enemy lived at a distance, he might again take his
cap to prove to his own friends and neighbours that he had killed
him. Robbery of the corpse by a third person was not to be feared;
since everybody within range, the dead man's relatives included,
rushed up at the sound of the shot, there was publicity enough to
prevent such an outrage. As for the supernatural dangers thought
to beset the bodies of persons dead in ordinary circumstances, it
was well known that Satan feared a rifle too much to approach the
body of the murdered man.

When describing how Albanian men used to shave their heads

except for a tuft on the crown, as a few old men and young boys still do, the Highlanders of north Albania asserted that a murderer had licence to cut off his victim's head. The tuft, they said, was left so that an enemy might conveniently carry the head when he cut it off; failing such a handle, he would thrust his finger into the dead man's mouth, an intolerable insult. The veracity of this story appears doubtful, since although the Highlanders, Slavs, and Turks all cut off heads, Albanians as far inland as Elbasan shaved their head save for the tuft on the crown, and it is unlikely that all anticipated murder by Slavs or Turks. Whatever the purpose, the tuft was not confined to Albanians, but was seen in 1926 worn by small boys in the Turkish villages in south Serbia where the population was of mixed Turkish and Bulgarian stock.

A murderer usually announced his crime to the victim's family by a crude message to fetch him from such-and-such a place and bury him. He was always expected to surrender the body, but if a feud was unusually bitter, the murderer might forbid the body to be buried in the cemetery in the ordinary way. If he was backed by enough men to make his ban effective, the body was buried in the secrecy of night. Sometimes he forbade it to be taken even at night to the cemetery; in that event it had to be buried elsewhere. A story comes from Sopot in Dibër. About 1893 Abas Kamber's enemy killed one of his men and forbade him to carry the body to the cemetery. Abas, strong though he was, could do nothing but bury it in the courtyard of his house. Just before it was lowered into the grave, the enemy repented and sent him leave to bury it in the cemetery. To show that he was not always prepared to do the enemy's bidding, Abas sent back the message that he would not dig up the body again and concluded that burial as it had begun.

Hiding the body was universally deprecated. When men stole a grazing cow, it was said they killed it, roasted and ate what they could of the meat and hid the remainder. But it was not to eat a man's flesh that they killed him and they must not conceal his body like the cow's. If they did, the feud was doubly embittered.

By rights a man was never buried where he was killed. Even if the spot were two days distant, or if, like Kol Mali's victim, he had lain three weeks undiscovered, he was carried home for burial. 'He had been theirs', his relatives said, and neither distance nor a natural repugnance could prevent them from doing their duty by him. In the northern mountains, in Mirditë and in Kurbin, a heap of stones was made where he was killed; on this every passer-by was expected to throw a green leaf, a blade of grass or a pebble while expressing a wish for the repose of his soul. In Shkrel, according to one informant, a stone was stuck at the head and another at the foot, as though the place was a real grave, but a *muranë* was not made. Any relatives who wished to mourn him went to his grave, not to the place where he had been killed. Exceptionally, what seem real graves may be seen near the meadows of Tërnovë above Zerqan; ten or twelve in number, each roughly outlined with stones, they are known as 'the murdered graves' and are said to contain the bodies of men who fell there in a long-past battle between the villages of Tërnovë and Sopot. Again exceptionally, when Muharrem Bajraktar of Lumë fled in 1934 to Yugoslavia, the Spahi family, his hereditary enemies, killed one of his servants. Muharrem said this man was not to be buried in Bicaj, his native village, but by the wayside where he fell, so that when he himself returned from exile he should see the grave and be reminded to take vengeance.

The ideal was to take vengeance as soon as possible. In Kurbin the piled stones served to make the dead man's kinsmen hasten to take vengeance, reminding them of his death and so 'heating their blood'. For the same purpose the Catholics of the north frequently buried the man in his blood-stained clothes; the Mohammedans, however, obedient to the dictum that all who profess their faith must go to the grave in a clean winding sheet, discarded this custom. A still stranger reminder of the need to take vengeance, a little bottle filled with the dead man's blood, was used all over north Albania and in Kosovë. This bottle the relatives looked at day and night. As soon as the blood 'boiled', i.e. fermented, they seized their rifles, cocked their skull-caps over one ear to show their determination, and rushed forth to kill the murderer. If the blood did not 'boil', they might accept a money indemnity instead of taking a life. In western Mat they dipped a rag in the dead man's blood; when it looked stained and brown, they knew the hour to avenge him had struck. None of these reminders was found as far south as Çermenikë and Shpat.

Public opinion also spurred the avenger on. A man slow to kill his enemy was thought 'disgraced' and was described as 'low-class' and 'bad'. Among the Highlanders he risked finding that other men had contemptuously come to sleep with his wife, his daughter could not marry into a 'good' family and his son must marry a 'bad' girl. As far south as Godolesh on the outskirts of Elbasan, he paid visits at his peril; his coffee cup was only half-filled, and before being handed to him it was passed under the host's left arm, or even his left leg, to remind him of his disgrace. He was often mocked openly.

All over north Albania it was permissible for the victim's kin to burn down the murderer's house. The veteran Mirash Nue of Vuksan in Shalë boasted that once he saved his house from this fate by sending a message to the avenger which ran: 'Spare the ashes on my hearth for the sake of the open house I've kept.' The avenger, touched by the reminder of Mirash's noted hospitality, yielded to the plea. In 1935 a Dibran took to the mountains after wounding a fellow-villager with whom he was at feud; on recovering, his victim did not dare to sleep at home in case he returned under cover of darkness to repair his bad marksmanship by setting fire to the house and burning him to death. In hot blood an avenger might in some places do as much material damage as possible to the murderer, burning his hay as well as his house, scything his ripening grain and harrowing over his growing maize. For fear of reprisals in kind he could nowhere harm his children or animals.

Burning down a murderer's house is said in Martanesh to have been a recent innovation, and in Dibër and Lumë to have been formerly much more common than in recent times. Various considerations suggest that the latter view is correct. The reason given in Lumë for the waning of the custom is that it grew progressively more serious as people abandoned the straw huts in which they once lived and built themselves stone houses; the huts were cheap and easy to rebuild, but the houses were not so easily replaced. With poverty as general and murder as frequent as they used to be, it is obvious that if burning the murderer's stone house and destroying his crops had been freely permitted, the life of the tribe could not have gone on. To restrict the attacks on property, sanctions were introduced. In Dibër an avenger guilty of incendiarism was banished in perpetuity by the community. In Krujë the crime was deprecated as doubly unwise; it might cause further deaths, so involving the avenger in further feuds, and women and children might be among the victims, in which case the avenger would be covered with disgrace. In Shpat an avenger who burned his enemy's house found the whole community against him as a man willing to burn women and children to death and to harm property; in Shpat property was so sacrosanct that one must not touch even 'the leaf of the leek' belonging to one's enemy.

When the community decided to burn out a man whom they had sentenced to banishment for committing a heinous murder, their numbers and their power to exclude him completely from the tribal life made it impossible for him to resist. It was otherwise with the victim's kin. For want of power to exclude the murderer from more than their own section of tribal life they could not make him submit tamely, and in their attempts to use force they were often baffled by the fire-resisting principles on which most mountain houses were built. With the walls of stone, only the roof and the outer door were inflammable, and with no matches available these could only be set alight by blazing brands, probably of pitch pine, brought from another house. If the murderer was a rich man, he lived in a house surrounded by a courtyard wide enough to keep incendiaries at a safe distance from both roof and doorway; one or two towers in the walls of the courtyard sufficiently protected its gateway. If the murderer was poor, his house had no courtyard. But like the rich man's, it consisted of two or more storeys, the stable on the ground floor and the living-rooms above. The roof was, therefore, too high for the avenger to throw firebrands among the rafters. The door was surmounted by machicoulis through which the defenders could shoot or pour boiling water, and loopholes at the corners of the living-rooms commanded the approaches; in cases of bitter feud the door was sometimes covered outside with tin plates. Windows in a stable being thought unnecessary, the door was the only break in the solid walls of the ground floor. Sometimes avengers who were weak in guns hired men to fire the murderer's house. These hirelings came especially from Mirditë, for Mirdites were notoriously brave enough to face the risk entailed and poor enough to think only of the money offered; this amounted to some thirty napoleons (£40 in the 1930's) per man.

When an avenger burned down the murderer's house in hot blood, his motive was to do the murderer as much damage as possible. When he burned it down in cold blood, his motive was to drive the murderer into the open to be shot at. A murderer not infrequently shut himself up in his house during the daytime and stirred outside only at night, so remaining beyond the avenger's reach. When his house was set on fire, he knew that if he remained inside the blazing building, his death was certain, and that if he came out, he had a sporting chance of escaping the avenger's bullets. He had, therefore, no choice but to leave the burning house. In the same way when gendarmes surrounded a house in which a desperate criminal was hidden, he preferred to run the gauntlet of their fire rather than wait tamely to be seized and led off perhaps to death as a menace to society. This was particularly true of Turkish times, when dangerous criminals were generally shot out of hand when arrested.

CHAPTER XXIV

BLOOD FEUD

III. EXPIATOR AND EXPIATION

In most cases of murder one life only was forfeit to the avenger; 'one for one' was the formula. This was irrespective of the social standing or the character of the victim. Hence the murder of a standard-bearer (bajraktar) was neither better nor worse than the murder of the least of clansmen, and that of a priest was neither better nor worse than that of a layman.

The formula of 'one for one' was disregarded only in a few cases. In Lumë, a district which prided itself on its 'spirit', 'two for one' was the rule when a man killed his social superior; nothing less would content his victim's injured pride. In most districts a man who suffered the more grievous forms of bereavement, losing his wife, guest or child at a murderer's hands, took double or even triple vengeance. In the Malësi e Madhe the victim's family, if 'strong' with all the pride that the epithet denotes, might kill two of the murderer's relatives if they found them together, though not otherwise. Spiro Toli of Shënjon, near Elbasan, a man as proud as any Lumjan of his 'spirit', felt so degraded when his brother was killed by a hireling at another's bidding, and that hireling a gipsy, that he killed both the instigator and the hireling. Pride, of course, was the ruling motive in every blood feud. By his successful crime the murderer had proved himself the better man, and the victim could not endure this inferiority and was bound to strike back in kind.

The person of the expiator seems to have undergone an historical development. Long ago, 'blood feuds went by the finger', that is to say, only the actual murderer, the man whose finger had pulled the trigger, was made to expiate his crime. Father Gjeçov aptly compares Deuteronomy xxiv, 16. In modern times the merging of the individual in his family was stressed as in the case of the avenger, and expiation might be made by any male who lived in the same house as the murderer and was in either the actual or classificatory sense his 'father', 'brother' or 'son'.

This rule was subject to several important reservations. The man killed in the murderer's stead must not be too old, feeble-minded, or physically frail to carry arms, for such men were counted women, and women could not be killed in blood feuds. If the avenger killed such a man, he lost caste, was publicly branded as 'low-class' and made it certain that the feud would not be closed. It was also illegal to kill boys who were still too young to carry arms, that is to say, under fifteen or in some cases twenty. In the Malësi e Madhe, however, it was held that one must take vengeance where one could, and that in default of an adult enemy one might kill a boy. Even in that region such a crime was not committed except by a very bad man or one who was frenzied with rage at the recent murder of a relative or otherwise. For instance, in 1933 a subaltern of the Alije family, whose wife had been carried off by another Dibran, refrained for some years from avenging the insult in the way demanded by mountain law. Taunted with this restraint at a chance meeting in a café, he put aside the civilization acquired during his military education in Albania and in Italy and rushed for his revolver. As he was unable to find the man who had taunted him, he lay in wait for the latter's schoolboy son, aged fourteen, and shot him dead.

The men of Shalë said that vengeance on a boy was commoner in Pult than in their own tribe; the men of Pult, they added contemptuously, were in every way their inferiors. Much the same was said by the tribesmen of Lurë of their neighbours in Mirditë and Kthellë, who returned the compliment in kind. In Lumë a man who took such vengeance was never again given the greeting 'Peace be with thee', which is every good Mohammedan's due from his fellows. The manner of such vengeance was inevitably very brutal. Thus two men from Shlak, when working in Bardhanjol, found the small son of their enemy and tore him in two; they are said not to have troubled to kill him first. More often the enemy wrenched the cradle off a woman's back and in her presence cut the infant's throat. A particularly nasty case was reported about 1932 from Shalë, one of the most backward regions of Albania. While two families were quarrelling about a piece of land, the wife of Grimës one day voiced her opinions so volubly in Gjelosh's house that he lost his temper and pushed her out. She fell down some steps by the door and bruised her hip. She showed the bruise to the gendarmerie, who were sympathetic enough to arrest Gjelosh and to imprison him for three months. The woman, who cared more for the violation of her honour by the push than for the bruise, was not satisfied and instigated her son, a boy of twelve or thirteen, to vindicate her honour by killing Gjelosh's son, who was of the same age. Since the boys habitually herded their goats together, her son found an opportunity of pushing the other boy over a rock and as he lay there helpless he stoned him till he died. Then Gjelosh, still in prison, paid a man to kill the little murderer. Grimës retorted by killing Gjelosh's remaining son and dooming Gjelosh's family to extinction.

Two instances, both from Beshkash in western Mat, in which a child was killed by a woman in revenge for the death of a relative, are recorded. In the first (about 1918) the only son of Pushko Zefi of Beshkash had been killed, and the cousins, who were his natural avengers, did not seem inclined to do their duty. Maddened by their inaction, the victim's sister, who was married in Perlat, took the opportunity provided by a visit to her old home and called at the enemy's house. On being left alone for a moment with a small boy in the kitchen, she cut his throat. Another woman in Beshkash, crazed by the murder of her grown-up son by Pal Dede Hajo, went to Pal's house and cut off the head of a little boy she found asleep in his cradle.

Since women do not have rifles or blood feuds according to the Kanùn, a woman could not possibly be killed to avenge a murder. It follows that when a woman avenged a murdered relative, she could not be killed in return, and indeed this did not happen very often. The tabu on killing a woman in any circumstances was reinforced by all the forces of public opinion and superstition. Killing a woman save when taken in adultery or incorrigible pilfering was the most disgraceful thing that an Albanian could do. Only one who came from 'a low-class family' would do it, he never again had any luck with his rifle and he could not hope to have his crime pardoned, but must wash away his crime with his blood. He need pay with only one life, but if his victim was a married woman, he could hardly hope to save it, for two or even three families sought to take it. The dead woman's husband wished to avenge his wife, her father his daughter, and, in Martanesh, her maternal uncle his niece. At Shënjon, near Elbasan, the father asked the husband if he meant to kill the enemy; if from cowardice or weakness he said no, the father at once set about tracking down the enemy. Since 'rifles can't weigh'—that is, discriminate—a woman was sometimes shot accidentally in a man's stead in spite of the tabu. In that unhappy event in Kurbin a woman in the murderer's family might be killed in return. If, too, a feud was unusually bitter, as was, for instance, the Kaloshi family one in Dibër, all barriers of law and disgrace were thrown down; 'kill at all costs' was the order of the day, and in its execution women and children were as likely as men to suffer.

This tabu on killing women had several sources. In the first place, a woman was 'a sack for carrying' things, i.e. she was the vehicle by which a family was carried on, and killing her might mean the loss of more than one man to her husband's family. Then she carried no arms, and therefore was classed with old men, children, and lunatics as safe from an avenger. Again, she was always regarded as an article of property, belonging in her maiden days to her father and afterwards to her husband; her father had the right to her work till she married, and her husband afterwards; in token of this work her father sold her dear, and her husband bought her dear. Articles of property could not be damaged in the course of blood feuds. There was also the feeling that it was a disgrace for a 'strong' man to kill anything so inferior as a woman.

The tabu on killing women was so strong that when one committed a murder, not she but one of the males in the family expiated the crime, if expiation were possible. Murders by women fell into two categories, the first outside and the second inside the family. In both cases the murderess might commit the crime on her own account or butt into a men's quarrel to avenge a murdered relative.

One more class of expiator remains to be considered. It sometimes happened that a man hired an outsider to kill his enemy. In the Breg i Matit some held that such a man was a 'witch', and since witches could not have blood feuds, he must go scot-free and his hireling suffer, like any other murderer. In most places, if the instigator could not be discovered, or if time was passing without vengeance being taken on him, the hireling was killed. These practices were exceptional, and in general the feud was credited to the principal rather than to the subordinate who fired the fatal shot.

Vanity as well as justice came into the question, for the instigator was usually a more important person than his instrument, and killing him brought the avenger more glory.

If expiation took the form of blood money, no distinction was made for age; the payment for a worn-out man of eighty or an able-bodied man of thirty was the same as for a boy of five or an infant of a few weeks. As when a life was taken for a life, no distinction was made for social standing or moral character; the payment for a bajraktar was the same as for a labourer. A female's 'blood', however, cost only half a male's. In the early days when these payments were determined, money was so distributed that the rich had a great deal, while the poor, who formed the bulk of the population, were all but penniless. The fear of having to pay a large sum in blood money was therefore a considerable deterrent against murder.

Blood money was accepted only in Mirditë and north Albania. Elsewhere it was scorned. 'Blood money and bride-price do you no good', said Lumë. 'We don't sell blood for money; that is a low thing to do', said Çermenikë, a boast repeated in Dibër in even stronger terms. In Labinot and Godolesh blood could not be washed away with money on the north Albanian system. In all these districts the formula after a murder was 'either pardon or kill'.

It must be admitted that neither lived up to its pretensions, the north being more truculent and the other districts less truculent than they claimed. In the Malësi e Madhe, for instance, only weak, low-class families would accept blood money; if other families did so, they were held to have 'disgraced themselves'. Indeed, a bajraktar's household, a voivode's or a 'leading family' should seek for fifty years, if need be, to kill the murderer of one of their men. On the other hand, a Çermenikë man sometimes accepted blood money, but if he so demeaned himself, his aim was to ruin his enemy and he fixed the price accordingly. In Dibër no man would accept blood money for a male relative unless it was accompanied by the present of a rifle as a conventional sign that he was still free to kill the murderer if he could. In Lumë a subtle use was sometimes made of blood money. Normally, when a life had been paid for a life, peace was made. But when an inferior killed his superior, the latter's relative would not make peace till he had killed two of the other's men. At the peace-making the first was paired with the original victim and for the second the superior's relative paid blood money.

Given the stigma attached to blood money, it was seldom paid except in lighter cases. After an accidental murder, for instance, honour was in most places satisfied by a money payment. For example, two men of Krujë were examining a revolver together, not knowing it was loaded, when it went off suddenly and killed one of them. The other was held guilty of murder, but in view of the circumstances escaped with a payment of twenty-five napoleons, the conventional six purses. If an animal killed somebody, the death was considered accidental and the payment of blood money sufficed. In Breg i Matit the grazing was good enough to carry a considerable head of cattle which wandered freely through the swamps, with consequent risk to the public from the bulls. If a man was killed by a bull which its owner knew to be dangerous, the latter had to pay blood money, failing which he was liable to be shot. If he did not know the animal's character, he was excused the payment of blood money but had to surrender the bull to its victim's relatives as a minor atonement.

Accidental though a murder might be, the murderer could not rely on saving his life with blood money. Especially while the crime was fresh, he was well advised to lie low until responsible men had weighed the case and confirmed its accidental character. After paying the money he was not absolutely safe unless he found a guarantor.

In Mirditë when blood money was accepted the murderer had also to pay fines of 100 rams and one ox to the tribe and of 500 grosh (piastres, i.e. one purse) to the family of the Hereditary Captain of Mirditë; the animals were eaten at a public banquet by the tribe. These fines were imposed on the murderer for disturbing the public peace. In cases of accidental murder, however, no fine was payable; the formula ran: 'The rifle which kills accidentally entails blood (really blood money) for blood, but not a fine or pursuit.'

The payment of blood money also solved the difficulties in certain cases of murder within the family where atonement had to be made, yet could not properly be exacted in the form of a life for a life. For instance, if two brothers in Shkrel had separate households, when one killed the other's wife for any but a question of honour, the victim's husband could not kill his own brother for her sake but had the right to exact blood money; after all, he had been unjustly deprived of his wife's services and must buy another wife. If a married woman in Shkrel were killed, again unreservedly, by some member of her husband's family, her son, if fifteen years of age or more, could not kill the murderer, his own relative, but exacted blood money. In Shalë another principle came into play. If the dead man's relatives did not succeed in killing the murderer within seven years, they accepted blood money. In places like Mirditë where a fine was exacted when blood money was accepted for a murder, no fine was payable in cases of wounding.

In Mirditë 'wounding went by the part'. If the wound was inflicted at the waist or upwards, even if the bullet only grazed the man's head, the aggressor had to pay three purses; if the wound was below the waist, he need pay no more than 750 grosh, i.e. 1½ purses. In Lumë if a wound left a man lame for life, the wound-money was assessed at seventeen napoleons, roughly four purses, or two-thirds of a man's value; if not, five napoleons were enough. In Krasniqë if a man was so wounded in the private parts that he could no longer be a husband, his assailant had to pay him twelve purses, double the price of a dead man. The doctor's expenses had always to be paid by the aggressor; in Martanesh these were customarily reckoned at 200–300 grosh (piastres), and if they were paid, wound money was sometimes not asked. In Mirditë the doctor's expenses were not fixed by custom but were due only when the victim's relatives regulated the matter, not when the headmen did so. In Çermenikë if a man wounded his enemy, that is to say, the man with whom he had a feud, he did not pay the doctor's expenses; if he accidentally wounded a friend or a neutral, he did. This rule was maintained by King Zog's government. Once an American missionary of Korchë had taken a class of boys for a walk in the country when one fell down a precipice and was gravely injured; the government refused to allow the American to leave Albania until the boy, months afterwards, was restored to health and the American had paid the doctor's bills.

As with a death, accident was no excuse. For example, in 1932 two men from Zdrâjshë in Çermenikë were cutting down a tree by the wayside, when a man from Neshtë, on his way to fetch maize, rode by. The woodcutters called to him to stop, but he paid no heed. As he passed, the tree fell, pinning him to the ground. He was carried home, where he lingered for three months and then died. After his death the woodcutters had to pay his family three purses for wounding him. Wounds inflicted by animals, though considered accidental, had also to be paid for. Those inflicted by dogs fell into a special category. In Shkrel the elders were summoned to assess the doctor's expenses, which were then paid by the animal's owner.

A murderer might also expiate his crime, voluntarily or involuntarily, by exile. If voluntarily, he ran away fearing for his life, but only a weak man who was personally a coward, or had few adult males in his family to keep the enemy at bay, consented to show the white feather.

Voluntary exile might be temporary or permanent. In the former case the murderer did not give up the idea of eventually making his peace with the victim's family and securing their permission to return home.

A normal exile's hope of ending his feud lay in several directions. The victim's family might become so weakened by other blood feuds that they knew themselves to be no longer formidable and sank their pride enough to accept blood money in full payment. They might even become poor enough to be tempted by the offer of money. Or they might consider an absence of ten or twenty years' duration as part atonement and for the rest content themselves with blood money. They might even, on the intervention of friends, forgive the crime outright. In Çermenikë, in the days when 'murder went by the finger' and a murderer's relatives could not make vicarious atonement for his crime, he commonly retired to another district for four or five years, after which the victim's family probably gave a conditional assent to his return. If he risked returning, he kept discreetly out of the way while mutual friends interceded for him. Occasionally they secured his pardon; more often he had to withdraw for a further period of four or five years. During this second absence the enemy's heart almost certainly softened enough to make his next return definite.

Voluntary exile might become permanent for several reasons. It might, for instance, be so protracted that the murderer grew used to his new surroundings and, ceasing to hanker for his old home, settled down where he was. Hysen Agë Jella, of Tirana, having killed Ramiz Bey Toptan, also of Tirana, fled to Bulqizë and took refuge with the noted brigand, Sul Hupi. Under the latter's protection and by reason of his own wealth and prestige, he acquired such a position in Bulqizë that when eventually the feud with the Toptans was closed, he did not return to Tirana, preferring to remain in Bulqizë.

Again, an exiled murderer sometimes prospered so much that

he found it to his interest to stay away permanently. If he found the climate or the soil of his new home kindlier, he might sell his paternal holding through an intermediary and with the proceeds buy land in his new home. Before he ran away, he had probably sent his wife to her parents, who no doubt lived in another village. There he visited her at intervals until he was installed in his new property, when he sent for her and their children, if any. A voluntary exile, it may be added, was content to leave his wife in his brother's charge; a compulsory exile took her with him. Good examples of voluntary exiles turned permanent from motives of advantage are provided by the many Bojdan families from Bicaj in Lumë, who in recent centuries involved themselves in blood feuds and fled to Kosovë. Their feuds were compounded in every instance, but the greater fertility in Kosovë was not to be resisted. To-day their descendants live scattered as far apart as Kaçanik and Blacë, near Skoplje. They still preserve memories of their kinship one with another and with Bicaj; in fact, till the break-up of the Turkish empire in Europe after the Balkan wars interposed new frontiers between the Albanian lands, they made occasional pilgrimages to the homes of their ancestors in Bicaj.

Sometimes an exiled murderer set up a small business, selling cigarettes and cleaning shoes, and made money as he could never have done in his mountain village. Sometimes, too, he entered the service of a rich man and in return for his devotion was given a grant of land.

The emergence of a central government which punished murder tended to increase the number of permanent exiles and to make the strong as well as the weak run away. An Albanian would face boldly enough the vengeance of his victim's relatives, but he detested being imprisoned by the government. A man of Bashabun, near Elbasan, killed a neighbour years ago. Blood money was paid, and so far as his victim's family was concerned, he was free to return home. Unwilling, however, to serve the short term of imprisonment to which the government would condemn him, he remained in exile in Bosnia. A Milot murderer remained in exile after the payment of blood money had closed the feud, because he feared imprisonment by the government. In an accidental meeting with his victim's brother, both forgot the closing of the feud and shot at each other, the brother killing the murderer. Then only the taking of the oath with twenty-four men cleared him from the accusation of taking government money to kill the murderer after he had taken blood money from the family.

The same fear of government action was at work in Kosovë, a province largely populated by Albanians but assigned to Yugoslavia after the Turkish empire broke up in 1912. A steady drift towards Albania proper went on among the Kosovars. Some were impelled by land hunger to go and take up the free land which the Albanian government had offered them; others came to evade Yugoslav justice. By contrast with the Albanian government, which did not yet punish severely homicide that was justifiable by tribal law, the Yugoslav government hanged most murderers. To avoid this ignominy, a Kosovar murderer preferred to emigrate, lock, stock and barrel, to Albania. Most interestingly, this emigration was the ebb of the tide that within recent centuries peopled Kosovë with Albanians.

Sometimes a murderer did not run away of his own accord, but was forcibly expelled by the community. Although when murder was not punished by government, only the weak ran away voluntarily, the community expelled a strong man as readily as a weak one. In tribal districts like Mirditë which contained several villages, the murderer's village could not expel him without the other villages' consent and help. If the village resisted the expulsion, the tribe as a whole had the right to 'proclaim' the village or to call in other tribes to bring it to reason. In small tribes like Nikaj the murderer's kinsmen could expel him independently of the tribe. In non-tribal districts like Shpat, where each village was a self-contained unit, it needed to ask no one before expelling a murderer.

A man sentenced to communal expulsion was always one whose crime struck at the roots of society as understood in the mountains. Perhaps he had violated the acknowledged sanctity of the 'pledged word' by killing his enemy during a public truce or even after making peace with him. Perhaps he had infringed the sacred laws of hospitality by killing his host or guest. Perhaps he threatened family solidarity by killing a cousin to get his land. Perhaps he had killed a man to steal his rifle and thereby as good as robbed him of his manhood, for a man without a rifle is as nothing, no better than a woman. Perhaps he had committed sacrilege by killing someone, possibly the priest himself, inside the territory of church or mosque, or by breaking into the church to steal.

For any such anti-social murder no ordinary vengeance, no pardon was possible. The community assembled and passed judgement in the time-honoured formula that so-and-so 'is burned, roasted, cut down and expelled from the tribe'. Without loss of time—probably immediately after passing sentence—they burned the man's house, killed, roasted and ate his sheep, goats and cows, cut down his trees, and drove him into exile. They further required him to make public confession of his guilt by himself applying the burning brand to his house. In Mirditë and elsewhere he had at the same time to make himself a public scapegoat, saying as he lit the fire, 'On my head be the ill-luck of the village and the tribe'. If he and the other men in the house who were qualified to represent him refused to set the house alight, the head of his clan bade his next nearest relative do so. The fire once started, the whole village or tribe kept it going until its work was done, for it was essential that the whole community should take part in executing the communal sentence. But they could not touch the fire until the criminal had lighted it. In the same way, the murderer had to be the first to apply the axe to his trees and vines; if he jibbed, his nearest relative took his place and the work was completed by the whole community. If he had a vegetable garden it was destroyed in the same fashion. On the same day all his edible livestock was roasted and consumed by the community at a public banquet. This was by way of a fine. He himself, with his wife and children, was escorted to the tribal frontier to make sure that he was not killed on the way. At the frontier he was ordered never to return again. In Shpat he was literally drummed out of the village; the community hired gipsies to lead the way beating drums, and all the men sang to mark their joy at getting rid of a bad character.

The community destroyed the murderer's house, fruit trees and livestock not to punish him directly for his crime, but to make it impossible for him to defy the sentence of exile by remaining in his home. For the essential feature of their sentence was the condemnation to exile, the expulsion of an undesirable, of one whose act had dishonoured the whole tribe and must be repudiated by the whole tribe. Since robbery was not their motive, the murderer was free to take his money with him; in any case, it could not be seen, securely hidden as it was in a purse in his armpit.

Sometimes the expulsion was for ever, sometimes for three, five, ten or twenty years, according to the crime. In Mirditë, presumably under church influence, the murderer of a priest was expelled for ever, and other anti-social criminals for five to fifteen years. In Martanesh the injured man might after an interval intercede with the local elders and secure a remission of part of the sentence; otherwise the murderer and his descendants must remain in exile. Several local traditions maintain that sentences of perpetual banishment were formerly much commoner. In Martanesh no such sentence has been pronounced for 200 years, and in Shpat none for 100 years. In Lurë any murderer used to be banished in perpetuity; witness the numerous families of Lurë origin who now live in Prizren, Tetovo, Reka and other places in Yugoslavia.

In Lurë when a man was sentenced to perpetual banishment, his nearest kinsmen, those who would have been his heirs in the event of his dying childless, divided up his land. His family was in fact reckoned as extinct so far as the tribe was concerned. In Mirditë also he was considered as dead to the tribe. Father Gjeçov gives two accounts of what happened there to his land. For ordinary expulsions it was left uncultivated and used for public grazing. When a man was expelled for breaking into a church or for killing a priest, his land was bought by his nearest kinsmen and the money given to the church. In Shpat again the murderer's nearest kinsmen divided up his land; but there the elders valued it and the kinsmen paid the murderer the estimated sum before he was drummed out; if they could not raise the money, the village found it, subject to recovering it later from the kinsmen. On the other hand, when a murderer was banished only for a term of years, his land everywhere remained uncultivated until his return, when he built a house and resumed cultivation. During his absence, his ownership of the land was uncontested, but he was not allowed to derive any profit from it. A voluntary exile was in a different position; he could empower a kinsman to work his land and throughout his absence to remit to him in his place of exile an agreed proportion of the profits.

When a man was expelled for good, the community signalled the same by tearing up the four corner-stones of the foundations of his house after they had burned it down. When his banishment was temporary, the corner-stones were left in place to await his return. Again when his banishment was perpetual, there could be no more giving or taking in marriage for him in the village; any engagements subsisting at the time of his expulsion were voided by that fact. When his banishment was temporary, his marriage engagements remained binding.

Even in cases of temporary banishment the murderer's separation from his tribe was thoroughgoing. For the specified period 'he could not light a cigarette in a single house of the tribe', as the men of Lurë put it. Nor could he, or his, return to borrow honey, that most important commodity where sugar is scarce. In Mirditë a tribesman who admitted him to his house for any of the above purposes was publicly 'burned, roasted and expelled' for breaking tribal discipline.

The banished murderer's obligation to take root whether he wished it or not in some alien spot is another of the factors which produced the many colonies of diverse origin in Albanian lands. The exiles, home-sick like exiles the world over, often gave the name of their ancestral village to their new settlement.

If the murderer did not choose to go into exile of his own accord, he was condemned by the avenger to virtual imprisonment in his house. Sometimes he shut himself up voluntarily; more often, especially in north Albania, he was peremptorily ordered to do so by the avenger. For the period of his 'imprisonment' fear that the avenger was lurking near prevented him from stirring outside during the daytime and restricted his movements to the night hours. If he left home, he had by dawn to find shelter under a friend's roof and he could not continue his travels until the next night fell. These disabilities were his so long as he eluded the avenger, and he might do so for years, as in the case of a native of Sheshaj who had been shut up by his enemy for twenty-five years. At Belsh in Dumre, as a result of this confinement, two men who had been shut up for twelve years were 'waxen and yellow as the dead'. They longed to walk in the sunlight and were bored indoors where they could do nothing to pass the time except strip maize and knit (most curiously, knitting is one of the staple occupations of the men, but not the women, in Dumre). But they could not help themselves, since it was certain death to step outside during the daytime.

Just as the murderer's house could not be burned down in case women and children perished in the conflagration, so his 'imprisonment' could not be allowed to stop the work of the family in case women and children died of starvation. There were several provisions for carrying on the work. The first was the law that women, children, servants and domestic animals must not be shut up. So in comparative security the able-bodied women, on whom fell the heaviest burden, tilled the fields, went to market, ground corn at the mill and fetched water from the spring and firewood from the forest. The boys and aged women herded the cows, sheep and goats. The servants took part in any or all of these tasks, but few households could afford the luxury of servants.

A social phenomenon alleged to be a by-product of this immunity of women and children is interesting. To-day a good proportion of the agricultural work of Albania is done by women, while the men idle; a generation ago the bulk of it was so done. The men of to-day excuse their idling by saying it is a habit formed when they or their fathers were shut up by blood feuds; whatever their natural inclination to work, they were then driven perforce into allowing their women to toil alone to feed the family. This plea may or may not be valid; as the frequency of blood feuds decreased, the men's industry increased.

In bad feuds the immunity of women and children was sometimes denied. Even to-day the women of Murat Kaloshi's household cannot stir outside his compound except under heavy escort; failing that, they would be shot without pity by his enemies. The numerous children in his household are growing up illiterate four minutes' walk from an excellent school; if they attended this school, a battalion of gendarmes or men-at-arms could hardly ensure their safety. Another bad case is to be found at Milot, where even the boys in the cradle in Gjin Bardhoku's house have to share the men's imprisonment. In Çermenikë the immunity of women was never absolute; there was always a danger that the avenger might lose his temper and kill them. Within living memory two women in Fenars, one of the more accessible villages in Çermenikë, once tried to plough and were discovered by the avenger. On their declining to desist as he bade them, he fired at them with unexpectedly fortunate results. He wounded both but only severely enough to make them fall to the ground while letting go the oxen. They made a speedy recovery and, each wound counting as half a 'blood', the avenger was considered to have taken vengeance. The two parties were then 'measure for measure' and made peace.

Again with a view to feeding the murderer's family an avenger

sometimes yielded to a friend's pleadings and allowed one or more
men in the 'imprisoned' man's household to come out and work.
The same friend went security to the murderer for the lives of the
man or men released. In Shpat, if one of the men imprisoned
died, the avenger sent word that one of those hitherto free must
shut himself up in his stead. It is not known whether this was the
rule in other districts or not.

In earlier times, according to vague traditions still current in
Çermenikë and Martanesh, only the actual murderer was shut up
and the other men in his household were free to work and to travel.
This tradition is supported by the history of the Balli family in the
village of Fenars. Seven generations ago, i.e. about 175 years ago,
Sali Balli of Martanesh killed a friend and was shut up by the
avenger, while his four brothers went free. He grew so bored in
his 'prison' that he ran away from Martanesh and settled in
Fënars, where he founded a family now headed by Isuf Balli. The
descendants of his brothers still live in the old home in Martanesh.

When an avenger felt too bitter to release indefinitely one or
more men in the imprisoned murderer's household, he was sometimes induced to make a minor concession. When all the men were
shut up, women were able to hoe, to carry manure, to sow seed, to
reap wheat and to harvest maize successfully, but they could not
plough—so it was believed in north, though not in south, Albania,
where the wives of many emigrants must to this day plough if
they and their children are to eat. There was therefore danger in
north Albania that if all the men were shut up during the ploughing
season, the family would, in spite of the women's efforts, starve.
This led to a ticket-of-leave system, called besë, literally 'pledged
word', 'truce', or kuvend, 'agreement'. At the instance of a mutual
friend the avenger granted the murderer leave for one or more men
in his household to come out and work his land for a stipulated
period, varying from three to twelve months. As so often, the forces
of public opinion reinforced the friend's urgings; indeed, it was said
of an avenger who refused his enemy leave to plough that he 'was
not to be entered in the register', i.e. could not be classed as a man,
and of one who did not that he was both brave and honourable.

In Dukagjin the kanùn of murder was so stern that neither the
murderer nor his womenfolk were allowed to work his land if the
avenger was strong. Indeed, the avenger often worked it and
carried home the produce, leaving the murderer's household

dependent on charity. At best the elders fixed a sum to be paid by the murderer for leave to work his own land: the money paid, the avenger gave his word not to molest him; or a 'strong' friend guaranteed his safety as he tilled his fields. This arrangement continued until he was killed elsewhere or the avenger consented to make peace.

Various devices were tried to outwit an avenger too venomous to make the smallest concession to his 'imprisoned' enemy. The commonest was for the murderer to let his land to a neutral on the usual Albanian terms of 'halves'. Once some men of Lurë, trusting to the prevailing immunity of women from attack, dressed in their wives' clothes and went out to work. They were soon discovered and compelled to return home. Frequently a woman was made to work alongside the men, the assumption being that from fear of accidentally hitting the women and so disgracing himself the avenger would not fire on the party. The man who murdered the brother of Kodhel Dede of Nezhar in Shpat belonged to a large family, the members of which went to work with a woman between every two men. Kodhel thus found it impossible to kill one of them and after a long period of years made peace. Sometimes a man's wife kept watch while he worked; if she signalled the enemy's approach, he seized his rifle and prepared to defend himself. During Kodhel Dede's feud with the Trepsanishti family he found himself long baulked by the vigilance of his enemy's wife. At last his chance came on the eve of 15 August. The wife had her mind set on making *melata* (sacrificial foods) for distribution on the festival, and, forgetting her husband who was at work on the threshing floor, she went home to make them. Kodhel, who had crept up through a maize field, shot her husband as soon as her back was turned. In the hilly landscape of Fulqet in west Mat a different sort of watch was kept. The 'imprisoned' men, aided by friends, dug a hole on top of a hill commanding a wide view. One of their best shots, rifle in hand, settled down in this hole ready to snipe the avenger if he tried to kill any of the men at work.

Work in the fields apart, an 'imprisoned' murderer might for short periods leave his house under escort of a friend. This friend had to be 'strong', otherwise the murderer might be killed by his enemy, a lasting disgrace to the man whose protégé he was for the time being. Sometimes murderer and avenger had a common friend who took the former out; in that case the friend ran less risk of losing his protégé, but even so he had to be fairly 'strong'. In Mat such a friend might take the murderer out three times with impunity. Afterwards he was sure to receive a message from the avenger which ran, 'Don't stir out again. Stay indoors. It was for your sake that I didn't fire.'

In the majority of cases the murderer neither ran away nor was shut up, but went about his normal business, taking certain precautions. An Albanian never despised his enemy; the strongest man will say, 'I am stronger than he is, but a rifle doesn't care for bravery, a rifle kills'. He remembers also that an enemy is ever on the watch: 'A wooden stake rots, but an enemy doesn't.' Yet another saying—this from west Mat—'Wood rots, a wrong doesn't'. 'A feud can't be forgotten.' 'A man with an enemy is like a hare sitting on its form, he must watch all the time.'

The first precaution a hunted man had to take at home was never to answer the door himself.

Since the laws of hospitality were rigid and seldom transgressed, a guest seldom killed, or was killed by, his host. Frok Gjeta of Kthellë, however, had lost his father at a guest's hands; three men had called and been unsuspectingly admitted; the old man was hospitably making coffee when they suddenly opened fire and killed him.

About 1910 some men called at a house in Orenjë, in Çermenikë, and were admitted by its widowed mistress as guests. They seized the only adult male in the house, her stripling son and, hanging him head downwards by a rope slung across a rafter, demanded money and avowed that they were avenging the murder of one of their kin by the family. The son said he had no money; the mother screamed that she had a little, but they hanged her son.

Another precaution commonly taken by a 'wanted' man was to live in a house of more than one storey. Such a house never had more than slits for windows in the ground floor and those in the upper room were square holes without glass, across which stone shutters were drawn at night. In Çermenikë the outside staircase that led down to the stables on the ground floor was always fenced in carefully with wood. For greater security the women lived on the ground floor protecting the men who lived above. If a man were rich enough, he built a high wall round the house; this gave him the freedom of his courtyard. In this case all the windows looked inwards on the court; the outer walls were blank save for the loopholes. A still richer man, or one with many enemies, had several doors in his courtyard wall and watch-towers at strategic points. (The turrets at each corner and in the middle of the long walls effectually commanded these entrances, and many loopholes in the walls provided space for many defenders to shoot from.) Shevqet Bey Verlaci of Elbasan had several posterns in his garden wall, each commanded by a watch-tower and each providing him in case of need with a possible means of escape.

Incidentally, back entrances in the mountains were useful for guests with enemies. These could enter unseen by other guests, among whom there might be one or more who would inform the enemy of his whereabouts, and so endanger his life. They were also useful if the master had sent a group of his followers to shoot his enemy; if they failed, they could creep in unseen by the guests; in case of failure on such an errand, they did not wish the attempt to be known.

A wanted man who wished to work in his fields might station a child herding goats or a woman minding a cow at a vantage point where an enemy could be detected and the watcher give him warning, so that he might seize his rifle and defend himself. As the enemy's trump card was surprise, he was likely to retreat when detected. Before the wanted man left the house the women and children would look through the windows to make sure no enemy was near. A man with blood on his hands might wish to go to the forest to cut firewood, a place too distant for his women to keep watch. In that case he might send a scout ahead to reconnoitre the road, and himself follow rifle in hand. In Zdrâjshë, Çermenikë, the communal hay-field was so far away that a wanted man made no attempt to go and cut his hay; the others, however, gave him his due share, though he had done nothing to earn it. A man who, in spite of risks, kept moving about might never stir outside, especially at night, without his rifle. He never told where he was going and travelled by an unlikely route and at unwonted times.

In the summer of 1935, to return from Tirana, whither he had been officially summoned, Murat Kaloshi of Dibër sent out an attendant to find a car willing to drive at once to Dibër, and within five minutes of its drawing up at the door of his lodging started. This was at 2 p.m., an hour when Tirana is plunged in sleep on a summer afternoon. He supped at the wayside inn of Lunik, an insignificant village without telegraphic communication, four or five hours from Tirana, travelled on through the night, and in the early morning as the car neared Peshkopi, he got out and walked home across country. (With him were a number of attendants armed to the teeth.)

Needless to say, such a man never announced beforehand the time of his departure, if his intention to depart could not be concealed.

An obvious precaution was never to stir outside the house. When a Dibër notable went to Tirana, he took at least six armed attendants along with him, who might or might not live with him permanently. The armed attendants of the Hereditary Captain of Mirditë were mainly young relatives of his who spent years with him, at once his clansmen and his relatives; their loyalty was beyond doubt. The bodyguard of Shevqet Bey Verlaci of Elbasan were generally peasants from his farms who had been long in his service. Less rich men who needed numerous attendants on their walks abroad drew them from their neighbours. Selman Nus Cohu, for instance, an attendant of the bajraktar of Lurë, lived at home and only joined the bajraktar when he or another member of his family needed him for a journey or some other cause. When Miftar Selmani of Lumë came to Tirana he brought a posse of armed neighbours who constantly changed as their services were required at home; some came with him for the outing, others out of bounden duty to requite the help he had given them in earlier times.

Men still poorer contented themselves with reinforcing the men of the household with a single permanent retainer. Such a man was the peasant from Shëngjerg who fled to Namid Çallaku of Fulqet after committing three murders, and in return for his board and an occasional tip protected his protector. In Mat it was also customary to go and stay for a month at a time with a friend who had need of an extra gun.

Failing armed attendants, a hunted man was not without protectors on his journey. In districts where women were immune a woman's company, on a journey as at work, was sufficient. When Shalë as a tribe was in blood with its neighbour, Mertur, a man from Shalë could safely go to Mertur with a woman born in Shalë or another tribe who was married in Mertur, for she counted as belonging to Mertur and the man was therefore her guest. On the other hand, a daughter of Mertur who was married in another tribe was no protection, for she had lost her Mertur nationality as it were by her marriage, and so her company did not in itself make the traveller a guest of that tribe. In Mat it was a protection to have a foreigner in front of you, for a foreigner was as sacred as a woman. This held for most districts of Albania.

The principle of the guest's sacrosanctity was often invoked. If a guest of an important man in Dibër had an enemy and was travelling alone, his host would give him an attendant when he left. This attendant must see him safely to his next destination; should any harm befall him on the way his powerful host would avenge him. The protection, and with it the obligation, of his host ended by nightfall, for he would by then have either reached home or become the guest of another man. His journey being thus limited to a day's duration, the mere fact of his being accompanied by the attendant would generally suffice to keep him safe, for within the radius of a day's journey, on foot, everybody knew everybody else, and on his being seen in the company of the attendant, it was at once recognized whose guest he had been and who his avenger would be.

There were interesting extensions of the principle. It was not necessary to have been actually a guest of the strong man for him to avenge the traveller's murder; it was sufficient to say one was about to be his guest. In the time of Lan Kaloshi, one of the Alijes on his discharge from detention as a hostage by the Turks was on his way to stay with the Lleshaj of Kander when he was killed by the powerful Ali Doçi. Although he had not actually become the guest of the Lleshaj, it fell to that family to avenge him. They, however, realizing that they were no match for Ali Doçi, told the family that the only way in which the murder could be avenged would be to declare that the victim had been on his way to visit Lan Kaloshi. They did this. Lan accepted the responsibility, and avenged the murder.

In Shalë a traveller, no matter whether native or stranger, could travel safely provided he called out some native's name in a loud voice. Scattered though the population of that mountainous valley might be, there was always some goatherd or cowherd within hail to report on whom the traveller had called; in case of need, that involuntary protector recognized that the man was travelling under his protection and took whatever steps were necessary.

It sometimes happened that a hunted man, when paying a visit

to a friend, found his enemy was his fellow-guest. This was natural
enough, for especially where both belonged to the same village,
hunter and hunted always had a number of mutual friends. All over
Albania the two enemies, being fellow-guests, did not molest each
other, but rather, out of courtesy to their host, talked together as
if nothing divided them. In the old days they would in Çermenikë
even shoot at a target together without turning their rifles on each
other. In Çermenikë the hunted man's immunity was not quite
complete, varying according to his behaviour. If he cocked his fez
to one side and held his head high, his enemy might kill him even at
their common host's in his exasperation at his effrontery. If, on the
other hand, the murderer pushed his fez straight to the back of his
head and kept his head down, his enemy would almost certainly
not touch him till both had left the house. Sometimes hunter and
hunted were invited to the same wedding or funeral feast. Then the
same rules of courtesy came into play. The enemies sat at one table,
ate out of the common dish, passed each other their tobacco boxes
and drank coffee side by side. If toasts were drunk among the
Highlanders, they would not drink to each other's health nor would
they willingly address each other, but otherwise they gave little sign
of their enmity.

CHAPTER XXV

BLOOD FEUD

IV. PEACE-MAKING

Peace was seldom made until the same number had been killed on both sides. If the first man was only wounded, and in revenge killed his enemy, the elders made the first pay wound money, half a blood, so as to make it 'one for one'. In the same way if three, say, were killed on one side and two killed and one wounded on the other, peace was made on condition that the latter side should pay one wound money; then two killed, one wounded, and one wound money paid made the equivalent of the three killed on the enemy's side. The killings and the woundings might be done in one engagement or might be distributed over a number of years, taking place in the swing backwards and forwards of the feud. Killing or being killed by a woman was sometimes not accepted in the reckoning. The virgin Emin of Orenjë in Çermenikë killed the man who had killed her father, and so made it technically 'one for one'. But her enemy refused to make peace, saying that a kill by a woman did not count and they were not yet therefore 'one for one'. In Shpat peace was never made until shots had been fired at least once by the relatives of the man first murdered; that done, it did not matter much whether the victims were 'one for one' or not.

Peace was always made through an intermediary. If it were directly solicited by the hunted, the enemy's triumph would know no bounds, and he would arrogantly refuse to grant the other's request. But he could not indefinitely turn a deaf ear to the pleadings of friends; to do so risked quarrelling with them. 'You've shot enough', they said, as though to convince him that he had vindicated his honour. 'Forgive him, we beg you', they added. At length he replied, 'All right, I've forgiven him'. Then both enemies were safe from gossiping tongues, that bogey of primitive communities, for no one could say that one or the other man was either brave or cowardly. Sometimes not private friends, but a whole tribe, through their spokesman, intervened.

The ceremony of ratifying the promise of forgiveness varied

from place to place. In Shpat the original criminal must take the initiative and go to his enemy's house, escorted for safety's sake by at least one friend. The enemy came to meet him in the open air, but did not offer him his hand, for a man reserves his hand for his friends. Then both went into the house, the coffee, the all-essential to a peace-making, was soon served, followed perhaps by a meal with meat. Both coffee and meal were 'like a funeral', enlivened by next to no conversation and with little cordiality of mien. A day or two later the enemy must go to the original criminal's house, and the same ceremonies were gone through. Alternate visits had to be paid for some time, until at last the original enemy declared that he had forgiven the other. A marriage very often cemented the peace-making. Occasionally the attempt to make peace broke down— one's gorge rose at the idea of making friends with the murderer. Then the whole evil story began again, murder alternating with murder.

The ceremonies in Çermenikë and Martanesh followed much the same lines. New elements were introduced farther north, for example, in Krasniqë. Accompanied by six to eight men, the man originally at fault, with his hands tied behind his back, went unexpectedly on a festive evening to his enemy's house. The host, as in duty bound, said, 'Come in!' and invited them to sit down. They refused to do so until in sign of forgiveness he untied his enemy's hands. He never refused, for he said, 'Better forgive, and forget one dead man than quarrel with ten living ones'. If he had not granted their request, the murderer's escort would never have visited his house again. That night the uninvited guest ate a meal at the involuntary host's house, and the next day the man forgiven carried them all off to his house, where he provided a meal with meat pasty and sweets. Forgiveness in Krasniqë was more easily obtained for a murder done in hot blood, and the ensuing friendship was more genuine; if the murderer had ambushed his enemy, peace was more difficult to establish and the resultant friendship less real. In Lumë the murderer was thrust into his enemy's house before dawn so that his enemy might not see him coming; no notice of his coming was given beforehand. If the host did not untie his hands, the friends who accompanied him refused to drink coffee; the host always yielded to the threat of this disgrace.

In Kurbin peace was made by the same methods as in Lumë and Krasniqë. The murderer, who had the sailor collar of his jacket

17   HAM

thrown over his head, a sign of mourning and penitence, as well as his hands tied behind his back, a sign of helplessness, remained standing near the door, while his friends sat down round the hearth. The host gave coffee to them, but not to him; his forgiveness was not yet assured, and without such assurance he could not drink his coffee. The friends pleaded with the host to untie his hands; they threatened as well as pleaded saying, 'If you like, forgive him—otherwise kill us along with him'. At length one of two things happened. The host consented to pardon the murderer, got up to throw down his collar and to untie his hands, and bade him sit down and drink coffee, saying, 'You are pardoned, friend'. More frequently, he said he could not at once pardon the man, but would give him a truce of six months, a year, or more; in sign of his mollification he probably gave him coffee, though he sent him away with his hands still tied behind his back and his collar over his head.

If the murderer were pardoned, a meal with meat was given in all but the poorest houses—these must content themselves with coffee. On the departure of the guests a further ceremony took place. The host saw the party off as he would on any other occasion. On leaving the house he took a hammer and chipped out a little cross on the door. Each of the others in turn took the hammer and chipped out a little more, first the host's party and then the visitors. The host said, 'God send us no more grief' and 'May he be forgiven'. Each guest said, 'Honour to you for pardoning him!' After chipping out his portion each dropped the hammer on the ground for the next man to pick up; this was to make sure of not handing on the feud to him. The last man on the murderer's side threw the hammer away, repeating, 'Honour to you for pardoning him!' The cross signified that the family had had an enemy, had fired shots; the more crosses on a door, the more valiant the family. In Kurbin there are houses with ten or twelve. Since the district is now predominantly Mohammedan, the chipping of the cross is an interesting survival from the time when they were all Roman Catholic. The following day or the next the enemy paid a visit with his friends to the murderer's, and was regaled with coffee and a meal with meat; in every case the chief intermediary was an honoured guest. It may be added that modernization has attacked the ceremonies; as early as 1930 a murderer from the Saseri family of Krujë refused to have his hands tied when he went to his enemy's to be pardoned; he said it was 'disgraceful', and the plea was allowed.

The Highlanders had still another method. They called a 'St John' an infant which had not yet been sent to have its hair cut by its godfather, it being believed that St John the Baptist was Christ's godfather. When the time for peace-making seemed due, the friends brought pressure to bear to secure forgiveness. This promised, they arranged to take the murderer on a certain day to his enemy's house, his hands again tied behind his back, and take a 'St John' in its cradle with them. Probably they did not bring the murderer into view; at most they kept him in the background. One of the visitors turned the cradle with the infant, who was, as always, well strapped in, upside down, saying to the host, 'Put it straight; Turn it right side up!' If he were willing, and few were not, for leaving the infant upside down might kill it and leave him with innocent blood on his hands, he turned the cradle right side up, saying, 'All right, I pardon him for the sake of God and the Saint'. Then he went and without another word untied the murderer's hands. Next he said, 'A pardon for my murder; a pardon for my father's (or brother's) murder; be it forgiven', and turned to embrace the murderer. Coffee was then served and drunk by all amid general conversation—the Highlanders are unusually lively. Having fixed a day when they would all go to eat a meal with meat at the murderer's house they took their leave. This meal at the murderer's concluded the proceedings; afterwards all went about their business; no cross was made on the enemy's door as in Kurbin.

Friends were not the only interveners. Occasionally the Turkish government took a hand, declaring on penalty of imprisonment, internment and burning out that all feuds more than seven years old were to be compounded by a money payment and not reopened. When during the 1914–18 war Austria-Hungary was in occupation of all north Albania, she also ordered blood feuds to be ended with a money payment; the resentment of Çermenikë at this attempt to force them to make peace on northern terms is still hot. Sometimes a whole community itself interfered. The procedure of west Mat was typical. When a man had been killed on either side and the feud was 'one for one', the neighbours took effective steps to prevent its continuance. They each forbade the avenger to come on his land to kill his enemy; if he did so, he would be considered a trespasser and would have a feud with the owner. If, after this warning, the neighbour saw the avenger trying to kill his enemy on his land, he shot at him, and if he killed him, he had no feud, for he had forbidden him to raise his rifle on his land.

Religious influences also were brought to bear on the two enemies. The Bojdani sheikh of Bicaj in Lumë often intervened when there was shooting, both before and after the murder was committed; telling both parties they were in the wrong, he induced them to make peace. There is no record known to the author of an Orthodox priest acquiring influence enough to end a feud, and a Roman Catholic parish priest, though not ridiculed by his flock as his Orthodox brother too often was, had no power to curse people who kept up blood feuds, and without such power he could not compose a feud. Even a bishop was powerless in such cases. Jesuits, on the other hand, had the power and on occasion exercised it; it is commonly believed to this day that they are sent by the Pope and they are correspondingly feared. Every ten years or so, summoned by the archbishop or the priest in charge, at the instance of the village, they toured the Roman Catholic districts, their main object being to compose blood feuds. In 1932 three priests went to Shkrel for the best part of a week. Due warning of their advent had been given, and all devout Roman Catholics were bidden to attend church every day. Banners depicting the flames of hell and the crimes which earned them were hung round the church and the sermons were in the same strain. On the second day these placed emphasis on the privileged position of Roman Catholics; in return for this good Catholics should settle their blood feuds rather than risk losing the blessing of the church for themselves and their families during their lifetime and after it burial in consecrated ground. On the third day the priests inveighed against keeping up grudges; those who cherished their blood feuds risked the curse of God. This meant that nothing would go right for them. They would be shunned by everyone—an engaged girl could not marry with the blessing of the Church, but only by civil marriage—if indeed her betrothed did not prefer to give her up, although this meant losing her bride-price. On this occasion in Shkrel the vehemence of the priests' exhortations and the fear of the consequences of the curse resulted in the termination of several outstanding feuds.

APPENDIX

LAWS PASSED AT GENERAL ASSEMBLIES
(TRANSLATED FROM THE ORIGINAL ALBANIAN)

I. Some Laws Ratified by the Prefecture of Shkodër.
(From Father Gjeçov, *Kanùn*, pp. 128–9.)

1. Bride-price is not to be altered. The amount fixed seven years ago remains in force. It is, therefore, 600 grosh, a sum which includes everything. Whoever acts contrary to this order will be fined 1000 grosh.

2. Girls will be betrothed by their father, or if they have no father by their brother and, failing him, by their nearest male cousin. Women are not to interfere in betrothals.

3. Every betrothal will be arranged openly not secretly, and there will be a go-between as witness. When the betrothal has been completed and rifles have been fired off in front of the betrothed girl's house, the men who have the right to betroth her will go to the parish priest in order to register the names of the betrothed pair, the registrar and the witnesses, together with all the circumstances. Whosoever does not abide by this decree will be fined 1000 grosh.

4. Whoever refuses to go through the marriage ceremony when the priest comes for that purpose will be fined 1000 grosh.

5. Whoever incites a married woman to run away will be fined eight purses.

6. Whoever gives a bride to a man who has divorced his lawfully wedded wife will be fined 1000 grosh.

7. Whoever shall dare to send away his lawfully wedded wife in order to take another woman in unlawful wedlock will be fined 1000 grosh.

8. Whoever sells his daughter or sister or other female of his blood relations will be fined, like the buyer, 1000 grosh.

9. On the basis of the ancient customs, which are still observed among the Christians of the mountains of Shkodër concerning betrothals, marriages, enticing of other men's wives, running away of wives and other similar causes of trouble, some laws have been enacted for the repression of the aforesaid evil acts and have been approved by His Lordship the Archbishop of Shkodër, Mgr Luigi Çurçi, and by the mountain chiefs. These laws after being weighed by the Government Council have been approved and ordered to be put into execution.

10. The government authorities therefore by this Decree order that the nine points above-mentioned shall be observed and put into execution without fail or opposition.

Issued by the Government Authorities of Shkodër
Shkodër, Albania
May 9th, 1864

L.S. Mareshali
Civil and Military Representative of the
Government with the Prefecture of Shkodër

ISMAIL PASHA

II. Solemn Pledge between Mnelë and Gomsiqe, February 13th, 1873.

(From Father Gjeçov, *Kanùn*, p. 118.)

At the meeting we are holding to-day we have decided to write out the following document in order to have it for reference.

We, the tribesmen of Mnelë and Gomsiqe, comprising 150 houses, have solemnly promised each other to hold ourselves ready and of one mind for every need that may eventuate.

The witnesses of this pledge are:

[Here follow the names of 15 tribesmen, headed by the bajraktar.]

Written this day of February 13th, 1873.

III. Laws Enacted by the Twenty-four Elders and Agreed by the Chiefs, etc. Written in the Village of Kastrat on November 2nd, 1891.

(From Father Gjeçov, *Kanùn*, p. 125.)

1. From Krue i Ri, which belongs to all Kastrat, up to She i Gurit; from Vorr Gjolaj to Breg i Gurrës, marching with Gjelosh Luce; from Shkamb Gropë Mollë to Brigje; from Gjekë Petroviqi to Çukë e Gurrës...whoever quarrels or fires a weapon within these limits will be fined 3000 grosh and 24 rams.

2. Whoever refuses to allow a woman to fill her water-pitchers at fountains and springs saying she has no right to a share of the water, will be fined 250 grosh and 3 rams.

3. Whoever calls another names in the above-mentioned places or calls another's mother and father names, will be fined, if he is full 15 years old, 250 grosh and 3 rams.

4. Whoever goes to do a mischief in a mill must, if he is full 12 years old, pay a fine of 250 grosh to the miller and 500 grosh and 3 rams to the chiefs.

5. Whoever moves the stones of an old boundary and puts them in a new place will be fined 3000 grosh and 6 rams.

6. No one is to frighten a flock sheltering from the heat in a place it was in first.[1] Whoever does this will be fined 250 grosh and 3 rams.

7. The mill question remains inviolate as always and neither the Vukpalaj nor the Gjolaj may start a *degamë*,[2] and any miller who takes more than 5 per cent of the flour will be fined 500 grosh and 6 rams.

8. Any man who cuts down a tree under which animals take shelter from the heat or cuts off a mill or an irrigation stream will be fined 500 grosh and 6 rams.

9. Other fountains and springs are left under the old law, that is to say, whoever destroys a fountain or spring or prevents another from filling water-pots will be fined 500 grosh.

10. Milling is by order of arrival. Any miller who mills for a man who comes later than another and breaks the order either out of favouritism or because corrupted by bribes will be fined 150 grosh and 3 rams.

11. Whoever admits a stranger to huts on a mountain pasturage will be fined 500 grosh and 6 rams.[3]

IV. Truce Sworn between Nikaj and Mertur on August 10th, 1892.

(From Father Gjeçov, *Kanùn*, p. 121.)

The two tribes have sworn a truce with each other:

(1) As from August 14th up to the day of Our Lady of Mertur.

(2) As from December 26th up to the day of St Sebastian.

> The guarantors of Flock and Shepherd, i.e. Nikaj and Mertur and the Bajraktars of Krasniqë and Gash.

V. Laws Enacted in Kastrat and Bajzë on November 1st, 1892 A.D.

(From Father Gjeçov, *Kanùn*, p. 126.)

At a general meeting held under the presidency of Brahim Beg the serxherde, Kasem Beg the bylikbash and the four and twenty chiefs (elders) of Kastrat, the following laws were enacted.

1. Whoever murders a man of Kastrat or of any of the other mountains will be fined 3000 grosh and 24 rams.

---

[1] This must be a mistranslation. The Italian version of the sentence runs: *che nessuno ardisa impaurire il bastiame gravido.*

[2] The Italian version of this very obscure clause is as follows: *Le disposizioni riguardanti i mulini rimangono inaltarate per sempre e non possono causare litigi nè fra il povero nè fra il ricco*, clearly referring to the principle, enunciated again in § 10, which compels the miller to treat all his clients on the principle of 'first come, first served'. It is possible that the Albanian version has been misunderstood.

[3] This refers to the letting of some of the tribe's scanty pasturage to strangers.

2. Wounding a man means a fine of 1500 grosh and 12 rams.

3. Whoever fines another without doing it through a General Assembly and by common consent, will be fined 1000 grosh and 10 rams.

4. Whoever disputes with another or calls him names or aims his rifle at him in the following places—Breg i Shpellës, Viri, and Krue i Ri —will be fined 1000 grosh and 10 rams.

5. Whoever breaks down another's hedge in order to make a patch for himself must pay 150 grosh (3 rams) to the owner of the hedge.

6. Whoever murders anyone on the high road will be fined 3000 grosh and 24 rams.

7. Whoever robs another's house or sheepfold will be fined 500 grosh and 5 rams.

8. Whoever dishonours a woman or an engaged girl will be fined 3000 grosh and 10 rams.

9. Whoever does not wish to engage elders and goes away saying 'May I never forgive you' will be fined 500 grosh and 5 rams.

10. Whoever lets his animals graze on another's land will be fined 250 grosh and 3 rams.

11. A man who will not hear of fencing in his portion of land, going halves in the fence with his neighbour, will be fined 250 grosh and 3 rams.

12. A man who does not meet his obligations at the term fixed will be fined 23 grosh.

13. Whoever steals an ox, a cow or a horse in his own village will be fined 500 grosh and 5 rams.

14. A man who does not respond to the village's call to come to a General Assembly or some other requirement of the village will be fined 250 grosh.

15. A man who closes a gap which has always been in the hedge will be fined 150 grosh.

16. The chiefs are to meet in General Assembly once a year, one week after St John's Day. Whoever does not conform to this decision will be fined 500 grosh.

17. 'Pledge elders' are not to take more than 10 grosh as their fee for a judgement, and commoners not more than 5 grosh.

18. Whoever murders his adversary after their feud has been compounded by order of the government will be fined 12 purses and expelled from the village and turned into a ghost.

19. A dog which enters a vineyard with a wooden collar on its neck may not be killed. A dog which enters a vineyard or field without a wooden collar may be killed.

20. Whoever brings a house-dog with him to church or to Shpellë will be fined 50 grosh.

Whoever brings pigs or sheep to Shpellë will be fined 50 grosh.
Whoever washes clothes at Shpellë will be fined 50 grosh.[1]
21. A man who leaves his sureties to pay his debt is to pay a fine of
225 grosh to his creditor and 150 grosh to the chiefs and 5 rams.

VI. Supplement dated 1894.

(From Father Gjeçov, *Kanùn*, pp. 124–5.)

1. Whoever takes a woman to live with him without marrying her or
runs off with a married woman or a girl shall pay 1000 grosh to the
Church, 500 grosh to the chiefs and 10 rams.

2. Whoever tears his face in mourning and lamentation for the dead,
shall pay 1000 grosh to the Church, 1000 grosh to the chiefs and 10 rams.

3. Whoever does not permit the chiefs and fine-collectors to carry
out a tribal law will be fined 500 grosh and 5 rams.

4. Whoever commits a murder during a truce or after the feud has
been compounded will be fined 6 purses and 10 rams.

5. Whoever fires a rifle in a house where there is a wedding shall,
whether he be a guest or the master of the house, pay 500 grosh and
5 rams.

The same fine shall be paid by whoever annoys another with abuse
at table whether at a dinner or a wedding.

6. Whoever acts contrary to these laws, whether he be chief, fine-
collector, or commoner, shall pay 3000 grosh.

> Brahim Beg *serxherde*
> Kasem Beg *bylikbash*
> Dodë Prençi bajraktar
> Zenel Shebani
> Gjokë Doda
> Keq Prela
> Zef Gjeka
> Prelë Toma
> Gjelosh Nika
> Vukusa' Leka
> Brahim Vuksani

[In front of each of these names there is a Turkish seal.]

VII. Solemn Pledge for Flock and Shepherd in Nikaj and Shalë, St Prende's Day 1894.

(From Father Gjeçov, *Kanùn*, pp. 119–20.)

1. As regards roads it has been enacted as follows:
From the fountain in Faqe to the crucifix in Brazhdë the road is

---

[1] (Note by Father Gjeçov: Shpellë is the place where Bajzë and district take
water.)

solemnly pledged to safety for whoever goes to spend the night in Nikaj or Shalë. If any tribesman of Shalë who goes along this road is killed by a tribesman of Nikaj, the guest of all Shalë is killed, from dawn of day till the fall of night. If any tribesman of Nikaj who goes along this road is killed by a tribesman of Shalë, the guest of all Nikaj is killed, from the dawn of day till fall of night.

Between the same points the road is safe for Shosh and Mertur and is under the protection of Nikaj and Shalë. If a tribesman of Shosh kills a tribesman of Mertur he kills the guest of Shalë; if a tribesman of Mertur kills a tribesman of Shosh, he kills a guest of Nikaj.

Whoever resorts to violence on this road must make an oath with twelve men taking the oath and twelve standing by.[1]

2. A flock and its shepherd are not to be killed by anyone; their safety is solemnly pledged and guaranteed. Any man who kills them must pay 20 purses or be killed and have his life equated to theirs.

3. If the pledge of safety is broken and a tribesman of one tribe kills during the period of pledge and guarantee and a tribesman of the other tribe does not so kill, twenty-four men of the tribe that had a man killed must take oath saying, 'You killed me when guaranteed'.

4. The whole road to Curraj up to the Krue i Ftofët (Cold Spring) is under a pledge of safety.

5. Mowers and reapers with scythe and sickle are under a pledge of safety in both summer and winter pasturages.

Cutters of pine slivers and timber are under a perpetual pledge of safety.

Shooters are under a pledge of safety from St Nicholas's Day in summer (May 9th) to St Nicholas's Day in winter (December 6th).

A man irrigating during the night is under a pledge of safety.

6. A house with hearth and flour-bin and the keep of a house are not under a pledge of safety.

Sheepfolds are under a pledge of safety.

7. If anyone goes out from the keep or the house in order to go to the sheepfold which is under a pledge of safety he must say, 'Look, man, we're going to the animals (or the fold), which are under a pledge of safety.'

8. As for women in Shkodër and Gjakovë:

If any of them wants herself to run away or to behave badly for the fun of it, good luck to her.

---

[1] (Note by Father Gjeçov: It was the custom in Dukagjin to make half, not all, of the jurors take an oath. If twenty-four jurors are ordered, twelve go and lay their hand on the Gospel and the other twelve stand listening with folded hands. In many mountain districts unless the principal person concerned excuses someone, it is the custom of all the jurors to go and lay their hand on the Gospel while repeating the words of the oath.)

If any man meddles with one by force he has meddled with a person under a pledge of safety.

If any man dishonours a woman or ravishes her he has meddled with a person under a pledge of safety.

The Gjklika family is not under a pledge of safety.

Ndue Lika's family is under a pledge of safety for its flock and shepherd.

9. Whoever touches sheep belonging to Nikaj or Shalë must pay 500 grosh or give a Martini rifle, the value of which is 500 grosh. He must also return two animals for every one stolen and pay 500 grosh to the owner of the stolen animals.

10. A detective is to receive 100 grosh for tracking down a sheep and twenty for tracking down a cow or an ox.

11. If a Nikaj or a Shalë man goes to a house to kill someone, he has leave to do whatever the fingers of his hand or the muzzle of his rifle can do. But chisels, wood and any form of iron are not to be used.

Whoever breaks this law, unless he is killed and buried, must pay 20 purses and until he pays them he must look out for his life. If he is killed, the matter must be left at a head for a head.

12. Whoever plays false to this pledge treating it with contempt or ignoring it must give an oath with 24 persons who must say they know nothing, as arranged by the other tribes. If he cannot give such an oath he must pay 20 purses like a man who kills another.

13. A borrower who owes money to someone must go to the head of his ward. If he does not give this head satisfaction, he must go to the Bajraktar. If he does not give the Bajraktar satisfaction he is without protection. He may be robbed and killed until he enters the way of the Bajraktar.

14. The roads from Shalë and Nikaj to Shosh and Mertur are guaranteed by Shalë and Nikaj and if they are cut, 20 purses must be paid.

15. The chapels (*koniqet*) of Nikaj and Shalë in which no candle is lit to St John, St Nicolas and St Bastian (Sebastian), are under a pledge of safety.

16. Complaints in Shkodër and Gjakovë are annulled.

VIII. Pledge for Flocks and Shepherds in Nikaj and Curraj, St John's Day, 1895.

(From Father Gjeçov, *Kanùn*, p. 120.)

1. Any man who kills a shepherd will have his house burned down and his land kept untilled for three years.

2. His neighbours will not have their houses burned down but must pay five purses, 1000 grosh of it for the master of the feud and three purses for the guarantors.

3. Nobody may help to bury a murderer till three years have passed unless the master of the feud wishes. When somebody does help to bury him five purses must be paid to the master of the feud, either in money or in beasts, as may be arranged among themselves.

4. A murderer is never under a flock-and-shepherd guarantee until the murder has been avenged or the feud composed.

5. A cutter of pine slivers and a reaper with sickle are under a pledge of safety from the eve of St Anthony to the eve of Our Lady of Alshiqe.

6. A mower with scythe is under a pledge of safety.

7. A shooter is under a pledge of safety from the eve of St Anthony to the eve of Our Lady of Alshiqe.

8. The Ndermajë—Livath i Math (Great Meadow)—Shalë road and the Kodër Plak—Shalë road are under a pledge of safety for flock and shepherd.

9. Whoever steals small animals must pay 250 grosh and return two for every one stolen.

Whoever steals a cow or ox must pay 500 grosh and return two for every one stolen.

10. Whoever removes the tiles of a house must pay 500 grosh.

11. If a debtor does not meet his obligations he is to be accused before the head of his ward. If he still does not meet his obligations, he has no pledge of safety and may be robbed and killed until he enters the right path.

Guarantors: 3 tribes.

IX. Resolutions Made at Kashnjet, Mirditë, on August 17th, 1904.

(From Father Gjeçov, *Kanùn*, p. 128.)

We, the tribe of Dibër, met for some business in General Assembly at Kashnjet and we have examined the business legally as required by God and the Canon of Mirditë.

1. Whoever murders one of his kin shall be expelled for fifteen years from the tribe, his land shall be left untilled and he shall pay a fine of 100 rams and an ox and have his house burned.

2. Whoever allows a man who has murdered one of his own kin to enter his house becomes as guilty as the murderer.

3. The kindred which does not take the lead against such culprits commits a fault against the whole tribe.

[Here follow the names of the leaders, headed by the bajraktar.]

In whatever business the tribe may have these people will take the lead of the whole tribe.

Witness:

Dom Ndue Melguzhi, Pepaj, parish priest of Kashnjet.

X. Decisions Taken on April 30th, 1905, by the Youth of Shalë.

(From Father Gjeçov, *Kanùn*, pp. 126–7.)

1. As from to-day up to Ash Wednesday the percentage on loans at interest is to be paid with 25 okes of grain. If this is not paid by Ash Wednesday, a percentage of 30 okes is to be taken by force from the debtor.

As interest 100 grosh or 100 okes of grain as the creditor wishes are to be paid. Let him take 100 grosh if it suits him, or if he says, 'I'll have grain', let them give him 100 okes of grain.

2. Grain is never to be given to anybody by a man of Shalë unless it is wanted for a funeral meal or it is desired to make a present of not more than 20 okes.

3. Raki is never to be produced by a man of Shalë at a funeral meal except during the seven weeks of Lent.

4. No man of Shalë is ever to give away more than 100 grosh either outside or inside the tribe.

A godmother is not to present a red *xhamadam* (sleeveless jacket).

No woman is to go to a wedding in a party of five or more and they are not to seek a woman outside the same house.[1]

5. Whoever fires the first shot in the yard of a church or inside its boundaries is to have his house burned and must pay 20 purses under the guarantee of flock-cum-shepherd and the youth of Shalë.

6. If a man disturbs a mass that is being said and if the priest, crucifix in hand, says, 'So-and-so has troubled me', the offender will have his house burned and must pay a fine of 2 oxen to the tribe.

7. Whoever touches Church property must pay a fine of 2 oxen to the tribe.

8. Whoever molests the Church servant must pay a fine of 2 oxen to the tribe.

9. If anyone borrows coffee and sugar from the priest for a funeral meal and does not return them to him within four weeks, and if the priest complains, he must pay a fine of one ox to the tribe.

10. Whoever steals an ewe, goat and cow from a man of Shalë and whoever does anything to his neighbour that disgraces him, shall have his harvest burned, his fields plucked bare and his grain panniers smashed. He will pay fines of one ox to the youth and 2 rams to the government representative.

11. These laws, enacted by the youth of Shalë together with the

---

[1] The last clause of § 4 is given as in Mrs Hasluck's MS., but there seems to be some mistake, as the corresponding passage in the Italian version of Father Gjeçov's *Kanùn* runs:

Lo shalano non può fare il compare più di 5 volte, e non può chiedere che si leghino in comparto più di 5 famiglie.

bajraktar, are perpetual like the law about fire[1] and other laws. Whoever breaks this law must pay an ox to the tribe and 300 grosh and a ram to the government's representative, otherwise he will have his house burned.

The Youth of Shalë
April 30th, 1905

XI. Laws Enacted by the Tribe of Kurbin on August 5–7, 1906.
(From Father Gjeçov, *Kanùn*, p. 129.)

1. Whoever joins the government police shall have his house burned and be excluded from funeral gatherings and hospitality.

2. A man who goes to complain to the Turkish government about a Christian shall pay a fine of 1000 grosh.

3. A man who steals from his neighbour or breaks into his house must, if he denies doing so, give his oath with 12 compurgators. If he proves to be a robber, he must pay a fine of 1000 grosh, and return to the owner of the house two for every article stolen.

4. If an ox is stolen and the accused denies the theft he must give his oath with 6 compurgators. If on enquiry he proves a thief, he must pay a fine of 500 grosh and return to the animal's owner two oxen for the one stolen.

This judgement holds also for a horse and a mule.

If a cow is stolen and the theft denied, the accused's oath needs three compurgators. If he proves a thief the penalty is returning two for one to the owner and a fine of 250 grosh. So too for a donkey.

If a bell-goat or a bell-wether is stolen two for one to the owner and a fine of three rams. If the theft is denied the oath must be given by the accused and all the males in his house.

For every small animal two for one to the owner and a fine of two rams. If the theft is denied the oath is with all the males in the accused's house.

5. Setting fire to a house[2] means a fine of 2500 grosh; to an animals' fold, a haystack and a hedge, a fine of 1500 grosh and returning two for one to the owner.

6. A man who does not come to a General Assembly when summoned by the village elder will be fined one ram.

7. If word is sent to the elders to come to a General Assembly anyone who does not come must pay a fine of five rams. If he has an excuse this will be weighed by the other elders.

[1] The Italian version already alluded to (Gjeçov's *Codice di Lek Dukagjini ossia Diritto Consuetudinario delle Montagne d'Albania*, Tradotto dal P. Paolo Dodaj, Roma, 1941) here reads *il mugnaio*, 'the miller' (cf. supra p. 263).
[2] The Italian version reads *La violazione (per furto) del focolare domestico*, and taking fire from a neighbour's hearth without permission is frequently taboo among primitive peoples.

8. As for jurors, in every crime committed in Kurbin, a murder excepted, the jurors must give their oath, saying, 'That it has been stolen from you, I don't know'.[1]

9. What an informant says is said with an oath of how it was in mind.[2]

10. If a man quarrels deliberately with another and without informing the village elder, he will be fined 500 grosh.

If he informs the village elder and the latter asks for a pledge of good behaviour from the one who is oppressing the other and this man refuses to give it, he will be fined 500 grosh.

If the village elder cannot put things right he gives both men a month's grace and informs the other elders who shall settle the quarrel in accordance with the local law.

11. Anyone who gives food or admittance to his house to a Christian or a Mohammedan who is a policeman in the service of the Sultan shall be fined 1500 grosh.

12. If a man breaks a pledge of security given and taken in the presence of elders and commoners in Kurbin, the elders and commoners are under an obligation to burn his house and to expel him from the tribe.

Written in Delbinisht, Kurbin, at the spring of water under the mulberry tree near the Archbishop's palace on August 5th, 6th and 7th, 1906.

Gjin Pjetër Mark Pervizi of Skuraj, Kurbin, senior elder among the 45 elders of the environs of Krue, in the name of the elders and commoners.

Also present at this General Assembly and registrars of the aforesaid laws:

Mgr. Nikollë Kaçorri, witness.

Father Shtjefën K. Gjeçov, Franciscan, witness.

XII. Letter from Shalë dated May 12th, 1907.

(From Father Gjeçov, *Kanùn*, p. 127.)

1. Greetings from the bajraktar of Shalë, the notables and youth to you, chiefs and youth of Theth. We beg to inform you that the undermentioned laws have been enacted by the tribe of Lower Shalë. We let you know, asking if you too will abide by these laws. We laid down the

---

[1] The Italian version of clause 8 runs: *Il dorere del giurato per tutto ciò che accada nel territorio di Kurbini, salvo che nelle cause di uccisione, consiste nel giuramento di non cognoscere il colpevole.*

[2] The Italian translator has *La deposizione del delatore deve essere accompagnata dal giuramento.*

laws and gave our oath to abide by them and not to break them. The laws are as follows:

2. Pecnikaj enacted a law that when a man is murdered the murderer's heir shall find the guarantors and has three days of guaranteed safety. He has to go with the head of his ward to the victim's representative who shall give him a pledge of security for a week[1] and the murderer's 'brethren' shall bring forward two guarantors. If the victim's representative objects, he shall be left to nominate one and the murderer's 'brethren' shall nominate the other.

Whoever murders someone after the enacting of this law and the swearing of this oath has his safety guaranteed for three days.

Whoever commits a murder murders on his own responsibility and his own risk a person under the protection of Pecnikaj and will have a feud and will never be forgiven for that murder and if anyone kills him he does so by order of the whole tribe of Shalë.

3. Although this law was laid down by Pecnikaj, Lotaj, Abat and Bobi concur.

4. As representative for witnessing Theth's oath all Shalë has chosen Tahir Deli, who was at this meeting of the General Assembly.

5. Whoever murders someone in Shalë—apart from the actual murderer—must not burn his house.[2]

6. In case he burns his house[2] he must pay for a fine of four Martini rifles to the Youth of Shalë and must pay twice the value of the house and the damage done to the owner of the house.

7. If, after the 'brethren' of the murderer have gone to their homes, anyone goes to break into one of their houses either to burn it or to kill its men, he must pay to its owner and the Youth 20 purses and a life for a life.

8. Mules are under the protection of the Youth and anyone who takes them takes them subject to the appropriate penalty.

9. What is written in this letter is guaranteed by the bajraktar and the Youth of Shalë and the government's representative.

10. From Prekë Ndue Mashi to Ndue Ulë Bobi whoever pilfers a neighbour's unmilled grain must pay a fine of one ox to the Youth of the tribe and a ram to the government's representative.

XIII. Covenant of Mat.

(From the Albanian Newspaper *Tomori*, November 7th, 1942.)

1. The people of Mat, comprising 5000 families, hereby pledges itself either to denounce to the competent authorities or itself to arrest

[1] The Italian version above referred to seems to omit this provision for a week's security from revenge.

[2] According to the Italian translation the house of the murderer only shall be burned, and if anyone else's house is set on fire the murderer shall pay the specified fines.

any political intriguers against the present régime who may be found within its territory.

2. If, after the conclusion of this covenant, one man kills another with or without just cause, his family shall be punished by the people of Mat with banishment from Mat for three years and his property, both movable and immovable, shall be confiscated and become state property.

3. The same penalties shall be imposed on any man who runs off with a betrothed girl or a married woman.

4. When a domestic animal has been stolen and the thief cannot be found, the village to which the tracks lead must either pay the animal's value or prove that the tracks lead away from its land.

5. Whoever aids criminals and gives them food and shelter renders himself liable to the penalties detailed in clause 2.[1]

6. Whoever carries arms of any description without declaring them renders himself liable to the death penalty.

7. Whoever spreads false rumours about the policy of the State, public security or public finances to the detriment of the present régime and its policy shall be punished as laid down by the Lieutenant-General's decree No. 185.[2]

8. The people's representatives are to regulate and to examine all complaints which may be made concerning land, irrigation, water, roads and forests and if a commission succeeds in settling a dispute between two persons, the decision of the commission shall be inviolable. If it is contested, the contestants shall take the matter to the proper court.

9. Land in Mat is generally held without regular title-deeds and ownership is proved by nothing but a written receipt (*senet*) and a meal according to the local custom. It appears that lately the ownership of properties bought 5, 10, 20 or 30 years ago with a receipt and a meal, as witnesses also confirm, is often disregarded or if regarded, is a constant source of disorders and murder. To put an end to such quarrelling the local Commission must not meddle with exchange of land so made until the Government has registered all the land according to the laws concerned.

10. The chairman of the Commission shall be the local sub-prefect, and its members the political secretary of the sub-prefecture, the gendarmerie commander, the Fascist Albanian militia's commander, and the representatives of the people who assist in drawing up the present covenant.

11. It is learned that Communists or, as some call them, Bolshevists, have made their appearance among us. We must get rid of these persons,

---

[1] (Author's note. At this time the term 'criminals' included not only transgressors of the law but also patriots resisting Italian rule.)

[2] (Author's note. No copy of this decree can be found.)

HAM

whether they be young or old, and must not let them exist within the boundaries of the district of Mat. If there are any such persons, the people of Mat, together with the local authorities, must destroy them, not only with the rifle, but also with the fist. For no one can endure a person who is a traitor and has neither character nor morals. The entire people must disown such men and attack them with all its strength until it destroys them root and branch.

12. By statutory law the Albanian and the Italian peoples are brothers with the same mother and the same father. That is to say, the two peoples have the same father who is the King Emperor and the King of both Albania and Italy. So we shall destroy anyone who insults the King by talking against him and we shall punish the fellow as specified in clause 2.

13. This Covenant which we have made at a plenary meeting of the people of Mat is to remain valid until the end of the General War, and anyone who breaks it is to be considered a traitor to his country and to the régime, that is to say, a betrayer of his fatherland and the régime.

> Sgd. Beqir Sitki Hasa
> Chairman of Commission
> Sub-Prefect of Mat.

INDEX

Women (*cont.*)
  8, 249, 250, 251, 252, 253, 256; theft
  by, 42, 204, 208–9; theft from, 205
Work, men's, 24, 25, 26, 28, 30, 31,
  248, 249; women's, 25–30, 41–2, 63,
  248, 249, 250

Ymer Tullumi, 32, 35
Young Turks, 120–1
Yugoslavia, 1, 3, 13, 81, 112, 115, 126,
  244, 246

Zadrimë, plain of, 1

Zdrâjshë, 29, 117, 214–15, 241, 252
Zef Bardhoku, 117
Zef Doçi, 124, 126, 127–8
Zef Nika, 32
Zerqan, 67, 69, 112, 118, 206; litigation,
  140, 142, 144; oath-taking, 166, 167,
  168, 169, 170, 172, 173, 175, 177, 181,
  182, 184, 185, 189, 193; roads, 83,
  92; witness, 196, 197, 198, 201
Zog, King, 1, 19, 126–9, 208, 241
Zogolli family, 2
Zogu family, 10

For EU product safety concerns, contact us at Calle de José Abascal, 56–1°, 28003 Madrid, Spain or eugpsr@cambridge.org.

www.ingramcontent.com/pod-product-compliance
Ingram Content Group UK Ltd.
Pitfield, Milton Keynes, MK11 3LW, UK
UKHW012329130625
459647UK00009B/174